The Ethnic Dimension in American History

VOLUME ONE

THE ETHNIC DIMENSION IN AMERICAN HISTORY

VOLUME ONE

James Stuart Olson

Sam Houston State University

ST. MARTIN'S PRESS • New York

Library of Congress Catalog Card Number: 78–65207
Copyright © 1979 by St. Martin's Press, Inc.
All Rights Reserved.
Manufactured in the United States of America.
32109
fedcba
For information, write St. Martin's Press, Inc.,
175 Fifth Avenue, New York, N. Y. 10010

Cover design by Jack McCurdy

Maps by Clarice Borio, New York City

ISBN: 0–312–26613–8

To my father and mother, and
To our Norwegian, Swedish, and English ancestors

Preface

As a boy, I returned to California from a visit with my Norwegian and Swedish grandparents in Minnesota to discover that Jerry Pete, a Navajo boy, had moved next door. For the next ten years we were friends, even though I could never fathom the pull that the reservation in Arizona exerted on him and his family. My neighbor on the other side, Sammy Mester, was an Italian-American boy who attended the St. John Bosco parochial school. In my own elementary school the principal was Edward Beaubier, a descendant of French immigrants; and our family doctor was Zoltan Puskas, a tyrannical, Magyar-accented refugee from Hungary. George Beatag, a Rumanian-American, was my fifth-grade teacher, and I remember his proudly telling me that in all of America there was only one Beatag family. In high school my English teacher was Mitsue Maeda, who first told me of the Japanese-American relocation camps of World War II; and on the football and basketball teams I played with Dave Ronquillo and Ron Alvarez (Mexican-Americans), Sam Abajian (Armenian), Dean Chikami (Japanese), Michael James Patrick Clark (Irish), Tom Overholtzer (German), Mike Tortolini (Italian), and Dirk Bogaard (Dutch).

Eventually I married Judy Mehr (Swiss-American), and we lived for several years in Rocky Point, New York, a largely Italian colony on suburban Long Island. Among our friends and colleagues were Paul Bottino (northern Italian), Reed Johnson (Swedish), Herbert Zolot

(Russian Jew), Roberta Brown (English-Japanese-Polynesian), Eleanor Toon (Polynesian), Dirk Hooiman (Dutch), Olga Hooiman (Serb), Kaethe Paetz and Herbert Holtzer (German Jew), Joseph Marasco (Italian Jew), Wini Marasco (Japanese), and Heinz Phaff (German). In the history department at Sam Houston State University I have taught with scholars like Richard Yasko (Polish), James Hagerty (Irish), and Edward Chien (Chinese). Our students come from the Mexican-American barrios and black ghettos of Houston and Dallas; the German, Czech, Polish, and Cajun farming colonies of western Louisiana and eastern Texas; and the English and Scots-Irish neighborhoods of small southern towns. In the evenings my wife teaches English to Kiem Pham (Vietnamese), Emiliana Lopez (Ecuadorian), Etelvina Floyd (Panamanian), Samira Saqr (Egyptian), Maythe Al-Fohaid (Saudi Arabian), and Fatomeh-Aminian (Iranian).

What really is extraordinary about all this is that my odyssey with American pluralism is probably the rule rather than the exception. Most people who have lived in the United States for even a short period of time also have friends and acquaintances with a similar variety of ethnic backgrounds. And the American past, at virtually every turn in our history, profoundly reflects that pluralism, as will, no doubt, the American future.

For years I have taught the course "Ethnic Minorities in American History," but I was never able to find a text which exactly filled my needs. There has been no dearth of literature on American ethnic history; indeed, the topic has been a national obsession since the early 1960s, and the "Roots" and "Holocaust" television spectaculars in 1977 and 1978 clearly illustrated the continuing American fascination with the ethnic past. There are hundreds of volumes about individual ethnic groups; many others on such topics as abolition, riots, wars, relocations, laws, and social movements; and still others on immigration, religion, racism, nativism, and American culture. My teaching problem, however, was that no single text attempted a real synthesis. I wanted a book that not only described Afro-American, native American, Hispanic American, and European-American group life but also placed all of those accounts in the larger context of United States history. In *The Ethnic Dimension in American History* I have tried to fill that need.

Writing the book has been a formidable challenge. Problems of space and organization have been the most serious, and no single ethnic group has been given enough coverage to do it justice. But my purpose has not been to give comprehensive coverage to every ethnic group; such a project would fill libraries. Instead, I wanted to construct a reasonably complete picture of the major groups that have peopled America and show how their presence here has affected public policy. It will no doubt appear to many readers that I have given too much coverage to Indians, blacks, Hispanic Americans, and Asians (fourteen chapters) and too little to the white ethnic groups (eleven chapters). Actually, in terms of words, as much space has been devoted to white ethnics as to racial minorities. But given the size of the white majority, that may still seem too little. There was a reason for my decision. Since I wanted to survey the range of public debate through United States history, and because so much of that debate centered on the racial minorities, I decided to discuss blacks, Indians, Hispanic Americans, and Asian-Americans within each appropriate chronological period. The book is not just a history of American ethnic groups; it is also an ethnic history of American public life, and as such justifies expanded coverage of certain groups.

Several major assumptions governed my approach to the ethnic history of the United States. First, I am convinced, as many others are today, that the "melting pot" has not overtaken us and will not create an ethnically homogeneous society for many centuries. The forces of assimilation, of course, are as powerful today as ever before, but shifting coalitions of racial, ethnic, religious, and cultural values continue to create a pluralistic society. Second, I believe that the main sources of ethnicity are internal. Although discrimination and hostility from other groups may stimulate a sense of unity, the most powerful feelings of fidelity and security spring from the values and symbolic associations of the groups themselves. Internal perspectives, not external pressures, explain the continuity of group life in the United States. Finally, I believe that ethnicity is the central theme of American history, more important than the lack of an aristocracy, the existence of the frontier, the abundance of natural resources, the entrepreneurial impulses, or the isolated security behind two oceans. From the earliest confrontations between Europeans and native Americans in the 1600s to the United States Supreme Court's decision in the Bakke case, the pluralism of American society has shaped the course of public debate.

A number of people have helped me in the writing of this book, and I would like to express my appreciation to them. Many colleagues at Sam Houston State University read portions of the manuscript and offered suggestions that improved it. I am grateful especially to Lee Olm, David Anderson, John Payne, William Haynes, Thomas Camfield, Robert Shadle, Joseph Rowe, Gary Bell, Charles Frazier, and Barry Hayes. At St. Martin's Press, Bert Lummus and Carolyn Eggleston were especially helpful. I am deeply indebted to the hundreds of students who have passed through History 382 and provided invaluable insights into their own ethnic American histories. Finally, I am grateful to countless friends and strangers who have responded so graciously to my incessant questions about their surnames, family histories, and perspectives on American life.

James Stuart Olson
Huntsville, Texas

Contents

Part II: AMERICAN ADOLESCENCE, 1776–1890

Introduction: Ethnicity and Ethnic Relations in America

Because of their ethnic heritage and ideological values, Americans tend to think that the United States is more beset by ethnic conflicts than other countries. But ethnic politics in America is part of a global phenomenon. Today people everywhere are searching for identity and equality, and as "colored" people replace old deferences with new demands, white elites are witnessing an erosion of their traditional authority. The United States is clearly not the only country with ethnic problems.

What does set America apart is its ethnic diversity; a nation of minorities, it defies generalization. Within its boundaries nearly every major racial, religious, nationality, and language group on the planet has tried to achieve economic security and social order. Along with material plenty and economic success, ethnic pluralism is one of the organizing principles of American history and remains today a dominant theme in the way most Americans interpret their environment.

A precise definition of ethnicity is difficult because no set of characteristics is common to all groups; feelings of loyalty and community within groups rest on a variety of ties. In general, however, an ethnic group is a collection of people self-consciously united by physical similarities, cultural traditions, or common visions of the past and future. Skin color has been an especially powerful factor in the United States. Africans, native Americans (or Indians), Asians, and Hispanic Americans· have often been segregated, excluded from wealth and power because of their darker skins. Blacks who three centuries ago came from African tribes with enormous differences in language and religion evolved into an ethnic community because of their common racial heritage and common destiny in America. Indians, Asians, and Hispanic Americans have also slowly acquired a self-conscious vision of mutual dependency within their communities.

Differences in nationality, religion, and language define group membership even more exactly. Europeans viewed native Americans as one group, but the Indian population consisted of hundreds of separate communities with completely different languages, religions, and customs, each tribe fired by an independent sense of destiny. The bonds of earth and soil, of region and locale, are central to community consciousness; people feel close to friends and neighbors, comfortable with others from their corner of the world. The region binding together immigrants to America was sometimes a country, as for the Irish; a province, as for the Germans and the Japanese; or even a village, as for the Italians and the Syrians. Language reinforces ethnicity. People sharing a verbal and gestural heritage communicate and resolve conflict more easily. Religion also unites people, sometimes even when they come from different backgrounds. The German, Galician, Russian, Hungarian, and Rumanian Jews immigrating to the United States all shared a historical and religious consciousness that was central to their ethnic identity.

In addition to customs, language, nationality, and religion, the immigration process itself contributed to the ethnic consciousness of European immigrants. In the peasant villages of the Old World life was closely circumscribed by personal relationships—in the family, church, and fields. People knew one another and felt secure. But that sense of community was lost in the migration to the industrial cities of the New World. Thus the pilgrimage helped create ethnicity. In the foods they ate, the holidays they celebrated, the way they raised families, and the subtle nuances of taste, morality, and religion, the immigrants found symbolic associations to preserve some of the way of life they had left behind.

Shared characteristics—whether of race, nationality, language, or religion—do not always produce ethnicity, however. Race was crucial in transforming African cultures into an organic whole in America, but it did not do the same for native Americans. Although Russian Jews and Russian Slavs, or the Irish and Scots-Irish, shared similar national origins, they never evolved into a cohesive ethnic community in America. The Irish and the English shared the same language but not the same sense of community; indeed, they were cultural enemies through much of American history. And although most Irish, Poles,

Czechs, Slovaks, Italians, Croatians, Slovenes, and Lithuanians were Roman Catholic, religion did not unite them ethnically. In short, shifting combinations of race, nationality, language, culture, and religion organized ethnic life in America, creating hundreds of culturally independent communities.

American Approaches to Ethnic Diversity

Over the years Americans have tried to cope with the heterogeneity of their society, seeking ways to fulfill egalitarian ideals while preventing ethnic conflict. The traditional and most rigid approach to diversity was "Anglo-conformity," the conviction that minorities should adopt the values of white Protestants. By rejecting and then forgetting their backgrounds, new immigrants and Indians would blend into the larger society and ethnic conflict would disappear. In the Dawes Act of 1887, for example, Congress tried to force native Americans to become small farmers by breaking up reservation land into small holdings. After World War I the "Americanization" movement sought to divest immigrants of their cultural heritage. Throughout the Southwest, teachers discouraged Mexican-American children from speaking Spanish in school. But minorities resented demands that they give up their ethnic identities. Had they done so, the surrender of language, religion, and culture would have left them naked in a strange environment, unable to interpret or adapt to their surroundings. A widely accepted ideology until 1945, Anglo-conformity with its implied derogation of other cultures has today fallen into disrepute.

A second view of cultural diversity was that America would act as a vast "melting pot" and a new culture would emerge from the amalgamation of minority groups. In 1909 the English playwright Israel Zangwill described the American melting pot:

> There she lies, the great melting pot—listen! can't you hear the roaring and the bubbling? There gapes her mouth—harbour where a thousand mammoth feeders come from the ends of the world to pour in their human freight. Ah, what a stirring and a seething—Celt and Latin, Slav and Teuton, Greek and Syrian, black and yellow . . .*

By embracing all groups and envisioning a new culture, the melting-pot ideology was more generous than Anglo-conformity, but its objectives were the same—cultural fusion and social stability.

But the melting pot produced no single culture shared by all Ameri-

*Israel Zangwill, *The Melting Pot* (New York, 1909), pp. 198–199.

cans. Indeed, it was naïve to think it ever would. For complete assimilation to have taken place, ethnic groups would have had to discard their cultural heritage, intermarry freely, lose their sense of national and religious peoplehood, and encounter no prejudice from other Americans. Obviously, assimilation stopped short of amalgamation, even though mass culture, mass education, economic prosperity, and geographic mobility have touched most people living in the United States. For immigrants, acculturation to American society (in the form of language, dress, transportation modes, holidays, use of the mass media, and consumerism) took place over several generations.

Frequently the first immigrants from a particular region experienced a period of culture shock when prejudice and the strangeness of American life threatened and confused them. To control their lives and deal with the new environment, they established their own schools, clubs, churches, newspapers, magazines, and fraternal societies, and largely confined their social life to those organizations. When the second generation adopted English and other American customs, ethnic organizations tried desperately to preserve Old World languages and loyalties. Intergenerational conflict in the immigrant communities was common, and native-born ethnics resented their parents' "parochial" attachment to the past as much as the parents disliked their children's "rebelliousness" and "disloyalty." The second generation's devotion to American customs often became exaggerated in response to their parents' conservatism. Then in the third and fourth generations major changes occurred: the Old World language was all but lost, membership in ethnic organizations was declining rapidly, acceptance of American ideas was becoming more complete, and many members of the group were acquiring middle- and upper-class status. Conflicts and fears about identity subsided and the descendents of the immigrants developed a comfortable interest in their heritage.

Although the pace of acculturation varied from group to group, it did set the stage for some forms of assimilation. At work, school, or in suburban neighborhoods the descendents of the immigrants established relationships with people from other ethnic backgrounds, and as these relationships developed over time, familial assimilation through intermarriage occurred more frequently. Over several generations of marital assimilation, forms of identificational assimilation based on groups much larger than the original immigrant groups appeared. Millions of Africans merged into a single Afro-American culture; Sicilians, Abruzzians, Calabrians, and Neapolitans evolved into Italian-Americans; Prussians, Bavarians, Hessians, and Palatinates became German-Americans; and Welsh, Scots, and English immigrants gradually formed an Anglo-American community.

Sociologists Ruby Jo Kennedy and Will Herberg believe that national-ity mergers produced a triple melting pot of community identities based on Protestantism, Catholicism, and Judaism. Protestant immigrants from England, Germany, and Scandinavia have intermarried freely, and their descendents have lost touch with some of the more obvious expressions of their cultural heritage. This is especially true in the newer cities of the South and West, and in suburbs everywhere, where post–World War II migrations have blurred the ethnic distinctions so com-mon in the East and Midwest. Jews from Germany, Russia, Poland, and Hungary merged into a self-conscious Jewish community. And among the Roman Catholic immigrants from Ireland, Germany, and eastern Europe, intermarriage has produced a large Roman Catholic group identity.

But distinctions based on race, religion, and class continue to sustain strong group identities. For blacks, Indians, Asians, and Hispanic Amer-icans, there has been little marital assimilation, either with one another or with the larger European society. Discrimination based on color largely barred these people from most personal relationships with whites, so racial divisions remain the most visible separation in Ameri-can society. Most Americans identify themselves in broad ethnic terms as whites, blacks, Indians, Asians, or Hispanic Americans. Within broad categories based on color, Americans also group themselves along reli-gious lines. Millions of whites, proud of their Protestant, Catholic, or Jewish heritage, deliberately confine intimate relationships to members of their religious group. Asians and Indians may group themselves on the basis of Christian or non-Christian beliefs, and Hispanic Americans divide into Protestant and Catholic groups. And finally, within color and religious groupings, class divisions further retard assimilation. Sociologists are now, for example, describing a new "underclass" of desperately poor people alienated by extreme poverty from the rest of American society. Some Puerto Ricans in the South Bronx, some blacks on the South Side of Chicago, some Mexican-Americans in East Los Angeles, and some whites in Appalachia are so emotionally and cultur-ally isolated that they feel affinities only for others in their racial, religious, and class status. Because of social ostracism, personal choice, or unconscious emotional needs, then, most Americans still claim membership in an ethnic community. The melting pot may be bub-bling, but it is still a long way from creating an America of one race, one religion, and one culture. Pluralism, not complete assimilation, is the reality of life in the United States.

Recognition of that reality gave rise to the advocacy of cultural pluralism. Accepting each person's right to political and economic opportunity, cultural pluralists also uphold the right to affirm a special heritage. They exalt ethnic differences as the genius of American society, for although ethnic diversity guaranteed cultural conflict, it also prevented class conflict by dividing workers along ethnic lines and helped to stabilize American politics. Promoting equality and diversity, cultural pluralism is more tolerant than Anglo-conformity and more realistic than the melting pot.

Historians too are reconsidering ethnicity. For years most historians ignored ethnic minorities or treated them as troublesome, inferior people. According to many textbooks written before World War II, black people were happy, irresponsible children destined to serve white civilization. Either as noble savages or cruel beasts, native Americans were important only to measure the inevitability of white expansion. If blacks and Indians found a place in these textbooks, Mexican-Americans were invisible. Few scholars mentioned them. Finally, the immigrants from southern and eastern Europe were often dismissed as hopelessly backward though hardworking and colorful people. Until the 1940s, American history was primarily a history of white American Protestants.

But the history books changed as ethnic minorities pushed for equality after World War II. Some historians passionately condemned slavery, nativism (antiforeign sentiments), anti-Semitism, and anti-Catholicism. Even then, black people were usually significant only as the slaves of white racists; native Americans only as victims of the frontier juggernaut; or Slavs and Italians only as the butts of nativism. Ethnicity was still nothing more than a ghetto response to discrimination. Exaggerating the disruptive impact of the social environment on ethnic groups as well as the appeal of Anglo-American culture, historians focused on torment and conflict as the sources of ethnicity, ignoring cultural continuity with the Old World, the power of chain migrations, the intensity of religious nationalism, and competition among the immigrants themselves. They failed to see that ethnicity was as much a reconstitution of Old World visions of order and security as it was an accommodation to American society.

Recently this view too has been revised. Black society is studied as an independent, organic culture. Once seen as a morally disintegrating matriarchy, the black slave family is now believed to have been a relatively stable, two-parent institution. Historians are taking new interest in native American cultures as complex, tenacious ways of life. The whole field of Mexican-American history has opened up. And scholars are now revising old interpretations of migration, nationalism, ethnicity, and assimilation in European immigrant communities.

Cultural pluralism implies, of course, the indefinite survival of ethnic subcultures and their inevitable accompaniments—suspicion and prejudice. Prejudice is a state of mind in which a person negatively stereotypes the people of other groups, using his own background as the positive point of reference. And as long as prejudice exists, discrimination will continue as people act upon their emotional fears.

Forms of Discrimination

Discrimination assumes many forms. One form is verbal abuse. Some people may tell ethnic jokes; others repeat them maliciously. At its worst, verbal abuse is bitter and hateful. When Jackie Robinson first played with the Brooklyn Dodgers, he received intense abuse from fans and other players. In 1957, when the federal courts desegregated Central High School in Little Rock, Arkansas, black children encountered bitter verbal attacks as well as threats of violence. Verbal abuse also occurs when blacks use the terms "honkies" or "kikes."

Avoidance is another form of discrimination. Schoolchildren may consciously, or even unconsciously, segregate themselves at dances, games, and free periods. In restaurants and other public places Americans may congregate racially. The white flight to the suburbs is an example of avoidance; so are the antibusing protests in Detroit and Boston.

Discrimination can also involve unfair treatment of others, through either private or legal means. Segregation is formal discrimination, whether sanctioned by private custom or legal authority. Private restrictive practices are still common. Some private elementary and secondary schools in the South, for example, do not admit blacks, while fraternities, sororities, churches, clubs, and neighborhoods sometimes exclude certain ethnic groups. Restrictive practices go on in the labor market. Some minority groups have been relegated to menial, low-paying jobs. Even now black people are excluded from some of the most powerful construction unions. Federal courts are trying to decide where the right of one person to exclude others privately stops and where the right of the "others" to join begins. It will be a matter of controversy for years.

When the exclusion of certain groups is sanctioned by law, it is *de jure* segregation. From the 1880s through the early 1960s, southern blacks were subject to "Jim Crow" laws in schools, housing, hospitals, jobs, theaters, parks, restaurants, and transportation lines and depots. In the Southwest, Mexican-Americans were once unable to vote or hold public office because of restrictive laws. In the early 1900s Japanese-Americans were segregated in California schools, and during World War II they were confined in relocation camps. At one time or another most ethnic groups have faced housing discrimination because of residential covenants and special zoning laws.

Although today *de jure* discrimination is dead, a more insidious form of institutional discrimination involves admission and promotion procedures in government, business, and education. Admission and promotion in colleges, universities, medical schools, law schools, civil service, and private corporations frequently depend on successful performance on achievement tests. The tests, however, are usually written by white middle-class scholars and are often culturally biased. People from poor, rural, and non-English-speaking backgrounds cannot perform as well on the tests as middle-class whites. Although there is no overt discrimination—every applicant is judged according to his or her test score—the cumulative results favor whites. Since it is all but impossible to construct culture-free tests, other solutions to the problem have been proposed, but they are extremely controversial. If, on the one hand, admission and promotion quotas are established for minorities, whites can legitimately claim that they are the victims of reverse discrimination. But if traditional criteria continue to be used, admission to the top schools and the most lucrative and influential positions in business and government will remain in the hands of middle-class whites. Considering the debate over the end of *de jure* segregation in the South, the controversy over institutional discrimination and affirmative action promises to be even more prolonged.

Finally, discrimination can become violent. A Nazi group may vandalize a synagogue, or the Ku Klux Klan may burn a cross in the yard of a black family. A Puerto Rican youth gang may wage "war" against a black youth gang, while both groups may harass whites. An enraged mob may join in a race riot over an alleged crime. Adolf Hitler's annihilation of 6 million Jews is the most destructive example of discrimination in recent history. American history is free of outright large-scale genocide, except perhaps in the warfare waged against native Americans in the nineteenth century, when white attitudes at battles such as Sand Creek and Wounded Knee came frighteningly close to a genocidal mania.

Sources of Prejudice

The intensity of prejudice depends on several conditions. In American society color has been critically important. Northern Europeans (especially Protestants) have usually been readily accepted by the white majority, and discrimination against them has been comparatively mild. Discrimination against darker-skinned southern Europeans, such as the Italians or the Greeks, has been more pronounced, as it has been for

Chinese, Japanese, and Filipino immigrants. And for the darkest-skinned people—blacks, some Puerto Ricans, native Americans, and Mexican-Americans—the road to success has been strewn with obstacles.

Cultural differences also contribute to prejudice. Presbyterians have been more tolerant of Baptists than of Catholics, and Protestants in general more tolerant of Christians than of Jews. Shared cultural values, such as language and religion, guarantee more tolerance. Spanish-speaking Puerto Ricans feel a greater affinity for Spanish-speaking Mexican-Americans than they do for English-speaking Anglos. It is not surprising that blacks, Indians, Hispanic Americans, and Asian-Americans have had more difficulty than other groups in dealing with whites in the United States.

Economic interests are another source of prejudice. Where one group is economically dependent upon exploiting a minority, prejudice will be more intense. Slavery is a good example. The southern economy before the Civil War depended on black slaves, and white planters opposed emancipation. Economic reality reinforced prejudice. Today, in the fruit and vegetable farms of California and southern Texas, the need for farm laborers has generated similar feelings about Mexican-Americans. The same was true for unskilled Chinese laborers in the nineteenth century and, to a lesser extent, for Scots-Irish indentured servants in the eighteenth century.

Economic mobility and job competition influence social tensions. In the textile factories of nineteenth-century New England, Irish and English workers bitterly resented Italians, Greeks, and Syrians because they depressed wages. Industrial workers hated black strikebreakers in the 1930s, and Mexican-American farm workers were alarmed at the immigration of Filipinos in the 1920s and 1930s. Today many whites resent federally mandated affirmative action programs.

Demography affects ethnic relations. If an ethnic group is small and scattered, prejudice is less intense. When 115,000 Vietnamese refugees settled widely across the country in 1975 and 1976, Americans expressed few misgivings. If, on the other hand, the ethnic group is large and concentrated, the sense of insecurity is much greater in the larger society. In antebellum South Carolina and Mississsippi, slaves outnumbered whites, and whites relied on harsh disciplinary codes to control them. Where whites outnumbered blacks, relations were more relaxed. Few people worried about Irish immigration before 1840; but when the potato famine brought millions of Irish Catholics, many Americans became concerned, a nativist movement developed.

Geographic mobility is just as important. When one group encroaches on the territory of another, confrontation is inevitable.

Native American history is one illustration; as white farmers moved west, Indian-white relations deteriorated. The migration of black families to northern cities during World War II led to several racial clashes, the most serious of which took place in Detroit. Today when black families move into an Irish neighborhood in south Boston or a Polish neighborhood in Chicago, it often precipitates a wave of resistance or home sales.

Finally, social problems intensify discrimination. Wars, depressions, or vast social upheavals create unusual tensions. Worried, fearful, and unable to solve their problems, people look for someone to blame, ultimately accusing innocent people. In Germany during the 1920s, Jews were blamed for inflation, unemployment, and national humiliation. Old Bostonian families blamed Irish Catholics for all sorts of problems during the 1840s, and many people made life miserable for German-Americans during World War I.

During the past twenty years, as minorities have protested poverty and discrimination, the United States has become the object of world criticism. And there is ample room for criticism. But the problem must also be placed in perspective. For three centuries literally hundreds of different racial, religious, and nationality groups have striven for success in American society. And that ethnic competition has occurred in a society in which egalitarianism is a national religion. Controversy is not at all surprising. Everyone expects equality and justice because the political culture of the first English immigrants demanded it. Everyone claims an equal right to "life, liberty, and the pursuit of happiness" and demands that the polity deliver on its promise. Considering America's unique mix of cultural pluralism and egalitarian philosophy, perhaps the nation has done rather well in dealing with the problems of ethnicity.

SUGGESTED READINGS

Ahlstrom, Sydney E. *A Religious History of the American People*. New Haven, Conn.: 1972.

Allport, Gordon W. *The Nature of Prejudice*. New York: 1958.

Dinnerstein, Leonard, and Reimers, David M. *Ethnic Americans: A History of Immigration and Assimilation*. New York: 1975.

Glazer, Nathan. "Liberty, Equality, Fraternity—and Ethnicity." *Daedalus*, 105 (Fall 1976), 115–127.

Gordon, Milton. *Assimilation in American Life: The Role of Race, Religion, and National Origins*. New York: 1964.

Gossett, Thomas F. *Race: The History of an Idea in America*. Dallas, Texas: 1963.

Greeley, Andrew M. *Ethnicity in the United States: A Preliminary Reconnaissance*. New York: 1974.

————. *Why Can't They Be Like Us: America's White Ethnic Groups*. New York: 1971.

Handlin, Oscar. *Race and Nationality in American Life*. Boston: 1957.

Higham, John. "The Immigrant in American History." In *Send These to Me: Jews and Other Immigrants in Urban America*. New York: 1975.

Kelley, Robert. "Ideology and Political Culture from Jefferson to Nixon." *American Historical Review*, 82 (June 1977), 531–562.

LaGumina, Salvatore J., and Cavaiolo, Frank J. *The Ethnic Dimension in American Society*. Boston: 1974.

Marty, Martin E. "Ethnicity: The Skeleton of Religion in America." *Church History*, 41 (March 1972), 5–21.

Nash, Gary B., and Weiss, Richard, eds. *The Great Fear: Race in the Mind of America*. New York: 1970.

Rischin, Moses. *Immigration and the American Tradition*. Indianapolis, Ind.: 1976.

Rose, Peter. *They and We: Racial and Ethnic Relations in the United States*. New York: 1964.

Seller, Maxine. *To Seek America: A History of Ethnic Life in the United States*. Englewood Cliffs, N.J.: 1977.

Smith, Timothy L. "Religious Denominations as Ethnic Communities: A Regional Case Study." *Church History*, 35 (June 1966), 523–543.

Sowell, Thomas. *Race and Economics*. New York: 1975.

Stein, Howard F., and Hill, Robert F. "The Limits of Ethnicity." *American Scholar*, 46 (Spring 1977), 181–192.

Wittke, Carl. *We Who Built America: The Saga of the Immigrant*. Cleveland: 1939.

Part I
COLONIAL ORIGINS, 1607 – 1776

In the sixteenth century, political, economic, and religious upheavals were disrupting the lives of millions of people in western Europe. Nation-states were emerging in Spain, Portugal, France, and England as local monarchs extended their territorial authority; entrepreneurs were searching for lucrative business opportunities; and frustrated people were about to rebel against the Roman Catholic Church. The convergence of nationalism, the Commercial Revolution, and the Reformation would soon shake Europe to its foundation and send thousands of people across the Atlantic in a determined search for economic opportunity and religious security.

North America's first colonists had to cope not only with a harrowing ocean voyage and often hostile inhabitants, but also with their own religious rivalries and political expectations. Virginia had its "starving time"; the Plymouth colonists braved a horrible winter in flimsy wooden huts; and New England shuddered in fear during King Philip's War. Eventually the colonists adjusted to the environment, transforming scarcity into abundance and hope into confidence. On the shores of the New World, America played host to cultural pluralism, individual rights, and the beginnings of political nationalism; all three ideas were destined to become ideological standards for the world.

Cultural pluralism revolved around religious diversity. Compared with the rest of the world in the eighteenth century, British North

America seemed an island of toleration in a vast sea of bigotry—even though Congregationalists, Presbyterians, Anglicans, and Catholics were hardly known then for open-mindedness. Because America was settled by many groups, not just one, political loyalty was never identified with any one set of religious beliefs. There was, to be sure, a powerful Protestant spirit, but in the absence of a national church, American culture was nonsectarian. Love of country never implied love of a particular church.

Religious pluralism led slowly to toleration. Jews, Catholics, Friends (Quakers), Separatists, Congregationalists, Presbyterians, Baptists, Methodists, Dutch Reformed, Lutherans, and German Reformed all tried to save souls in colonial America, but no single group had an absolute majority. All were minorities, and to protect its own security each had to guarantee the security of others. Tolerance evolved slowly, even torturously. Virginia prohibited Jewish immigration in 1607; Governor Peter Stuyvesant of New Netherland imposed discriminatory taxes on Jewish merchants in the 1650s; and Pennsylvania tried to prevent Jews from voting in 1690. The Maryland Toleration Act of 1649, which promised freedom of worship for all Christians, was temporarily repealed in 1654. Massachusetts Puritans expelled Roger Williams and Anne Hutchinson for heresy in the 1630s and persecuted Quakers throughout the 1600s. Nor was any love lost between Anglicans and Scots-Irish Presbyterians in the South. Still, religious conflict slowly succumbed to the reality of life in America. Each denomination drifted toward toleration out of necessity, and crusades to win converts were largely voluntary affairs by the late 1700s. Freedom of religion was becoming a hallmark of American democracy.

As the colonists came to terms with diversity, they institutionalized the natural rights theory of the English philosopher John Locke—that governments were only temporary compacts protecting individual claims to life, liberty, and property. The colonists agreed with the English Whigs that power was evil, governments dangerous, and restrictions on political power absolutely necessary. Such basic American concepts as separation of powers, checks and balances, federalism, and a bill of rights would eventually circumscribe power and exalt the individual rather than state or church. Offering abundant land, economic opportunity, and geographic mobility, the New World reinforced individualism, and natural rights became the secular religion of America. The European colonists worshiped God in different ways but paid homage to themselves with remarkable consistency: they possessed "unalienable" rights, and the purpose of government was to sustain those rights.

Early American politics inaugurated the first successful colonial rebellion in modern history. By 1776 the colonists had concluded that England was fulfilling Locke's warnings about the dangers of concentrated political power. They believed that the British writs of assistance, the Sugar Act of 1764, the Stamp Act of 1765, the Townshend Acts of 1767, the Tea Act of 1773, and the Intolerable Acts of 1774 violated individual rights instead of protecting them. Parliament had thereby surrendered its legitimacy as a government of the colonies. The Declaration of Independence and later the Constitution formally established natural rights as a basis for governance. In the nineteenth and twentieth centuries, when colonial peoples rebelled all over the world—Latin Americans against Spain, Indonesians against the Netherlands, Algerians and Vietnamese against France, Indians against England, and Angolans against Portugal—the American Revolution was one of their models. As a goal of colonial societies everywhere, nationalism won a great victory in colonial America.

The colonial period, then, established three great ideas—freedom of religion and its implied respect for cultural pluralism, the natural rights philosophy, and political nationalism—as standards for American society. Nothing would test those standards more severely than racial, ethnic, and religious diversity. When nationalism unified Americans politically, ethnic pluralism divided them culturally. At the same time, the natural rights philosophy promised justice and equity to everyone. The tensions between political nationalism, cultural pluralism, and egalitarianism would be the central dynamic in United States history.

Chapter One

The First Americans

Although small bands of Europeans or Asians may have crossed the oceans to the Americas, most native Americans, scholars argue, descended from Siberian hunters who migrated to North America many thousands of years ago.

Sometime between 40,000 and 32,000 B.C., glaciers covered Canada and the northern United States with an ice sheet thousands of feet thick. These huge glaciers froze up millions of cubic miles of ocean water, dropping the worldwide sea level by hundreds of feet. As the sea retreated into glacial ice, the shallow ocean floor of the Bering Sea surfaced, leaving a land bridge (called Beringia) more than a thousand miles wide connecting eastern Asia with Alaska. Vegetation grew on what had once been the ocean floor, and animals from Siberia and Alaska slowly occupied the new land. Nomadic Siberian hunters followed the big game, and each season their villages moved farther east until, thousands of years later, the migration was complete. On several subsequent occasions warming trends melted enough ice to cover Beringia, temporarily separating the two continents. "Siberians" became "Americans" in a series of major migrations between 40,000 and 11,000 B.C..

Unable to drift deeper into the continent because of the ice sheets covering much of North America, the hunters remained in Alaska for generations. But during the warmer periods, when the Beringia land bridge narrowed or disappeared, the continental glaciers retreated down both sides of the Canadian Rockies and opened an ice-free corridor through the Yukon and Mackenzie river valleys. Thousands of small hunting bands moved south to what is now the United States in between the cold spells that sealed the corridor. Finally, around 11,000 B.C., the Ice Age ended, the glaciers melted, Beringia disappeared under three hundred feet of water, and the hunting groups in America were permanently separated from Siberia.

For the next fifteen thousand years native American hunters spread across the Western Hemisphere, from the Arctic Circle to the tip of South America, and from the Pacific to the Atlantic. Separate bands split repeatedly from one another, and as people in different regions adapted to the land and the varying climates, their ways of organizing life and looking at the world proliferated into hundreds of different cultures. Some tribes remained nomadic, dependent on the natural environment, while others learned to grow their own food and liberated themselves from the need to search for it constantly. This agricultural revolution led to more sedentary life styles, increases in food production and population, social and religious development, and more complex divisions of labor based on sex and status. Some of the agricultural communities developed elaborate social, economic, and political systems.

On the Eve of Colonization

Throughout United States history white people have stereotyped native Americans as "Noble Red Men," innocent children of nature, or fierce, bloodthirsty savages. But in fact, when European settlers first came to the New World, the native American communities had advanced far beyond their Siberian ancestors. Native American societies in 1500 A.D. ranged from the primitive foraging tribes of southern California to the advanced Aztec and Inca civilizations of Mexico and Peru. Although some historians and anthropologists believe the land may have supported several million people, most agree that on the eve of colonization there were only about a million Indians living in what is now the United States. They were divided into more than six hundred separate tribal groups speaking more than two hundred languages, and occupied seven major regions: the northeastern woodlands, the southeastern forests, the Great Plains, the Great Basin, the northern plateau, the southwestern desert, and the Pacific coast.

The tribes of the Northeast lived between the Mississippi River and the Atlantic coast, north of the Carolinas and the Ohio River Valley. In New England they included the Penobscots, Pennacooks, Pequots,

Narragansetts, Mohegans, Massachusetts, and Wampanoags. In the Hudson River Valley the Five Nations of the Iroquois Confederacy— composed of the Mohawks, Oneidas, Onondagas, Cayugas, Senecas, and later the Tuscaroras—reigned supreme. And between the Great Lakes and the Ohio River were the Eries, Conestogas, Sauk and Fox, Ottawas, Kickapoos, Shawnees, Chippewas, Peorias, Menominees, and Miamis. Except for the buffalo hunters of the Illinois plains and the nomadic foragers of the far north, they lived in settled agricultural villages and cultivated corn, squash, and beans in communal gardens. They lived in wigwams or bark houses separated by streets and surrounded by protective stockades, and hunted game for both food and clothing. Except for the highly centralized Iroquois Confederacy of New York and the Algonquian-based Illinois Confederacy, each tribe was independent.

The southeastern tribes lived between the Mississippi River and the Atlantic coast and south of the Ohio River Valley. They included the Cherokees of North Carolina and Tennessee; the Seminoles, Timucuas, and Calusas of Florida; and the Choctaws, Chickasaws, Creeks, and Alabamas on the Gulf Coast. Most were sedentary farmers who raised corn, beans, and tobacco; hunted small game; and gathered nuts, seeds, and wild rice. They lived in farming towns of mud-plaster homes.

A different native American society emerged on the arid short-grass plains of what are now the Dakotas, Montana, Wyoming, eastern Colorado, western Kansas, Oklahoma, and the Texas panhandle. The Blackfeet, Dakotas, Sioux, Crows, Cheyennes, Arapahos, Com-

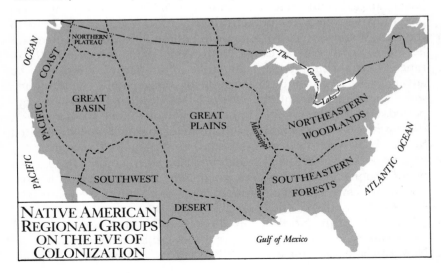

anches, Pawnees, and Kiowas were nomadic hunters whose social and economic life revolved around the buffalo herds. Bearing their portable tepees, they were constantly on the move. The buffalo provided them with meat, which they ate fresh or dried. Buffalo skins gave them their blankets, moccasins, clothes, and covering for their homes. Buffalo hair and tendons became thread and string for their bows. The buffalo stomach became a water bottle. Buffalo horns were used as cups and spoons. The hunters even turned the buffalo tongue into a hair brush and buffalo fat into hair oil. The sixteenth-century acquisition of the horse from the Spaniards vastly increased their range, improved the success of their hunts, and reinforced their nomadism.

For the Indians who lived in the Great Basin, the area between the Rocky Mountains and the Sierra Nevadas that includes present-day Utah, Nevada, southern Idaho, eastern Oregon, and eastern California, life was primitive. Water was precious, agriculture difficult, and the people extremely poor. Roving bands of Utes, Paiutes, Gosiutes, Monos, Panamints, Paviotsos, and Shoshones populated the region. With little agriculture there were no permanent villages, and small groups of extended families subsisted on small game, berries, roots, nuts, seeds, and insects. Here survival was problematical and prosperity unknown.

The plateau Indians—Flatheads, Spokanes, Yakimas, Nez Percés, Wallawallas, Chinooks, Modocs, and Klamaths—lived between the Rockies and the Cascade Mountains. The heavily wooded mountains and high plains of western Montana, Idaho, and eastern Washington were a generally nonagricultural environment. Most tribes hunted for small game, gathered berries and roots, and fished for the giant salmon. Relatively poor and politically decentralized, they lived in semipermanent villages along the major salmon rivers and streams.

Two cultures developed in the Southwest. One was made up of the Navajo tribe, which rose to power at the "four corners" junction of Utah, Arizona, New Mexico, and Colorado; and of the Apaches, who were dominant in southeastern Arizona and southwestern New Mexico. Both tribes were fierce, nomadic hunters who often raided neighboring settlements. They lived in tepees when moving through open country and in brush shelters in the mountains. The second culture was the sedentary, even urban societies of the Hopis, Zuñis, and Pueblos of Arizona and New Mexico. Despite dry weather they raised corn, squash, and beans; they also domesticated poultry, sheep, and cattle, wove cloth, and built towns of many-storied adobe dwellings into rocky hillsides. Labor was specialized, the social structure complex, and their cultures as sophisticated as that of any tribe in the United States.

Two more groups appeared on the Pacific coast. In southern California more than a hundred tribes—including the Yuroks, Salinas, Athapascans, Miwoks, and Chumosh—lived in nomadic villages and gathered acorns, seeds, shellfish, roots, and berries. Most were excellent artisans. In northern California, Oregon, and Washington another coastal culture included the Chinooks, Umpquas, Coos, and Tolowas. Though they were nonagricultural, an abundant supply of fish and game permitted the development of stable communities. They built gable-roofed plank homes and, unlike most other Indians, believed in private property.

Native American cultures had enormous variety. While the Plains Indians wore buffalo skins and the Basin Indians not much at all, the Pueblos were highly skilled weavers of blankets and clothing. The Plains and California Indians were nomadic, but the Iroquois and the Zunis lived in permanent, settled communities. Most northeastern, southeastern, and southwestern tribes raised corn and squash, while other tribes were hunters or gatherers. The Utes lived in primitive lean-tos and the Pueblos in multistoried buildings. Some Indians worshiped the "Master of Life"; others paid homage to ancestors, or animal spirits, or to the elements. Thus when the European settlers arrived, there were already hundreds of different ethnic groups in America.

Native Americans and Europeans: The Cultural Confrontation

The misunderstanding and persistent friction between New World natives and Old World immigrants grew out of competitive, mutually exclusive perspectives. In their approaches to life, death, and the earth, native Americans and Europeans were poles apart. To many Europeans the measure of a person was largely economic, a function of how much wealth had been accumulated. In many native American communities status was noneconomic, dependent upon courage and loyalty rather than on material possessions.

On attitudes towards the natural environment, the two peoples differed as well. White settlers mainly wanted to make a better living for themselves; they intended to use the wilderness, to convert nature into property, status, and security. The land was not sacred to them, and the earth had no transcendent meaning. But for native Americans the environment was holy, possessing a cosmic significance more important than its material riches. They viewed the earth as a gift of the gods which had to be protected and worshiped. Consequently the Indians lived in a symbiotic relationship with the environment, using resources without exhausting them. Chief Smohalla of the Wanapum tribe expressed this view of the environment when he said:

> God . . . commanded that the lands and fisheries should be common to all who lived upon them; that they were never to be marked off or divided, but that the people should enjoy the fruits that God planted in the land, and the animals that lived upon it, and the fishes in the water. God said he was the father and earth was the mother of mankind; that nature was the law; that the animals, and fish, and plants obeyed nature, and that man only was sinful.
>
> You ask me to plow the ground! Shall I take a knife and tear my mother's bosom? Then when I die she will not take me to her bosom to rest.
>
> You ask me to dig for stone! Shall I dig under her skin for her bones? Then when I die I cannot enter her body to be born again.
>
> You ask me to cut grass and make hay and sell it, and be rich like white men! But how dare I cut off my mother's hair?*

The use and ownership of land was the source of the most important environmental conflict between native Americans and Europeans. Impatient with native American economic values, whites considered Indian land-use methods inefficient, incapable of getting the most out of the soil. That fact alone, some believed, justified taking the land, peacefully if possible but violently if necessary.

In addition, the idea of private property was alien to most Indians; giving one man exclusive, perpetual control of land was as inconceivable to them as giving him the air or sky. The Reverend John Heckewelder, a Moravian minister, complained about an Indian's horses eating grass on his land. The Indian said:

> My friend, it seems you lay claim to the grass my horses have eaten, because you had enclosed it with a fence: now tell me, who caused the grass to grow? Can you make the grass grow? I think not, and nobody can except the great Manni-to. He it is who causes it to grow both for my horses and for yours! See, friend! The grass which grows out of the earth is common to all; the game in the woods is common to all. Say, did you never eat venison and bear's meat? . . . Well, and did you ever hear me or any other Indian complain about that? . . . Besides, if you will but consider, you will find that my horse did not eat all your grass.†

---

* *Fourteenth Annual Report of the Bureau of American Ethnology* (1896), pt. 2, p. 721.
† John Heckewelder, *Account of the History, Manners, and Customs of the Indian Nations, Who Once Inhabited Pennsylvania and the Neighboring States* (Philadelphia, 1819), p. 86.

This sketch of an Indian village in North Carolina, drawn by John White in 1590, reveals the compexity of native American society. (The Granger Collection)

This view was inconceivable to most of the settlers, and they began almost at once to displace the Indians, pushing them toward the vacant lands of the West.

The ethnocentrism of the Europeans also guaranteed conflict with native Americans. Convinced of their own religious and moral superiority, the Europeans approached native Americans from two different but equally destructive social perspectives. Some looked upon the Indians as savages requiring no more ethical consideration than the beasts of the field. By denying Indian humanity and creating negative stereotypes, they could rationalize the economic and military assaults on native American society. But other Europeans accepted the humanity, if not the cultural equality, of the Indians. Instead of annihilating them, these colonists wanted to transform native Americans into settled farmers who believed in private property and Christianity. Though more humane than the other point of view, this missionary impulse proved equally detrimental to native American society.

There were, of course, exceptions to the rule. In 1635 Roger Williams enraged the civil magistrates of Massachusetts by denying their Puritan authority and accusing them of violating native American rights. Insisting that the Indians owned the land and could keep or dispose of it at will, Williams went against the grain of European opinion, and the Boston magistrates expelled him from Massachusetts. A half-century later, in Pennsylvania, the Quakers tried to pursue an evenhanded policy toward native Americans. A persecuted people dedicated to nonviolence and the belief that all men and women were children of God, the Quakers wanted a colony in which everyone could live in harmony. They respected the Delaware Indians' right to the land and purchased it from them only after the most careful negotiations. Word spread, and in the 1690s and early 1700s the Tuscaroras, Shawnees, and Miamis all migrated to Pennsylvania. But as Scots-Irish Presbyterians, German Lutherans, and English Protestants pushed west and squatted on Indian land, traditional views triumphed in all the colonies.

Indian Resistance

Although the first years of colonial life were peaceful, the tranquility was short-lived. As soon as the Indians realized that more and more colonists would come to take more land, they began to resist. For years the Algonquian-speaking tribes of Virginia and North Carolina, linked together in a loose alliance under the leadership of Powhatan, had assisted the Jamestown settlers. Important cultural exchanges took place from the very beginning of the Chesapeake colonies. While Europeans excelled in transportation and the use of iron for tools and weapons, the Indians were far more advanced in regional geographic knowledge and economic adjustment to the land. The Powhatan tribes were quick to make use of English kettles, traps, fishhooks, needles, and guns, and they passed on to the English their knowledge of fishing; raising tobacco, corn, beans, squash, rice, and pumpkins; and using herbs and dyes.

In 1622 the peace was shattered. Powhaten had died in 1618 and a more aggressive relative, Opechancanough, had replaced him. During the next few years, as tobacco production became more profitable, the white population increased. Political relations changed dramatically. Feeling the enormous pressures of white civilization, the Indians began to fear it. On March 22, 1622, they attacked colonial settlements throughout Virginia, killing 347 people and destroying dozens of villages. More than a third of the white settlers died. Throughout 1622 and 1623 the English settlers pursued the Indians relentlessly, crushed the Powhatan Confederacy, and annihilated most of the native Americans who had participated in the uprising. Rather than trying to assimilate the remaining peaceful Indians, the colonists imposed a scorched-earth policy. Arbitrary treaties and forced land sales removed the Indians still living in the eastern counties.

Sporadic conflicts erupted throughout the next few decades, most notably in 1644, when Opechancanough himself rebelled, but Virginia would never again be threatened with extinction. After Opechancanough's rebellion the Virginians dealt with the Indians differently. Tired of wars and of native American resistance to English culture, the Virginians "reserved" land north of the York River as a permanent Indian homeland. For the next thirty years the reservation policy worked, and the two peoples even established a valuable fur trade. But it was only a temporary expedient. As the white population increased, pressure to open up the reservation land to settlement became increasingly strong. Convinced that the reservation policy was the only way to guarantee peace, Virginia Governor William Berkeley refused, but white settlers moved north anyway. Nathaniel Bacon, an English-born member of the colonial council, demanded the opening of reservation lands, greater militia protection for western settlers, and wars of extermination against the Indians. Berkeley still refused, and in 1676 Bacon took matters into his own hands. Marching against Jamestown, his supporters slaughtered peaceful Indians along the way and burned the colony's leading settlement. Bacon's Rebellion was over by 1677 and so was Indian resistance in Virginia. Divided politically and vastly outnumbered by Europeans, native Americans were weakened militarily; and by 1680, with a thousand Indians left out of an original population of more than thirty thousand, the clash of cultures was over in Virginia.

In New England the pattern of European land pressure, tribal rivalries, and ethnic conflict was repeated. With a proud sense of mission the Puritans had set out to build the kingdom of God in the New World. Squanto, a Pawtuxet Indian, had helped the Pilgrims in 1620, and for a few years the hatred of the Narragansetts, Wampanoags, and Pequots for one another prevented Indian resistance. When a smallpox epidemic wiped out thousands of native Americans in 1633 and 1634, the Puritans interpreted it as an act of God, proof that Christianity would triumph in the New World. But the Pequots were not convinced. They had moved into southern New England late in the 1500s and ever since the founding of Massachusetts and Connecticut, they had worried about Puritan expansion. Occasional acts of mutual brutality occurred between 1631 and 1636; but in 1637, when the Pequots allegedly killed several whites in Connecticut, the colonists retaliated with a vengeance. It was a bloody affair. Puritan armies drove to Long Island Sound, shooting and burning more than six hundred Pequots. By 1638 the Pequot tribe was nearly destroyed.

Some forty years later New England experienced one of the most savage racial conflicts in American history. Born in 1616 near what is now Warren, Rhode Island, King Philip became chief of the Wampanoag tribe in 1662. Resentful of white settlements, violations of land titles, and assaults on individual native Americans, he attacked on July 4, 1675. Joined by the Narragansetts, Nipmucs, and Penobscots, the Wampanoags eventually destroyed twenty New England towns and killed more than three thousand people. It was only a temporary victory, however, for in the battle of Great Swamp in December 1675, Philip saw a thousand of his warriors die. He too was killed late in 1676. By 1678 a colonial army had cleared southern New England of Indians. opening the area to white settlers.

In the South the conflict continued. Along the coastal plains of North Carolina, the Tuscaroras had lived peacefully for years, raising hemp, corn, and orchard fruits; but, despairing of white encroachment on their land, they killed 130 colonists in 1711. Two years later more than a thousand Tuscaroras were dead and another seven hundred sold into slavery in the West Indies. The Yamasees of South Carolina rebelled in 1715. Exploited in the fur trade and frightened of white immigration, they joined the Creeks, Catawbas, Appalachees, and Santees and killed more than four hundred colonists. Not until the Cherokees joined the whites in 1716 did the rebellion end. The Yamasees and Creeks retreated into the wilderness.

Tension between Indians and whites was intensified by Anglo-French rivalry. Both France and England wanted the Ohio Valley, and the Indians were caught in the middle. Except for the Iroquois, most Indians were loyal to the French because the French did not pose quite the threat of the English. French settlements in Canada were not nearly as large as the English colonies; and because the French were more interested in trade and commerce than in agriculture, they did not usually push the Indians off their land. The centralized authority of the Roman

Catholic Church and its interest in converting Indians guaranteed more humane treatment than that generally provided by English Protestants. It was only natural for the Indians to cast their lot with the French.

During the eighteenth century the French and English fought four colonial wars in North America: King William's War (1689– 1697), Queen Anne's War (1702-1713), King George's War (1740-1748), and the French and Indian War (1754– 1763). In each case the English and most of the Iroquois fought the French and other northeastern tribes. Not until 1763 did the French admit defeat and cede Canada. The Iroquois reaped the prestige and spoils of victory, but thousands of English, Scots-Irish, and German settlers began pouring across the Appalachians to take land from defeated "French-loving" Indians. Settlement pressures and unscrupulous land speculators angered the Indians, especially Pontiac, chief of the Ottawas. In 1763 he led the Ottawas, Delawares, Miamis, Kickapoos, and Shawnees against white settlements in the Ohio Valley. To mollify Pontiac and relieve the pressure on the western tribes, the British Parliament issued the Proclamation of 1763, prohibiting further white settlement in the region. After three more years of fighting, Pontiac signed a peace treaty with England. Except for some tribes in upstate New York and along the Gulf Coast, most of the Indians had been pushed from the Eastern Seaboard. Between 1766 and 1776 Indian relations improved with the British government and deteriorated with the colonists, and during the American Revolution most Indians would consider England their ally, again joining the loser in an international conflict.

The Indians had resisted the colonists almost from the beginning, but their resistance was doomed to failure. For one reason, the European population dwarfed them. Except for the first half of the seventeenth century, the Indians were always outnumbered. They might win some battles but they could never win the wars. Worse, they had no immunity to European diseases. Smallpox, influenza, scarlet fever, whooping cough, and diphtheria decimated Indian communities. Between 1607 and 1776 the European and African population in the British colonies grew to about 2.5 million people while the Indian population dropped from a million to about 600,000. Even when Indians had temporary superiority in numbers, intertribal rivalries—often exploited by the colonists—prevented the formation of effective, long-lasting confederacies. Finally, the westward shift of the white economy destroyed the Indians' habitat and upset the ecological balance of their communities. As the white population increased, the small game disappeared, the buffalo herds were slaughtered, and the land itself was denied them.

In spite of all this, native Americans continued to resist European civilization in many ways, and the presence of whites never resulted in acculturation. Historians and pulp writers have immortalized resistance, and in the colonial period the Powhatan tribal uprisings of 1622 and 1644, the Pequot War of 1637, King Philip's War of 1675, the Tuscarora War of 1711–1712, the Yamassee War of 1715, and Pontiac's Rebellion of 1763 symbolize the Indian refusal to accept white encroachments passively. Some tribes remained as cultural islands in the colonial society, usually confined to reservations; but even there, where white missionaries had unfettered opportunities to Europeanize the native Americans, they clung tenaciously to their own culture.

SUGGESTED READINGS

Chamberlain, J. E. *The Harrowing of Eden: White Attitudes Toward Native Americans.* New York: 1975.

Corkran, David H. *The Creek Frontier, 1540–1783.* Norman, Oklahoma: 1967.

Craven, Wesley Frank. *White, Red, and Black: The Seventeenth Century Virginian.* Charlottesville, Virginia: 1971.

Debo, Angie. *A History of the Indians of the United States.* Norman, Oklahoma: 1970.

Denevan, William. *Native Population of the Americas in 1492.* Madison, Wisconsin: 1976.

Farb, Peter. *Man's Rise to Civilization as Shown by the Indians of North America from Primeval Times to the Coming of the Industrial State.* New York: 1968.

Hagan, William T. *American Indians.* Chicago: 1961.

Jacobs, Wilburn R. *Dispossessing the American Indian: Indians and Whites on the Colonial Frontier.* New York: 1972.

Jennings, Francis. *The Invasion of America: Indians, Colonialism, and the Cant of Conquest.* Chapel Hill, N.C.: 1975.

Johnson, Richard R. "The Search for a Usable Indian: An Aspect of the Defense of Colonial New England." *Journal of American History,* 64 (December 1977), 623–651.

Josephy, Alvin M. *The Indian Heritage of America.* New York: 1968.

Lurie, Nancy O. "Indian Cultural Adjustment to European Civilization." James M. Smith, ed. *Seventeenth Century America.* Chapel Hill, N.C.: 1959.

McNickle, D'Arcy. *Native American Tribalisms.* New York: 1973.

Oswalt, Wendell H. *This Land Was Theirs: A Study of the North American Indian.* New York: 1966.

Sanders, William T. and Marino, Joseph P. *New World Prehistory: Archaeology of the American Indian.* New York: 1970.

Washburn, Wilcomb E. *The Indian in America.* New York: 1975.

Wise, Jennings C. *The Red Man in the New World Drama: A Politico-Legal Study with a Pageantry of American Indian History.* New York: 1971.

Chapter Two

The Europeans: Westward Expansion

The Europeans who moved to the New World were a special people, courageous enough to face an unknown wilderness, restless enough to leave the ties of home, and confident enough to believe they could succeed in such a daring enterprise. Some left Europe to escape poverty, jail, or persecution, and others to reform the world. Some wanted to save the souls of the Indians, and some sought challenge and adventure. Most came to America, however, for religious freedom and economic success; they intended to plant the kingdom of God and build a better life.

From the beginning, North America attracted different groups. In 1624 the Dutch West India Company established a trading post on the Hudson River in New York. Spanish and Portuguese (Sephardic) Jews, Belgian Protestants (Walloons), Puritans from Massachusetts, French Huguenots, and black Africans all lived in New Amsterdam before the English took over in 1664. The Swedish West India Company deposited Finns and Swedes along the Delaware River in 1638. A failure economically, New Sweden was annexed by New Netherland in 1655. After the Edict of Nantes—which had granted religious toleration to the Huguenots—was revoked in 1685, several thousand French Protestants immigrated to America. And after the union of Scotland and England in 1707, Lowland and Highland Scots began coming to the New World.

Early America was already a polyglot society, a cross-section of western Europe. But for all this diversity, three groups dominated the early migrations to British North America: English, German, and Scots and Scots-Irish settlers came in such large numbers that by 1776 they were the most visible and influential people in the thirteen colonies.

The English Settlers

The British colonies reflected the social, economic, and religious changes of seventeeth-century England. Since the early Middle Ages, English economic life had been remarkably stable, with farmers tilling the soil for landlords and closed trade and craft guilds controlling commerce in the towns. But the rise of a money economy and inflation created new social problems. Landlords increased rents to compensate for higher prices; and because commodity prices were not keeping pace with those of manufactured goods, tenant farmers were squeezed between their incomes and costs. Many began looking for new economic opportunities.

At the same time, the Commercial Revolution created a class of business entrepreneurs looking for profits. Highly successful in textiles, banking, and foreign trade, they reinvigorated economic life in England. During the 1500s they had accumulated excess capital; they anxiously sought new investments and were willing to assume great risks. Few ventures seemed riskier than colonization; but if the Spanish plunder of Aztec and Inca treasures was any indication, potential returns were immense. Their pursuit of wealth, along with the desires of more humble people for a better life, created a fascination with colonization. If the lower and middle classes were willing to settle abroad, the merchant capitalists would finance them.

England was also the scene of intense religious debate in the seventeenth century. Ever since the 1530s, when Henry VIII rejected Roman Catholicism, the Church of England had been a powerful institution. After 1558 church and state were a single entity, with religious and political loyalty different sides of the same coin. England was a spiritual battleground. Roman Catholics balked at Henry's break with Rome and the subsequent protestantization of the church by Edward VI and Elizabeth I, and the Quakers rejected all varieties of political, social, and religious authority. Zealous Anglicans persecuted both groups, and many Catholics and Quakers looked to America as an escape.

Puritanism was another powerful force. Committed to cleansing the social order of evil and corruption, Puritans rejected the hierarchical structure of the Church of England, repudiated free will for predestination, and believed in the inherent evil of man. That was the "Puritan dilemma," for while taking a dim view of human nature, they nonetheless felt called to perfect society. Eventually some Puritans decided that England was not ripe for purification and that perhaps in America a perfect community could be realized. Theirs was not an escape to America; the Puritans wanted to prove that a righteous community could succeed. It was an "errand into the wilderness."

Chesapeake Bay and New England

The first two European population centers were along the Atlantic coast, one at Chesapeake Bay and the other in New England. In 1607 a small band of settlers arrived at Chesapeake Bay, sailed thirty miles up the James River, and established Jamestown, the first successful English colony in America. Although some of the colonists hoped to convert the Indians, most had more secular interests in mind. Some dreamed of their own farms, while others planned to export valuable commodities to the mother country. Most of their hopes went unfulfilled until 1612, when John Rolfe "discovered" tobacco; after learning to improve the quality of the "noxious weed," the colonists made it the economic backbone of Virginia. By 1624, even though more than five thousand people had come to Virginia since 1607, only thirteen hundred were still there, the others dead or returned to England. Starvation, disease, and Indian hostility made life difficult; but through courage, tenacity, and luck, the remaining colonists survived.

Two hundred and fifty miles north, other English colonists founded Maryland. In 1632 Charles I granted George Calvert, the first Lord Baltimore, a huge tract of land between Virginia and Pennsylvania. A recent convert to Catholicism, Calvert sought a haven for his persecuted brethren and a fortune through land sales to incoming settlers. Religious idealism and economic enrichment were perfectly compatible for Baltimore. Maryland attracted both Protestant and Catholic farmers, artisans, and servants; and since the Catholics were a minority, the second Lord Baltimore drafted the Toleration Act of 1649, providing freedom of religion to all Christians to protect those of his faith. Tobacco plantations became central to the economy; at first they were worked by indentured servants from England, later by great numbers of slaves brought from Africa. By 1650 the two Chesapeake colonies were successful outposts of English civilization.

The New England colonies were established between 1620 and 1640. More concerned with religion than their Chesapeake neighbors, the New England immigrants were equally interested in succeeding economically. The northern colonies formally began in 1620, when the *Mayflower* unloaded a small group of English Separatists who founded

Plymouth Colony. The most radical of the Puritan sects, the Separatists believed that the Church of England was too hopelessly corrupt to be reformed, that Anglicanism was little more than Catholicism, and that only a complete break could restore true religion. Anglican persecution and their own intolerance for spiritual "deviations" explain their impulse to move constantly—to become "Pilgrims." Living first as nomads in England and Holland, they committed the ultimate act of separation by abandoning the Old World for America, where the kingdom of God would be free of "popish" distractions. Despite the hostile environment of the North Atlantic coast, they survived economically by farming and fur trading and emotionally by the absolute conviction of their righteousness.

The great Puritan migration commenced in 1629. Convinced of the terrible majesty of God and hoping for salvation, they wanted to establish the first sinless society in human history. Like the Separatists in Plymouth, the Congregationalists who founded Massachusetts Bay Colony believed in local church autonomy rather than authoritarian hierarchies, but unlike the Separatists they thought the Church of England could still be saved. Mainstream English reformers committed to social change, they left England to live where God's holy kingdom and the civil polity could be one. Boston, their "City on a Hill," would impress people back home and help reform Old World institutions. Between 1629 and 1640 more than twenty thousand people migrated to the "Bible Commonwealth" in Massachusetts, and they prospered from the very beginning, eventually absorbing Plymouth in 1691.

Three more New England colonies grew out of the first two. The Puritans had immigrated because they wanted religious freedom for themselves, not for anyone else. The Bible Commonwealth in Massachusetts was an oppressive coalition of church and state, an intolerable environment for free spirits. One such spirit, in the person of Thomas Hooker, led a group of settlers from Boston to the Connecticut River Valley, where they founded a new colony in 1636. At the same time, Roger Williams, expelled by Puritan leaders for criticizing church authority and whites' treatment of the Indians, established Providence Plantation—the colony of Rhode Island. And on the coast north of Boston, enterprising merchants and fishermen founded several fur and fishing villages in the 1630s. They were attached to Massachusetts until 1679, when they became the colony of New Hampshire.

New England was ethnically homogeneous, unlike American settlements that were to come. The people worked as small farmers, middle-class merchants, craftsmen, and fishermen. Unlike the commercial, cash-crop economy of Chesapeake Bay, New England built ships; exported fish, furs, timber, and rum; and shipped freight to England and the West Indies. Perhaps it was their intense religious faith that helped give New Englanders their remarkable optimism and sense of an American destiny.

The Middle Colonies

Between 1640 and 1660 the English Civil War discouraged colonization, and the composition of the Chesapeake and New England colonies remained essentially unchanged. But with the restoration of the monarchy in 1660, there was a new enthusiasm for colonization. During the next twenty-five years two new population centers developed in America, one between the Hudson and Delaware River Valleys and the other south of Virginia. By 1689 the British colonies had more than 210,000 people.

The English presence in the middle colonies began in 1664, when Charles II ceded to his brother, the Duke of York, a tract of land running from the Connecticut to the Delaware River Valley. This grant included New Netherland and New Sweden. Envious of the rich Dutch estates along the Hudson River and the deep harbor at New Amsterdam, the duke assembled a naval fleet during one of the Anglo-Dutch wars. It sailed into the colony, and the English peacefully assumed political control, renaming the area New York. A ready-made colony of ten thousand Puritans, Jews, blacks, Dutch, and Swedes, New York was the most ethnically diverse of the North American settlements.

Satisfied with his new possessions but worried about governing all of them, the Duke of York deeded the land south of New York to John Berkeley and George Carteret in 1664. They advertised for new colonists for their "Jersey" property, and the original Dutch, Swedish, and English settlers were soon joined by hundreds of Puritan families from New England. In 1674 Berkeley sold his share, known as West Jersey, to two Quakers; the Carteret family sold East Jersey to Quakers in 1681. By 1689 more than ten thousand people lived in the two Jerseys, and in 1702 England joined East and West Jersey into a single colony. New Jersey had an English majority of Anglicans, Puritans, and Quakers, and a minority of Finns, Swedes, Danes, Dutch, Germans, and French Huguenots.

The middle colonies expanded in 1681, when Charles II, to repay a debt to Admiral William Penn who had died, granted Penn's son, William, a tract of land west of the Delaware River. Several thousand settlers from New Sweden, New Netherland, and New England were already there, but Penn wanted to provide a refuge for persecuted

Edward Hicks' painting of William Penn's treaty with the Indians illustrates the careful, magnanimous approach the Quakers adopted in their relations with native Americans. (The Granger Collection)

Quakers. The Society of Friends, as they called themselves, were peculiar by seventeenth-century standards. By emphasizing the "Inner Light" between God and man, denying the legitimacy of political authority, and preaching pacifism, they invited hostility. There was little in William Penn's background to suggest that he would join this ridiculed and persecuted minority, but he had been a Quaker since he was a young man.

Born into the turbulent world of London in 1644, Penn came from a wealthy family. His father, a British naval hero, gave William a privileged, secure childhood. Penn attended Oxford, was a guest at the coronation of Charles II in 1661, and traveled extensively in France and Germany. He was tall, brilliant, handsome, and rich. Then, astonishingly, he seemed to throw his life away. Sometime in 1666 or 1667 Penn underwent a profound religious transformation, possibly precipitated by the London fire of 1666 or the great plague of 1665. Acquainted with several Quakers, he found the Inner Light and in 1667 was arrested for being a Quaker. Dumbfounded and enraged, his father begged William to renounce the new faith, but Penn refused. Between 1667 and 1681 he went to prison several times and became increasingly committed to the tenets of his faith.

William Penn guaranteed all the people of Pennsylvania religious freedom and humane treatment, and the colony attracted settlers from all over Europe and from other colonies. Only four years after he received his grant there were nine thousand colonists in Pennsylvania, and by 1700 there were more than twenty thousand. The Quakers brought to their new home a quiet faith in the dignity of all people, a repugnance for slavery, and a deep love for the human community.

The middle colonies were the breadbasket of the New World. With rich soil, good harbors, and navigable rivers, New York, New Jersey, Pennsylvania, and Delaware (which was under the executive control of Pennsylvania until 1776) produced wheat, rye, corn, and livestock— enough to feed themselves and export to New England, the South, and the West Indies. Economic prosperity and religious toleration were magnets that attracted Dutch, German, Scots, Irish, and English settlers as well as Quakers, Dunkers, Moravians, Puritans, Anabaptists, Schwenkfelders, Jews, Catholics, Lutherans, and German Reformed. They formed one of the eighteenth century's most cosmopolitan societies.

The Southern Colonies

Another population center developed along the Atlantic coast south of Virginia. In 1663 Charles II ceded land in the Carolinas to eight wealthy English proprietors, who planned to produce wine, silk, and olive oil. Not until 1670 did large numbers of people settle there. Many were frustrated English farmers from Barbados, where the introduction of slave labor had driven small sugar planters out of business. They settled in the southern reaches of the territory and established a plantation economy based on rice and indigo. Late in the seventeenth century settlers arrived from New York, New England, and the West Indies, but population growth was slow, and as late as 1700 only seven thousand people lived in southern Carolina.

Northern Carolina grew even more slowly. Without a good harbor, the colony was unable to fully develop the plantation system so characteristic of the South. Most settlers were poor tobacco farmers. Only about three thousand Europeans lived there when, in 1712, the crown separated the northern Albemarle region from the southern settlements, naming the two colonies North and South Carolina. During the seventeenth century the Carolinas were overwhelmingly English and Anglican, as ethnically homogeneous as New England.

Georgia was the last of the thirteen colonies. At the time England wanted a buffer colony protecting Virginia and the Carolinas from Spanish Florida. James Oglethorpe, an idealistic English general, was interested in establishing a refuge in America for poor people. Political and personal goals merged in 1732 when Georgia was chartered. Oglethorpe carefully screened prospective settlers and selected the "responsible poor"—hardworking men who, if some came from debtors' prisons, had been there through no fault of their own. As in the other southern colonies, the first settlers of Georgia were primarily English.

Common Bonds

The English colonists shared a perspective on life that transcended their differences. They were flexible, innovative, able to look beyond tradition and custom; America's characteristic optimism, transiency, and pragmatism originated with those first immigrants. In England many of them had deferentially accepted a rigid class structure as the natural order of things, but the American experience undermined that idea. It was the more easily undermined because the one social class that did not join the great migration was the English nobility. America lacked an aristocracy. Well-to-do landowners, political officials, merchants, and clergymen had usually risen from humbler circumstances, and their ties to the yeomanry were fresh. It was a fluid upper class, and poor people hoped to enter it themselves some day.

A belief in progress reinforced the expectations of the middle and lower classes. Many, perhaps a majority, of the colonists of the seventeenth and eighteenth centuries came as indentured servants. Because of labor shortages in most colonies, large landowners and merchants recruited workers by advertising the great opportunities of life in America. Prospective colonists mortgaged their futures, agreeing to work a certain number of years in return for passage to America, room and board, and severance pay after fulfilling their contract. Eventually they became the backbone of the large middle class. Since land was easy to acquire, most ended up as independent farmers, a status which would have been impossible for them in England. Others apprenticed themselves and ultimately became paid artisans. The middle class was always expanding, and the servant class was constantly changing as newer immigrants replaced liberated indentured servants. Membership in the lower class seemed a temporary station. Faith in upward mobility became part of the national ideology of a hardworking, confident people.

Only the middle colonies had large non-English minorities before 1689. Then the colonial population began to change, increasing tenfold by 1776. In the intervening years English immigration continued, but hundreds of thousands of other settlers arrived as well. Two new groups in particular, the Germans and Scots-Irish, immigrated during the eighteenth century, and along with the English became the foundation of American society.

The German Settlers

Between 1618 and 1648 the Thirty Years' War between the Catholic leaders of the Holy Roman Empire and the Protestant leaders of Germany, Denmark, and Sweden reduced much of Germany to misery, ravaging the countryside, destroying crops and livestock, and killing millions of people. From 1689 to 1713 the War of the League of Augsburg and then the War of the Spanish Succession brought more suffering to Germany. In addition, the small, decentralized German states of the seventeenth and eighteenth centuries were governed by princes who levied heavy taxes and periodically tried to expand their territory. Political instability deepened the frustrations that the wars of Europe had already bequeathed to Germany.

Germany also suffered from religious controversies: Catholics, Lutherans, German Reformed, Quakers, Dunkards, Moravians, and Mennonites were all struggling for survival or supremacy. Lutheranism was a German counterpart of Anglicanism. Authority-conscious and tied to the German elite, Lutherans believed in salvation by grace rather than works. The German Reformed Church was in many ways the counterpart of Puritanism. Its members too believed in predestination and argued that Lutheranism, though the creation of the Protestant Reformation, still resembled Roman Catholicism too closely. German pietists, such as Quakers, Dunkards, Moravians, and Mennonites, generally occupied the bottom of the social ladder, as did their Quaker brethren in England. They eschewed theological subleties and authority systems for a personal God with whom all men could communicate. Not surprisingly, they encountered the wrath of Catholics, Lutherans, and the Reformed, who looked upon them as threats to the social order.

Politics complicated religious life. If a Catholic prince suddenly took control of a Lutheran principality he might begin persecuting local Protestants. Lutherans might do the same in a Catholic state. It was no wonder many Germans yearned for the peace and stability they expected in the New World.

In the 1680s colonial agents advertised the fertile soil, political stability, and religious freedom of America. William Penn visited the Catholic Rhineland in 1682 and invited harassed pietists to come to Philadelphia. With Francis Pastorius as their agent, they purchased forty thousand acres outside Philadelphia and began immigrating in 1683. Known as Germantown, their community was the first German settlement in America. Thousands of German Quakers, Dunkards, Amish, Mennonites, Moravians, and Schwenkfelders soon followed. They came to America for religious freedom and, much to their joy, found it.

German immigration became a more complex affair in the eighteenth century. Between 1707 and 1709, after another French invasion and severe winters in the Palatinate, the trickle of German immigrants became a flood. Fifteen thousand German Lutherans came to London in 1708 and 1709, and from there most went on to settle in Pennsylvania and New Jersey. Nearly three thousand of them, under the leadership of Conrad Weisar, moved to the Mohawk Valley of New York and a thousand went down to North Carolina. During the 1720s another fifteen thousand Germans came to Philadelphia, followed by fifty thousand in the 1730s. In 1731, for example, Archbishop Firmian of Salzburg ordered all Protestants to leave the city, and more than thirty thousand people fled. Politics and economics, as well as religion, brought most of the eighteenth-century German immigrants to America.

During the early 1700s most Germans settled in southern New Jersey and eastern Pennsylvania. But as the valleys of the Delaware and the Susquehanna filled, land became more expensive, and new immigrants moved down the Appalachian front into the Cumberland Valley of Maryland and Virginia. There were a number of German settlements near Baltimore and Frederick, Maryland, by 1730, and in 1734 Robert Harper and a group of German immigrants founded Harpers Ferry in western Virginia. German settlers fanned throughout the Shenandoah Valley in the 1730s and by 1750 had reached the frontier of North Carolina, joining their compatriots who had settled there in 1709, and from there moved eastward to the Piedmont. Perhaps half the eighteenth-century German settlers went to the southern colonies, ending forever the English homogeneity of the South. By 1776 there were nearly 250,000 people of German descent concentrated in Pennsylvania and New Jersey and scattered through the western sections of Maryland, Virginia, North Carolina, South Carolina, Georgia, and upstate New York.

The Germans became a prosperous people whose stereotype of orderliness, cleanliness, and hard work is legendary. To this day southeastern Pennsylvania is known as "Dutch" country, since *Deutsch* was the German language and *Deutschland* their original home. With their large barns, neat houses, clean yards, flower gardens, well-built fences, and fine cattle, many of these German farms were models of thrift, efficiency, and profit. Although their native soil had been rich, feudal obligations, often requiring peasants to work several days each week for the landlord, had pressed hard on small farmers, and to support their families they had to extract everything the land could yield. It was no wonder they were such hard workers. As free farmers in America, with fine land and no landlords, no feudal obligations, no heavy taxes, they made their farms into the most productive in the New World. And because of their desire to be self-reliant, they preferred subsistence, self-supporting farming over the large commercial farms or plantations of the English and Scots-Irish, which were dependent on export markets.

The Germans settled in groups, kept to themselves, and did not assimilate easily. Because their homeland was divided into separate principalities, they lacked a national perspective, and their political loyalties remained locally oriented. Years of war had left them wary of strangers, and the petty princes of Germany had made them suspicious of politicians. The English saw them as reluctant to associate with non-Germans, remaining loyal to their language, churches, and communities.

For these reasons as well as economic ones, German immigration was not entirely welcome among the English majority. Germans constituted one-third of the Pennsylvania population by 1776, and even the enlightened Benjamin Franklin was afraid German customs might triumph there. In 1753 he remarked:

> Why should the Palatine Boors be suffered to swarm into our settlements, and by herding together, establish their language and manners, to the exclusion of ours? Why should Pennsylvania, founded by the English, become a colony of Aliens, who will shortly be so numerous as to Germanize us instead of our Anglifying them . . . ?*

English colonists required the Germans to take loyalty oaths to the king, and throughout the colonial wars suspected them, erroneously, of being pro-French. For the most part, however, the two groups kept their distance, and in the America of the 1700s that was still possible. In the future common bonds would link the two peoples. Both were white and sensed a community of interest against native Americans and blacks. Common physical characteristics would contribute greatly to assimilation in the nineteenth and twentieth centuries. As to religion, the German pietists respected the English Quakers in the middle colonies; and because the other eighteenth-century immigrants were generally Protestants, the Germans shared a heritage with them. Religious hostility between different Protestant sects was still intense, but in the future

---

* John Bigelow, ed., *The Complete Works of Benjamin Franklin* (New York, 1887–1888), II, pp. 297–298.

Protestantism would serve to bring them together. And in addition, after centuries of political repression, the Germans were cautious politically. They usually cooperated with local officials, which mitigated some of the insecurity and prejudice of the English settlers.

The Scots-Irish Settlers

Nearly three hundred thousand Scots-Irish left northern Ireland for the colonies in the eighteenth century. Their ancestors had departed from Scotland in the early seventeenth century and settled in Ulster, fought with the English against the Irish Catholics, and then established their own communities on the "Emerald Plantation."

Life in the sixteenth century had been difficult for these Scots. Except in the eastern Lowlands, near the English border, Scottish soil was thin and rocky, with marshes and lochs everywhere. Years of wasteful timber use had left much of the Lowlands a treeless, barren land where even the wild game had disappeared. Scotland was a feudal society; independent noblemen and town gentry manipulated tenant farmers, farm laborers, and poor workers, and before 1550 a constant state of war with England disrupted the lives of Lowland Scots. Finally, there was continual quasi-civil war between Lowlanders and Highlanders, for whom life was even more primitive and desolate. The Highland Scots survived in part by raiding and plundering the Lowlands.

Many Scots wanted to leave, and early in the seventeenth century an opportunity appeared. For centuries English kings had tried to subdue Ireland, but the Irish had resisted and the English had frequently abandoned the project. When James I assumed the English throne in 1603, he invited the generally Protestant Lowlanders to settle in Ulster, promising them low rents, long leases, and religious toleration. They jumped at the chance. Between 1610 and 1640 more than forty thousand Lowland Scots crossed the Irish Sea to colonize Ulster.

Other Lowlanders emigrated after 1660. Ever since the Reformation the Church of Scotland (Presbyterian) had dominated the Lowlands. The Scots were Calvinists who believed in God's decision to redeem a few and damn everyone else. They strongly objected to the regal ceremonies, clerical elitism, and hierarchical church governments of Catholicism and Anglicanism. In 1660, when Charles II forcibly created Anglican bishoprics in Scotland, the Lowlanders resisted violently. The "killing times" commenced. Thousands of Scots died and thousands more fled to Ulster, where Anglican landlords still promised toleration.

For the Scots as for the English, the major problem with Ireland was the Irish. After their defeat by English soldiers and settlement by the

Lowlanders, the embittered Ulstermen hid themselves in the woods and fought a guerilla war. The Scots were persistant, however, hardened by centuries of deprivation. That the natives were Roman Catholics only stiffened the Lowlanders' resolve; they turned the war into a religious crusade against the Irish "heathen." By 1650 more than six hundred thousand people were dead, most of them Catholics, and in the process the English and Scots had almost destroyed the Irish political and social order. Irish farmers had been pushed into tenancy on the worst land.

From the English settlers the Scots learned to drain the marshes, and by planting American potatoes they increased agricultural production enormously. Throughout the meadows of northern Ireland the Scots grazed sheep and built a prosperous textile industry. Dairy farms and cattle ranches flourished. Presbyterian ministers came with the settlers, and by 1680 the Lowlands had built a new life for themselves.

Unfortunately, they were too prosperous. As the Ulster economy matured, it competed with vested interests in England. Alarmed about shrinking markets and falling prices, English merchants and landowners persuaded Parliament to close England to Irish cattle and dairy products in the 1690s. English textile manufacturers lobbied until Parliament passed the Woolens Act, which eliminated foreign markets for Irish cloth by restricting exports to the British Isles. The textile industry in Ulster collapsed. More hardships were in store. Throughout the eighteenth century famines plagued Irish and Scots-Irish farmers alike; in the winter of 1740–1741 nearly five hundred thousand people starved to death. To recoup their financial losses, Anglican landlords began breaking Scottish land leases and raising rents. Tithes on the land, already offensive because they were destined for the Church of England, rose with the rents.

Persecution of the Scots made matters worse. The Test Act of 1673 required Presbyterians to pledge allegiance to the Church of England as a prerequisite for holding civil and military positions, teaching school, or attending college. All Presbyterians loyal to their consciences were denied access to power and influence in English society. And during the reign of Queen Anne, in the early eighteenth century, the Anglican Church began enforcing religious conformity throughout the British Isles. English officials refused to recognize Presbyterian marriages, and couples were often prosecuted for "living in sin" even though they had been married for years. The Scots-Irish were outraged.

As in Germany, a contingent of ship captains and real estate agents visited Ulster to promote emigration. The troubled Scots-Irish were ready listeners. If they could not pay their own way to America, the agents sent them as indentured servants, promising free land along the frontier once their contracts were fulfilled. To farm tenants working for absentee landlords, the prospect of land ownership was irresistible. The exodus began in 1717 and 1718.

The several thousand Scots-Irish who settled in New England were not welcomed by the Puritans. New England had no labor shortage and did not need new immigrants. The Puritans felt no affection for Presbyterians, and the latter bitterly resented having to attend the Congregational Church and support it financially. After 1720 the Scots avoided New England and headed for the middle colonies. Most disembarked in Philadelphia, where free farmers headed west while indentured servants remained behind to fill their contracts. The price of land in southeastern Pennsylvania soon pushed them into Maryland, Virginia, and the Carolinas. By 1730 the Cumberland and Shenandoah Valleys were filling with Scots-Irish farmers, and between 1730 and 1760 the Carolinas' population doubled as Lowlanders moved east from the mountains to settle the Piedmont. By 1776 the southern colonies were divided between the English settlements in the east and the Scots-Irish and German communities in the west.

Relationships between the Scots-Irish and the English and the Germans were complicated by geographical separation and cultural differences. Like the Germans, the Scots-Irish settled in separate communities, usually on the frontier, where they established their customs without resistance. Normal social intercourse between the Scots-Irish and the English did not often occur. That was fortunate. The Scots-Irish remembered Ulster and the Lowlands and had little affection for the English or their American cousins. And they were militantly Presbyterian. Wars against Ulster Catholics and Anglican discrimination against the Church of Scotland had only reinforced their religious commitment. Had they settled among Anglicans in the eastern cities rather than in the wilderness, there might have been more trouble between them.

Social tranquility, however, did not always make for good will. The English at first appreciated the Scots-Irish because their presence on the frontier was a protective buffer between native Americans and the eastern English communities, but soon they grew complacent, content for the Scots-Irish to struggle with the Indians. The Scots grew angry about eastern insensitivity—so closely related to the old country English feeling of superiority to the "uncivilized" Scots—and demanded assistance against the Indians. They felt shortchanged, convinced that eastern and English interests were disproportionately represented in the colonial governments. Insurgent political rebellions erupted in Scots-Irish communities. These were not, of course, purely ethnic rebellions, but because so many Scots-Irish participated, there were ethnic dimensions to them. In 1763 a group of Scots-Irish settlers known as the Paxton boys, terrified by Pontiac's Rebellion, slaughtered twenty peaceful Conestoga Indians in western Pennsylvania and then sent a delegation of angry frontiersmen to Philadelphia demanding military protection. They won more representation in the colonial assembly and consequently more protection. The "Regulator" movement in North Carolina consisted largely of Scots-Irish settlers resisting eastern tax collectors, land speculators, and politicians. The rebellion lasted only from 1767 to 1771, but relations between the two groups remained strained for years.

Scots-Irish and German relations were somewhat different. Because of language and religious barriers, the two communities were separate, even when they occupied neighboring valleys. While the Germans were politically cooperative, the Scots-Irish were politically independent and quick to rebel against what they saw as injustice, so much so that the English population considered them out of control. Still, the availability of land in America permitted separate communities, and the Germans and Scots-Irish shared little socially. Both, as westerners, had a political resentment toward easterners, even though the Germans were not as vocal about it as the Scots-Irish.

In spite or because of their stereotype of being pugnacious and stubborn, the Scots-Irish made lasting contributions to American society. Ever since the Reformation, when John Knox called for a literate clergy and Bible-reading congregations, the Presbyterians had revered education. Throughout the cultural wasteland of the frontier South and West, they established grammar schools to educate their children. Of the 207 colleges founded before the Civil War, the Presbyterians were responsible for at least forty-nine of them, including Hampden-Sydney College, Washington and Lee, Dickinson College, and Princeton. Their commitment to education merged with similar views by New England Puritans to generate the national belief in education as a natural right.

The Scots-Irish approach to religion helped shape the American character; for them, right and wrong should be clear, and it was the obligation of the righteous to guarantee social morality. People were responsible for their own behavior as well as that of their neighbors; tolerance for evil or compromise with it was unthinkable. They condemned Sabbath-breaking, card-playing, gambling, dancing, sexual licentiousness, and frivolity; and American culture would in many ways reflect that perspective. The Scots-Irish also contributed to the egalitarian philosophy. Their struggles against the English had left them keenly sensitive to individual rights, and life on the frontier had obliterated most social distinctions. Presbyterianism reinforced social democracy by criticizing the Catholic view that priestly power flowed from the hierarchy down to the people. The Scots-Irish argued that local congregations should elect representatives to general administrative convocations because power flowed naturally from the masses up through the hierarchy. It was only a short step from religious democracy to political democracy, and the Scots-Irish were among the first to take it.

The Growth of American Nationalism

Assimilation was retarded in colonial America because of language barriers, cultural diversity, social and geographical segregation, and political competition. Contact between the English, Scots-Irish, and Germans was limited. But there were common bonds. For most colonists the journey to the New World was a one-way trip; they would never go home again. Continued immigration infused the old culture with new vigor, but loyalty to the Old World slowly decayed. The passage of time and the birth of native generations weakened emotional ties to Europe. For English, German, or Scots-Irish descendants, the New World was home.

Economic reality gave them a common perspective as well. The availability of land created similar social structures in all the new communities of Europeans. Most Americans became small farmers with considerable independence of the ruling gentry. They owned land and enjoyed the security that accompanies property. Accepting what would later be called the Jeffersonian ideology of a nation of farmers and artisans, they saw themselves in democratic terms. Regardless of national origins, they were part of the middle class and shared an economic and social community of interest with one another. Economic interests often transcended ethnic differences, exerting similar effects on all the members of a class, regardless of ethnic origins. The new Americans had begun to sense a common destiny.

Finally, racial conflict and foreign enemies unified the European colonists. In the South all whites shared a racial unity transcending cultural differences, even though the English and Scots-Irish were much more willing to own slaves than the Germans. Throughout the colonies, especially on the frontier, fear of Indians brought Europeans together. The presence of the Spanish in Florida and the French in Canada did the same. In particular, the French and Indian War and the events leading up to the Revolution united many colonists. The French and Indian War was especially difficult for Germans and Scots-Irish living along the frontier. It posed a real dilemma for German-Americans. Since the 1680s the German Pietists, like the English Quakers, had tried to fulfill their ideals of Christian brotherhood by treating the Indians as equals. They had purchased land at a fair price and tried to avoid military confrontation. But the French and Indian War left them no choice but to fight. German communities in the Mohawk Valley, led by Captain Nicholas Herkimer and his German volunteers, defeated the Indians, in 1757 and 1758. Other German militiamen joined the Scots-Irish to defend the Pennsylvania frontier, and served under Colonel George Washington in Virginia. When forced to fight, the Germans did well, especially against a French enemy. In many ways the French and Indian threats forced Germans out of their isolation and into cooperation with Scots-Irish and English colonists.

The Scots-Irish also fought determinedly. As in Ulster, they had carved homes out of the wilderness, and this time they meant to keep them. They participated in every major engagement of the war, attacking the Indians or the French at every opportunity. In the process English-Americans developed a grudging respect for the courage and tenacity of the Scots-Irish.

The American Revolution also unified many colonists. The English-American community was deeply divided—ranging from the militancy of Lexington and Boston to the complacence of occupied Philadelphia—but Germans and Scots-Irish tended to be loyal to the revolutionary cause. Despite political isolation, the Germans harbored intense antiroyal sentiments and sympathized with colonial complaints about tyranny. As they took up arms against the British, the German volunteers sang:

> Englands Georgel Kaiser König
> Ist fur Gott und uns zu wenig.
>
> Old England's Georgie, emp'ror king
> For God and us is a trivial thing.

A number of Americans of German descent distinguished themselves in the Revolution. Several German regiments mustered in New York, Pennsylvania, and Maryland and won the praise of General Washington. Nicholas Herkimer was a militant proponent of American rights, leader of a New York Committee of Safety, and commander of four battalions of German-American soldiers. By delaying the British advance through New York in 1777, he contributed materially to the victory at Saratoga. He died in the campaign and remains today a martyred hero in German-American history. Johann Peter Muhlenberg served on a Virginia Committee of Correspondence and in the House of Burgesses, raised a cavalry regiment for George Washington, and rose to the rank of brigadier general.

Few Americans were more anti-English than the Scots-Irish. Except for considerable Tory sympathy in the Carolinas—based in part on the

oath of loyalty to the crown that many had taken in order to emigrate—
the Scots-Irish were ardent American patriots. Scots-Irish sentiments
were so intense that some of the British thought the American Revolution was essentially a Presbyterian rebellion. In every colony, and in
virtually every engagement from Saratoga in 1777 to Yorktown in 1781,
the Scots were the backbone of the revolutionary forces. An anonymous
New England Tory described the Scots-Irish as the "most God-
provoking democrats on this side of hell." The Revolution gave the three
largest groups of European-Americans a common cause, forced some
political cooperation among them, and made them aware of their combined power. The beginnings of American nationalism were clear.

SUGGESTED READINGS

Ahlstrom, Sydney E. *A Religious History of the American People*. New Haven,
    Conn.: 1972.
Anderson, Charles. *White Protestant Americans: From National Origins to
    Religious Groups*. Englewood Cliffs, N.J.: 1970.
Bercovitch, Sacvan. *The Puritan Origins of the American Self*. New Haven,
    Conn.: 1977.
Boorstin, Daniel J. *The Americans: The Colonial Experience*. New York: 1958.
Bridenbaugh, Carl. *Vexed and Troubled Englishmen, 1590–1642*. New York:
    1968.
Bushman, Richard. *From Puritan to Yankee: Character and Social Order in
    Connecticut, 1690–1765*. Cambridge, Mass.: 1967.
Craven, Wesley Frank. *The Colonies in Transition, 1660–1713*. New York:
    1968.
———. *The Southern Colonies in the Seventeenth Century, 1607–1689*. New
    York: 1949.
———. *White, Red, and Black: The Seventeenth Century Virginian*. Char-
    lottesville, Virginia: 1971.
DeJong, Gerald F. *The Dutch in America, 1609–1974*. New York: 1975.
Demos, John. *A Little Commonwealth: Family Life in Plymouth Colony*. New
    York: 1970.
Dickson, R. J. *Ulster Emigration to Colonial America, 1718–1775*. London:
    1966.
Dunaway, Wayland F. *The Scotch-Irish of Colonial Pennsylvania*. Philadelphia:
    1944.
Ford, Henry J. *The Scotch-Irish in America*. New York: 1915.
Gollin, Gillian L. *Moravians in Two Worlds: A Study of Changing Com-
    munities*. New York: 1967.
Graham, Ian C. *Colonists from Scotland: Emigration to North America, 1707–
    1783*. Ithaca, N.Y.: 1956.

Hall, David D. *The Faithful Shepherd: A History of the New England Ministry in the Seventeenth Century*. New York: 1972.

Hostetler, John A. *Amish Society*. Baltimore: 1963.

Laslett, Peter. *The World We Have Lost*. London: 1965.

Leyburn, James G. *The Scotch-Irish: A Social History*. Chapel Hill, N.C.: 1962.

Morgan, Edmund S. *Puritan Family*. New York: 1944.

Nash, Gary B. *Quakers and Politics, 1681–1726*. New York: 1968.

Notestein, Wallace. *The English People on the Eve of Colonization*. New York: 1954.

O'Connor, Richard. *The German-Americans*. Boston: 1968.

Parsons, William T. *The Pennsylvania Dutch*. Boston: 1976.

Redekop, Calvin W. *The Old Colony Mennonites*. Baltimore: 1969.

Rippley, LaVern. *The German Americans*. New York: 1976.

Sloan, Douglas. *The Scottish Enlightenment and the American College Ideal*. New York: 1971.

Smith, James M., ed. *Seventeenth Century America*. Chapel Hill, N.C.: 1959.

Vaughn, Alden W. *New England Frontier: Puritans and Indians, 1620–1675*. New York: 1975.

Wood, Ralph. *The Pennsylvania Germans*. Princeton, N.J.: 1942.

Chapter Three

Black People in Colonial America

The ancestral homeland of most black Americans is the rain forest of West Africa, a broad stretch of land extending from the upper Guinea coast to the Congo River basin. The grasslands of the northern Sudan also furnished slaves to America. West Africa in 1500 was made up of a bewildering variety of cultures ranging from the sophisticated, literate Islamic nations of the northern Sudan to the nonliterate, agrarian states of the southern rain forest. Most of the slaves brought to North America were from the agricultural tribes of West Africa: the Ibos, Ewes, Biafadas, Wolofs, Bambaras, Ibibios, Serers, and Aradas. Some came from the large centralized states of Yoruba, Dahomey, Ashanti, Fulani, Mandingo, and Hausa, and hundreds of slave expeditions invaded the Islamic nations of the northern plains.

The northern Sudan was an early cradle of civilization comparable to societies of the Near East and the Indus River Valley. By the fifteenth century the kingdom of Songhay had risen to undisputed power in sub-Sahara Africa under the leadership of Askia Mohammed I. Between 1493 and 1529 he transformed Songhay into one of the major empires of the world, controlling much of West Africa south of the Sahara, from the Atlantic coast in the west, through the Niger and Benue river basins, to Lake Chad in the east. An orthodox Moslem, he ruled according to the Koran. He codified the legal system, established a centralized bureaucracy to govern his kingdom, formed an effective banking and credit system, and provided education from kindergarten through the

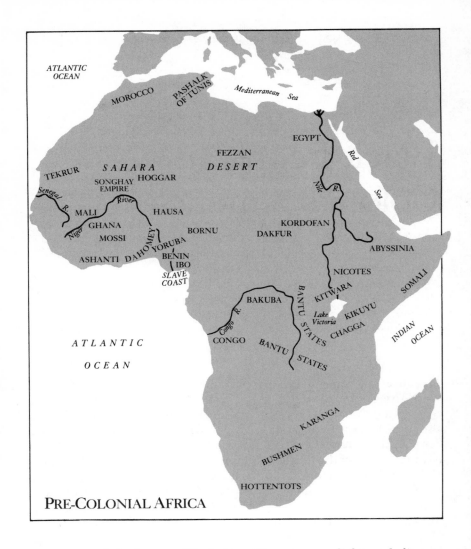

ATLANTIC
OCEAN

MOROCCO

PASHALK
OF TUNIS

Mediterranean Sea

EGYPT

FEZZAN
DESERT

Red Sea

SAHARA

Nile R.

TEKRUR

HOGGAR

SONGHAY
EMPIRE

Senegal R.

MALI

Niger River

GHANA

MOSSI

HAUSA

ASHANTI DAHOMEY YORUBA

BENIN

IBO

SLAVE
COAST

BORNU

KORDOFAN

DAKFUR

ABYSSINIA

NICOTES

SOMALI

KITWARA

BAKUBA

BANTU STATES

Lake
Victoria

KIKUYU

CHAGGA

Congo R.

CONGO

BANTU

STATES

INDIAN
OCEAN

ATLANTIC

OCEAN

KARANGA

BUSHMEN

HOTTENTOTS

PRE-COLONIAL AFRICA

University of Sankore at Timbuktu. He was an enlightened, literate
ruler.

Political power in Songhay rested on the royal family, whose authority
was not unlike that of the royal families in western Europe. Songhay's
economy was complex and specialized. Farmers raised sheep, cattle,
okra, sorghum, cotton, and a variety of garden crops. Artisans and
mechanics, organized into elaborate family craft guilds, manufactured
jewelry, tools, textiles, pottery, bronze castings, and farm implements.
Songhay miners produced copper, gold, bronze, and iron ore. A powerful merchant class, working the urban centers of Kumbi Kumbi, Timbuktu, Gao, and Kano, exported goods to Mediterranean nations. The
Songhay economy compared favorably with those in Europe during the

1500s, and the general population was as well off as the masses of western Europe. Songhay was also recognized in the sixteenth century as an intellectual center. Schools for young people could be found throughout the kingdom, and scholars from Africa and the Middle East gathered at the University of Sankore to study literature, languages, philosophy, law, medicine, and geography.

Though nonliterate and less sophisticated technically than Songhay, the smaller states of the coastal rain forest had advanced far beyond primitive nomadism. Yoruba, Ashanti, Dahomey, Mossi, and Hausa had a rich variety of cultural styles. Political authority usually rested in family networks which respected local prerogatives. The king was dominant, but his power was not absolute. In most cases the selection of a new monarch was made by an "electing family." Although the choice was limited to the immediate royal family, the electors did not have to choose the eldest son but could select the most capable male heir. Because the coronation of a new king required prior ratification by an "enthroning family," some community participation in politics was guaranteed. The king had to delegate authority to ministerial assistants drawn from the noble families; they performed many legislative and executive functions for him. Only rarely, as in Dahomey, did a king establish absolute centralized power.

The social structure was similarly decentralized; life revolved around the extended family. Kinship loyalties were strong, and individual identity was tied inextricably to family membership. As in most such societies, the problems of alienation and feelings of rootlessness were unknown. In a natural transition, people extended family ties into the next world, making ancestor worship an integral part of religion.

The economies of these states were generally stable. On coastal farms people raised yams, carrots, and potatoes; near the Sudanese grasslands they raised wheat and cotton. Others raised sheep and cattle, fished, and manufactured rugs, cloth, pottery, and iron tools. Private property was unknown to most Africans, so farmland was held in common and leased out on a temporary basis to families. The people were self-sufficient, labor was specialized, and their standard of living was well above that of primitive societies.

The people of West Africa lived productive lives. Their intense feelings of family loyalty and identification with the larger group made for a profound sense of community. Their political systems—whether in the kingdom of Songhay, the centralized despotism of Dahomey, or the village states of the coast—were generally stable. When Europeans moved into West Africa, they encountered highly developed societies whose political, social, and economic institutions were functioning reasonably well.

The Origins of Slavery

Slavery was both an economic and a social institution in America. With its fertile soil, long growing season, and navigable rivers, the South was ideal for a plantation economy. And with European demand for tobacco, rice, indigo, and cotton seemingly insatiable, commercial agriculture prevailed from the beginning. But commercial production of tobacco, rice, and cotton required a huge supply of cheap labor, and labor was scarce and costly. If southern farmers were to prosper, they needed workers who would not demand high wages, or be inclined to leave the plantation, or aspire to higher callings. It seemed impossible that free laborers would meet these requirements, particularly when most colonists worshiped the twin ideas of success and individual opportunity. Slave labor seemed to offer a solution.

True, there were white indentured servants, and plantation owners were not above exploiting them. But servants proved unsatisfactory. They were expensive. They sometimes escaped to the cities, where it was difficult to trace them. And they worked out their contracts in a few years and were free to go.

Nor was enslaving native Americans the answer. There were simply not enough of them. Only about 700,000 Indians were left by 1700, and not all of them were accustomed to a sedentary agricultural life. Nor, with their lack of immunity to European diseases, could the Indians survive contact with whites; epidemic death among native Americans was catastrophic. Finally, the Indians knew the land and could escape with relative ease. An economy based on slave labor required an abundant supply of easily recognizable people conditioned to settled agriculture and immune to European diseases. Americans turned to Africa.

The relationship between slavery and prejudice is complex. Some scholars believe slavery created prejudice—that debilitating involuntary servitude led to misconceptions about race and color. Others argue that slavery reinforced preexisting beliefs about racial inferiority. From their earliest contact with Africans in the sixteenth century, the English responded negatively, first with surprise and then suspicion; and long before plantations had created a demand for slaves, the English were prejudiced toward black people.

Color was important. For centuries Western society has instinctively attached meaning to various colors. Red, for example, suggests anger and green symbolizes envy. But the most powerful associations are those connected with black and white. Black has usually been linked with fear, evil, sin, death, and the unknown, and white with purity, chastity, light, spiritual essence, and truth. People still think of white as good and black as bad. A 1972 edition of Webster's New World Dictionary defines *black* as "totally without light; soiled; dirty; evil; wicked; harmful; disgraceful; sad; dismal; gloomy; without hope." Psychologists disagree about the emotional dynamics of color association. Some believe the aversion to blackness is tied to childhood fears of the dark—of loneliness and abandonment—while neo-Freudians argue that white people associate blackness with defecating, a repulsive act in Western society. In hindsight, perhaps these and other theories can be considered justifications rather than true explanations. Whatever the reasons, color is an element of racism.

But color association alone does not explain the origins of racism. Many Europeans fastened moral values to cultural differences. They examined African culture—homes, food, clothes, languages, and sexual practices—and decided that it was savage and primitive. They also disapproved of African religions. Sixteenth-century Protestantism left little room for toleration. To many Europeans, Africans were heathens, misguided children destined for hell. With its magic and mysticism, its worship of idols and ancestors, African religion seemed sacrilegious. Images of African heathenism reinforced white racism.

If the plantation created the need for involuntary servants, English racism turned American eyes to Africa as the source of slaves. That Africans were numerous, accustomed to settled agriculture, and relatively immune to European diseases made them even more likely candidates for slavery.

The Atlantic Slave Trade

The first African slaves were taken by the Portuguese in 1443. The Portuguese began the trans-Atlantic slave trade to supply their Brazilian sugar plantations. Late in the seventeenth century, after tobacco and sugar plantations were established in North America and the Caribbean, the English created the Royal African Company, ending the Portuguese and Dutch monopolies. From that time until its demise in the nineteenth century, the slave trade was dominated by the British.

There were three stages in the Atlantic slave trade. First, the slaves had to be captured, and European traders relied on other Africans to do this. Human bondage was nothing new to West Africa; for centuries West Africans had owned and traded slaves. But slavery was not a

African slaves, yoked in pairs, are forcemarched to the coast, where slave ships wait to take them to America. (The Granger Collection)

capitalist or a racist institution in West Africa. Most slaves were house servants who shared their master's race and whose opportunities for adoption or freedom were relatively good. Slavery was not the harsh, exploitive institution it became in the New World. And at first the slave trade was a casual affair; Africans sold their prisoners of war to the Europeans. By the eighteenth century, however, the trading had assumed economic importance and had become a major cause of war in Africa as coastal tribes competed to supply the New World plantations.

Moving captives from the interior to the coastal exchange posts was the second stage of the trade and was also handled by Africans. Along the way, slaves changed hands several times as African middlemen exacted their own profits. When they reached the coast, the Europeans bought them with rum, cotton cloth, guns, gunpowder, cowrie shells, brass rings, and pig iron.

After plying the African coast for several months acquiring cargo, the slave ship turned west and headed for America. This was the third stage—the "Middle Passage." Hundreds of slaves were crowded into the dark, damp holds of a slave ship for months at a time, with little or no exercise, subsistence diets, and no sanitary facilities. The mortality rate from flu, dysentery, pleurisy, pneumonia, and smallpox was devastating. Thousands died from "fixed melancholy," a form of mental depression so severe that the victims lost the will to live. Twenty percent of the Africans did not survive the voyage. Since perhaps 10 million slaves were taken from Africa to all the colonies in the Western Hemisphere between 1600 and 1800, it can be assumed that 2 million died in transit. It was, as one European trader recalled, "a dreadful business."

Slavery in Colonial America

Dutch merchants delivered the first Africans to Virginia in 1619. At that time Africans were legally indentured servants, and they were released after seven to ten years of work. Between 1619 and 1660, however, laws prohibiting interracial sex and the possession of firearms by black people began to appear in Virginia. The length of service for black servants was gradually increased, distinguishing them from white indentured servants. In 1661 the Virginia House of Burgesses called for lifetime servitude in certain cases and shortly thereafter declared that the children of lifetime servants inherited their parents' legal status. At first lifetime servitude was reserved for rebellious or criminal servants, but by 1700 it had become common throughout the country and meant hereditary servitude. Slave codes became more severe during the 1700s. Soon the law viewed slaves as property, people without civil liberties and subject to the absolute legal control of their masters.

Economic and social pressures hurt southern blacks. As tobacco, rice, and indigo plantations were developed, black indentured service seemed uneconomical. By requiring service for life, planters eliminated labor turnover and protected their investment. And as the black population increased, a sense of insecurity developed among whites. In the northern colonies, where black people numbered less than 5 percent of the population in 1750, there was little insecurity; but it was different in the South. Black people had comprised only 2 percent of the Virginia population in 1640, but they accounted for 31 percent in 1715 and over 40 percent in 1770. Similar situations prevailed in Maryland, the Carolinas, and Georgia. Whites feared the growth of the black population but believed it was economically necessary. Black indentured servitude was expensive and possibly dangerous. Black servants would someday be free, as would their children. Whites worried about the prospects of having thousands of free blacks living beyond the authority of the plantation. If all blacks were slaves, however, they could be controlled absolutely and, supposedly, would be less threatening to the white community. Not surprisingly, during the last half of the eighteenth century whites transformed black labor, replacing indentured servitude with lifetime hereditary slavery.

Deterioration in the treatment of slaves was especially severe in the South. In New England slavery was comparatively mild; slaves joined the Congregational Church, had their marriages recognized by the state, and received limited educations. To a lesser extent, New Jersey, Delaware, and Pennsylvania treated slaves liberally. In New York City, where blacks accounted for perhaps 15 percent of the population, racial tensions were more pronounced and the slave codes more severe. But for the middle colonies in general, with only 10 percent of the population black and the Quakers demanding humane treatment, race relations were better than in the South.

Changes in black status came just as the Africans were playing increasingly important roles in southern life. In the beginnings of colonial settlement, blacks and whites had to work closely together to survive. Since the climate and flora of West Africa resembled those of the South, blacks made conspicuous contributions to the economy. West Africans helped introduce rice cultivation to South Carolina, and Guinea corn was mixed with native Indian varieties. Experienced in animal husbandry, blacks were put in charge of the livestock. The use of gourds for drinking, grass and reeds for baskets and mats, and palmetto leaves for fans, brooms, and chairs all came from Africa. Familiar with swamps and marshes, Africans dominated fishing and passed on to Europeans their knowledge of temporarily poisoning rivers and streams with quicklime to catch fish. Europeans feared alligators, but Africans knew that, like the crocodiles back home, they could be used to protect livestock. Blacks also introduced the use of certain herbs and natural medicines to the colonies, dominated the fur trade as Indians disappeared, and served in the colonial militias well into the 1700s.

The basis of the southern economy, slavery provided whites with a degree of economic security; but at the same time it robbed them of their emotional security, troubling their consciences and disturbing their sleep. And yet, in an extraordinary paradox, slavery enabled white planters to join in the rhetoric of democracy; they could support civil rights for all whites, regardless of economic status, because Africans had come to occupy the bottom of the social ladder. With a readily exploitable slave caste, the whites could at least pay lip service to white democracy. Throughout southern history rich whites would manipulate the racial fears of poor whites, always holding out to them their elite social and political status as whites even though they were desperately poor. In this sense slavery permitted a plutocratic society to sustain a democratic ideology.

By the eighteenth century a distinct Afro-American culture had appeared. Many African traditions survived. Carrying infants by one arm with the child's legs straddling the mother's hips was an Old World custom, as was coiling, a method of sewing woolen trays. Special styles for braiding hair came from Africa, as did the wearing of head kerchiefs by black women. Except for isolated words (such as the West African "okay," which became "OK" to Americans) or the dialects of the most isolated Afro-American communities (such as the Sea Islanders of Georgia and South Carolina), few African words survived in America.

People from all over West Africa were thrown together in a melting pot which fused them ethnically. By the eighteenth and nineteenth centuries a fourth-generation Afro-American had little sense of tribal origins.

But although slaves spoke English, it was an English unique in pronunciation, grammar, and morphology. Some fusion with their native tongues occurred. Scholars speculate, for example, that the contemporary black phrase "dig the jive," meaning to understand what is going on, may be a combination of the Wolof term "deg," meaning to understand, and the English word "jibe." Black English also tended to eliminate predicate verbs, so that such statements as "He is fat" or "He is bad" became "He fat" or "He bad." Slave grammar neglected possessive constructions, saying "Jim hat" rather than "Jim's hat" or "George dog" rather than "George's dog," and it ignored gender pronouns and used "him" and "he" for both the masculine and the feminine. West African dialects had been similar to one another in structure, so in America the slaves used English words but placed them in a grammatical context which was both English and African in origin.

The West African roots of slave customs, family life, and religion are even clearer. In the black cultures of Guiana, Haiti, and Brazil, where slaves vastly outnumbered and rarely saw whites, African customs thrived; but in the United States, where whites outnumbered blacks and racial contacts were frequent, slaves adopted the outer forms of European social life but adapted its spirit to their own African and New World experiences. Threads of African secular culture survived in slave stories, games, dances, jokes, and folk beliefs and provided blacks with a rich verbal literature to express their joys and frustrations. Whites did not try to suppress that literature because it seemed trivial to them.

For years scholars believed that slave families were weak and matriarchal, but they disagreed about whether the source of the weakness was African society or the nature of slavery in America. But it is now accepted that if the native African family was polygamous and matriarchal, its American counterpart was monogamous and patriarchal. Most slave families consisted of two parents, most slave marriages were sound—when husband and wife were allowed to remain together—and most black children traced lineage through their fathers rather than their mothers. Still, the black family reflected its African origins. Although kinship systems were disrupted by the uprooting, blacks developed extended kinship ties in the United States. Elderly people were afforded a degree of respect unknown in white families; similarly, uncles, aunts, and cousins played more important roles in black than in white families. Under slavery the black family was a center of social life, not the debilitated institution many people have described.

The slaves adopted fundamental Protestantism, but they imbued it with an emotional spirit all their own. African musical rhythms and dances, voodooism and folk culture, and grave decorations survived in Afro-American culture; and since the idea of being possessed by a spirit was common in West Africa, the revivalistic flavor of fundamental Protestantism—with its handclapping, rhythmic body movements, public testimonies, and conscious presence of the Holy Ghost—appealed to the slaves. But while whites seemed preoccupied with guilt for sins, the slaves emphasized the redeeming features of salvation; while whites talked of eternal damnation, the slaves delighted in the story of the Jews' deliverance from bondage in Egypt. The result of both family mores and religious beliefs was a strong sense of group solidarity.

Despite their ability to rise above the dehumanizing effects of slavery, Afro-Americans were still embittered about their fate in the United States. Olaudah Equiano, an Ibo tribesman, expressed those feelings:

> Well may I say my life has been
> One scene of sorrow and of pain;
> From early days I griefs have known,
> And as I grew my griefs have grown.
>
> Dangers were always in my path,
> And fear of wrath and sometimes death;
> While pale dejection in me reign'd
> I often wept, my grief constrain'd.
>
> When taken from my native land,
> By an unjust and cruel hand,
> How did uncommon dread prevail!
> My sighs no more I could conceal.*

Slavery had profound effects upon the entire country, white people as well as blacks. In 1776, when the colonies rose up against England in defense of certain "unalienable" rights, more than 500,000 black Americans lived in bondage. Their plight would soon test the fabric of American values.

SUGGESTED READINGS

Bastide, Roger. *African Civilizations in the New World*. New York: 1971.
Craven, Wesley Frank. *White, Red, and Black: The Seventeenth Century Virginian*. Charlottesville, Virginia: 1971.

* Gustavus Vassa, *The Interesting Narrative of the Life of Olaudah Equiano, or Gustavus Vassa, The African* (London, 1794), p. 290.

Curtin, Philip D. *The Atlantic Slave Trade: A Census*. Madison, Wisconsin: 1969.

Davidson, Basil. *The African Genius*. Boston: 1969.

————. *Black Mother: The Years of the African Slave Trade*. Boston: 1961.

Davis, David Brion. *The Problem of Slavery in Western Culture*. Ithaca, N.Y.: 1966.

Degler, Carl N. *Neither Black Nor White: Slavery and Race Relations in Brazil and the United States*. New York: 1971.

Dillard, J. H. *Black English*. New York: 1972.

DuBois, W. E. B. *Black Folk: Then and Now*. New York: 1939.

Fage, J. D. *A History of West Africa*. London: 1969.

Foner, Philip S. *A History of Black Americans: From Africa to the Emergence of the Cotton Kingdom*. Westport, Conn.: 1975.

Forde, C. Daryll. *The Yoruba-Speaking Peoples of South-Western Nigeria*. London: 1951.

Forde, C. Daryll, and Jones, G. I. *The Ibo and Ibibio-Speaking Peoples of South-Eastern Nigeria*. London: 1950.

Franklin, John Hope. *From Slavery to Freedom: A History of Negro Americans*. New York: 1974.

Garrett, Romeo B. "African Survivals in American Culture." *Journal of Negro History*, 51 (October 1966), 239-245.

Gutman, Herbert. *The Black Family in Slavery and Freedom, 1750–1920*. New York: 1976.

Herskovits, Melville J. *Dahomey*. New York: 1938.

————. *The Myth of the Negro Past*. New York: 1941.

Jordan, Winthrop. *White Over Black: American Attitudes Toward the Negro, 1550–1812*. Chapel Hill, N.C.: 1968.

Levine, Lawrence W. *Black Culture and Black Consciousness: Afro-American Folk Thought from Slavery to Freedom*. New York: 1977.

Mannix, Daniel. *Black Cargoes: A History of the Atlantic Slave Trade*. New York: 1962.

Meier, August, and Rudwick, Elliott M. *From Plantation to Ghetto: An Interpretive History of American Negroes*. New York: 1970.

Morgan, Edmund S. *American Slavery, American Freedom: The Ordeal of Colonial Virginia*. New York: 1975.

Mullin, Gerald W. *Flight and Rebellion: Slave Resistance in Eighteenth Century Virginia*. New York: 1972.

Nash, Gary B. *Red, White, and Black: The Peoples of Early America*. Englewood Cliffs, N.J.: 1974.

Pope-Hennessy, James. *Sins of the Fathers: A Study of the Atlantic Slave Trade*. New York: 1968.

Rattray, Robert S. *The Ashanti*. Oxford, England: 1923.

Skinner, Elliott P. *The Mossi of Upper Volta*. Stanford, Cal.: 1964.

Wood, Peter H. *Black Majority: Negroes in Colonial South Carolina from 1670 Through the Stono Rebellion*. New York: 1974.

Summary

Ethnic America in 1776

As the historian Michael Kammen has written, colonial America was an "invertebrate" society of separate religious, ethnic, and racial groups lacking a "figurative spinal column." Economic individualism, abundant open spaces, and continuous immigration had created a pluralistic society. In 1776 perhaps 3 million people were living in what is now the continental United States. The 1.2 million people of English descent were the largest group. There were about 600,000 Afro-Americans, most of them slaves in the South, and 600,000 to 700,000 native Americans, by now living mainly in upstate New York, the Ohio Valley, the Southeast, and beyond the Mississippi River. The Scots-Irish and Germans, with 300,000 and 250,000 people respectively, were the other major ethnic groups in America. Finally, there were perhaps 200,000 French, Dutch, Belgian, Welsh, Scots, and Jewish settlers, most of them in the middle colonies.

The New England settlements were still ethnically homogeneous. After King Philip's War most native Americans had been driven into Canada and upstate New York or had died of European diseases; only 4,000 were left in New England. Without severe labor shortages, New England had only 16,000 blacks in a total population of about 700,000. The poor, rocky soil and Puritan intolerance of New England did not appeal to Scots-Irish or German immigrants. For all these reasons more than 97 percent of New Englanders were of English descent.

The middle colonies were more diverse. Although several thousand

Iroquois lived in western New York, the mid-Atlantic coast had been largely cleared of native Americans by 1776. Pennsylvania Quakers had cooperated with the Delaware Indians, but the pressure for land was so great that the Delawares had moved west of the Alleghenies. There were perhaps 60,000 blacks in the middle colonies out of a general population of nearly 700,000. Only in New York City, where 20,000 blacks lived, were race relations tense, and the slave codes especially harsh. But elsewhere in the middle colonies slavery was generally a dying institution, a victim of economic irrelevance and Quaker disapproval. Race relations in Pennsylvania and New Jersey were the most relaxed in North America. In eastern Pennsylvania more than 100,000 German settlers tended their fine farms, as did perhaps 25,000 more in upstate New York. Farther west, 75,000 Scots-Irish settlers were turning the frontier into farms. Along the Hudson River in New York, the Delaware River in New Jersey, and in New York City, several thousand Dutch colonists still retained the farms, estates, and businesses their ancestors had founded in the seventeenth century. The largest group, nearly 400,000 English colonists, led by the Quaker elite in Philadelphia and the Anglican elite in New York, controlled economic and political life in the middle colonies.

There were about 1,250,000 people in the southern colonies. As the number of plantations increased, most coastal Indians moved west, but there were still Cherokees, Choctaws, Chickasaws, and Creeks in the Southeast. Tidewater settlements had mixed populations, with black slaves outnumbering white owners in many areas. The result was a social paranoia that made life difficult for the 520,000 southern blacks. Farther west, particularly in the Piedmont and upper coastal plain, perhaps 110,000 German immigrants lived in farming communities, and in the back country approximately 200,000 Scots-Irish pioneers were pushing the wilderness westward.

Beyond the Alleghenies, English, German, and Scots-Irish settlers were opening up the Ohio Valley and the Southeast. As many as 100,000 Indians were still east of the Mississippi River, and west of it perhaps 550,000 more were living out their traditional lives oblivious to the European presence.

Despite more than a century of political and economic contact between the English, Germans, Scots-Irish, blacks, and Indians, they were still distinct ethnic communities in 1776. Although the French traveler John de Crèvecoeur wrote in 1782 that Americans were a "mixture of English, Scotch, Irish, French, Dutch, German, and Swedes," he was describing a mixture that did not exist as such. Some groups to be sure were no longer separate entities. The English settlements in Pennsylvania had absorbed New Sweden, and French

Huguenots were becoming part of wider communities everywhere. Nevertheless, most ethnic groups were not intermarrying or developing close social ties. On the eve of the Revolution, people were still divided by more than they shared.

Racial Divisions

The most basic division was racial. The history of North America differed dramatically from the Latin American experience. Ever since the Moorish invasions of Spain, Iberian society had interacted with nonwhite people, and by 1500 the Spaniards felt little ambivalence about miscegenation. Settlement patterns in Latin America led to even more mixing. During the early colonial period relatively few Spanish or Portuguese women migrated to America, so family life depended on the integration of Indian or African women into European households. The children of mixed marriages—mestizos (Indian-European) and mulattoes (African-European)—achieved a social status between that of upper-caste Europeans and lower-caste Africans or Indians. Spanish and Portuguese fathers openly claimed their mixed offspring.

But English America had no place for such mixing. Insulated from Africa and the European mainland, the English had had little contact with nonwhites, and their sixteenth-century meetings with Africans and Indians had been marked by fear and ambivalence. While sexual contacts between the races in Latin America were socially acceptable and necessary, such relationships in North America were seen as threats to the family and the social order. Although sexual contact frequently occurred between whites and blacks, it was a clandestine affair, disapproved of publicly and unsanctioned legally. Nor was there a mulatto class; such children were inevitably considered African.

For North American Europeans and native Americans, economic reality outweighed other considerations. In New England and the middle colonies the European and Indian communities met to make war or make money, but miscegenation was rare. Disease, war, and ecological change so thinned the ranks of native Americans that by 1776 there was little or no contact between most Europeans and Indians. Family life in the northern colonies was relatively stable, the sexes were numerically balanced, and sexual relations were racially contained. In the Carolinas and Georgia, however, until the sexual ratio balanced out later in the eighteenth century, European men often sought out Cherokee and Creek women. Still, these were exceptions; the two communities did not amalgamate. While most whites viewed Indians as primitive savages good only as military allies or fur trappers, the native Americans saw

Europeans as a selfish and destructive people. A mestizo class never emerged in the British colonies.

Sexual contact between Europeans and Africans in the South was a more complex affair because the two races lived together. Colonial officials began prohibiting interracial marriages in the seventeenth century; but if intermarriage was extremely rare, sexual liaisons were not. Mulatto children of white masters and black slave women appeared in every southern colony. Racial amalgamation did not imply assimilation, however, for legal status followed a matriarchal line. Children of white fathers and slave mothers were still slaves and legally defined as such. White fathers often freed their mulatto children, and these mulattoes made up the majority of free blacks. But fathers rarely claimed and raised mixed offspring, and interracial sexual relationships hardly ever created nuclear families. By forbidding interracial marriage but blinking at interracial sex, colonial officials conferred no special status on illegitimate mulattoes and increased the supply of slave labor.

Because of extreme declines in the native American population between 1607 and 1776, there was little opportunity for sexual contacts between Indians and Africans especially in New England, the middle colonies, and the Chesapeake colonies, where there were also few blacks. Runaway slaves often found refuge with Indian tribes; but only in South Carolina and Georgia, where the African and Indian populations were large, did the two communities coexist extensively. Creek, Choctaw, Cherokee, and Chickasaw Indians outnumbered Europeans in South Carolina and Georgia until well into the eighteenth century, as did African slaves. Frightened Europeans, worried about African-Indian conspiracies, prohibited blacks from traveling in Indian country, offered bounties to Indians for returning escaped slaves, and used black troops in the colonial militia to fight Indians. Even then, though, the Yamasees and Apalachees in Florida were known to harbor escaped slaves, and more often than not the slaves took Indian wives and disappeared into tribal society.

Ethnic Solidarity

The American environment provided Europeans with some common experiences. The vast open spaces, the labor shortage in many areas, and the absence of a state church or aristocracy provided Europeans with an unprecedented sense of freedom and opportunity. And because so many groups were living in the colonies, people simply had to give one another at least a grudging tolerance, even if only for the most personal reasons. Race united them against slaves and Indians; and foreign threats—the French in Canada, the Spanish in Florida, the Indians in the West, and finally the British Empire—also brought them together in the common defense. They gathered in local committees to protest British violations of their rights; they served in ethnic militia companies and then together in the colonial army; and after the Revolution they would come together in local politics. In the process, they associated with people from other backgrounds.

Still, for the most part each European ethnic group went its own way. In New England the Yankee culture of individual liberty, moralistic reform, technical ingenuity, and commercial acumen was already emerging; and throughout the colonies people of English descent felt superior to other ethnic groups. The English proprietors of Pennsylvania, for example, periodically wanted to restrict immigration from Germany and were dissuaded only because the colony's labor shortage was a more serious problem than its cultural diversity. They sponsored "charity schools" in German communities not only to teach reading, writing, and arithmetic but also to Anglicize the Germans. Though of necessity tolerant of other faiths, the English were nevertheless convinced that their Anglican, Congregational, or Baptist churches were the true vehicles for building the kingdom of God.

Of course, other groups felt the same way. The Swedish colonists in New Jersey and Pennsylvania burned trees to clear farmland, fertilized their land with the ashes, and built log cabin houses just as they had done in the Old World. They established Swedish Lutheran churches and parochial schools to preserve the old culture. But because the Swedes were so few and were surrounded by English, Dutch, and German settlers, they were unable to maintain a separate identity in colonial America.

The Dutch did better. In parts of New York City, up the Hudson River in New York State, and down the Delaware River in New Jersey, Dutch culture thrived. The steep-roofed wooden homes—with divided doors, built-in cupboards and cabinets, and blue-tiled fireplaces—were always near Dutch Reformed churches and Dutch parochial schools. The church was a community center and welfare association. Schools taught Dutch Calvinism and the Dutch language. In 1766 the Dutch built Queen's College (Rutgers University) to train the Dutch Reformed clergy in America. Because of their geographical concentration and their emphasis on the mother tongue, Dutch culture remained a powerful force in the middle colonies.

The Germans were another cultural island. Driven by memories of home, they had settled in heavily forested areas of rich limestone soil where they built their characteristically large homes surrounding a central fireplace and iron stove, large barns, and immaculate farms.

Conditioned to the Old World struggle to survive, they were thrifty, well-organized, provident, and efficient. Conditioned as well to political disaster and foreign invasions, they were suspicious of strangers and apparently apathetic about politics. German families were large, German women often worked in the fields, and because of powerful family and community loyalties, German children often settled near home after marrying. Only rarely did a German family move to another area in the South or West. German Lutheran, Reformed, and pietist churches dotted the German communities; and especially after the English had tried to convert them, the churches sponsored parochial schools to educate children in the language and faith of the Old World.

The Scots-Irish did not maintain the ethnic isolation of the Dutch or Germans. They too selected land that resembled their homeland, prizing river bottom land which was rich and not heavily wooded, preferably along the unsettled frontier where it could be bought cheaply. But neither family nor church could keep the ethnic community together for long. Scots-Irish kinship ties were weak, and families readily moved alone to distant places, leaving kin and friends behind. The Scots-Irish frequently held their farms for only a few years before selling and moving. And while they brought the Presbyterian Church to America, it could not unify them either, because the community was so scattered and the scholarly standards for its clergy so high. Although the Scots-Irish had by no means melted into oblivion by 1776, the fact that they were dispersed, spoke English, and were Protestants helped integrate them into the English community and set them apart from the Dutch and the Germans. Cultural assimilation was widespread by 1776, and more than half the Scots-Irish were intermarrying with other groups, usually to people of English descent.

In 1776, then, North America was a cultural kaleidoscope of three races and dozens of ethnic and religious groups. Assimilation, even among Europeans, did not occur. Not for another century would the cultural differences between the colonial Europeans disappear, and then only after massive new immigrations from the Old World.

SUGGESTED READINGS

Ahlstrom, Sydney A. *A Religious History of the American People*. New Haven, Conn.: 1972.

Bailyn, Bernard. *Ideological Origins of the American Revolution*. Cambridge, Mass.: 1967.

Bercovitch, Sacvan. *The Puritan Origins of the American Self.* New Haven, Conn.: 1977.

Boorstin, Daniel J. *The Americans: The Colonial Experience.* New York: 1958.

Chamberlain, J. E. *The Harrowing of Eden: White Attitudes Toward Native Americans.* New York: 1975.

Hartz, Louis. *The Liberal Tradition in America.* New York: 1955.

Heimert, Alan. *Religion and the American Mind from the Great Awakening to the Revolution.* Cambridge, Mass.: 1966.

Kammen, Michael. *People of Paradox: An Inquiry Concerning the Origins of American Civilization.* New York: 1972.

Kelley, Robert. "Ideology and Political Culture from Jefferson to Nixon." *American Historical Review,* 82 (June 1977), 531–562.

Kraus, Michael. *The Atlantic Civilization: Eighteenth Century Origins.* Ithaca, N.Y.: 1966.

MacLeod, Duncan J. *Slavery, Race, and the American Revolution.* London: 1974.

Main, Jackson T. *The Social Structure of Revolutionary America.* Princeton, N.J.: 1965.

Marty, Martin. *Righteous Empire: The Protestant Experience in America.* New York: 1970.

Nash, Gary B. *Red, White, and Black: The Peoples of Early America.* Englewood Cliffs, N.J.: 1974.

Potter, David M. *People of Plenty: Economic Abundance and the American Character.* New York: 1954.

Robbins, Caroline. *The Eighteenth Century Commonwealthman.* Cambridge, Mass.: 1959.

Schlesinger, Arthur Jr. "America: Experiment or Destiny?" *American Historical Review,* 82 (June 1977), 505–522.

Strout, Cushing. *The New Heavens and New Earth: Political Religion in America.* New York: 1975.

Wells, Robert V. *The Population of the British Colonies in America Before 1776.* Princeton, N.J.: 1975.

Part II
AMERICAN ADOLESCENCE, 1776–1890

If the eighteenth century gave America its cultural and political values, the nineteenth century tested them. Caught up in vast economic and social change, the young republic had to decide whether pluralism and liberty applied to all races as well as all religions. The community horizons of the early Protestant colonists were challenged by profound ethnic changes. In the eighteenth century, cultural conflict had largely involved white Protestants, and cultural pluralism had implied toleration for each Protestant denomination. But in the nineteenth century Catholic immigration from Ireland, Germany, and Quebec frightened Protestants, who had only recently learned to live with one another. At the same time whites had to decide whether blacks, native Americans, Mexican-Americans, and Chinese were entitled to freedom and equality. Americans would pass through the crucibles of cultural conflict and civil war searching for answers to those questions, and their basic values would emerge intact and expanded, ideologically more pervasive than they had been in 1776.

Economic changes created new subcultures in the United States. The transition from a mercantile and subsistence-farming economy to one based on industrial production, commercial farming, and resource extraction stimulated demand for land and labor, and millions of immigrants were drawn into that expanding economy. With jobs in the Northeast and land in the West, America seemed a beacon of opportunity, toleration, and freedom to small farmers and artisans in western Europe and southeastern China. Few social movements in modern history compare with the migration of 18 million people to the United States between 1820 and 1900. The Great Migration was like the eruption of a huge social volcano, and it transformed the human landscape throughout the Western world.

Although wars, revolutions, religious creeds, and political repression were important, economic unrest was the driving force behind emigration. The smallpox vaccine, the introduction of the American potato throughout Europe, and the absence of protracted war reduced mortality rates, and between 1815 and 1914 Europe's population increased dramatically. The German population, for example, grew from 24 to 68 million; the population of Sweden from 2.5 to 5.5 million; and that of Norway from 850,000 to 1.7 million. Europe's population jumped from 140 million in 1750 to more than 260 million in 1850, and to nearly 400 million by World War I. Farm sizes dwindled, and many younger sons and laborers had to give up hope of ever owning their own land. Even those with land were hard-pressed to improve their standard of living. As huge mechanized farms appeared in the United States and oceanic transportation improved, American wheat became competitive in European markets. World grain prices and the income of millions of small farmers declined. Except for the tragic potato blight in Ireland, these changes occurred little by little year after year. To supplement their incomes, European farmers had to find extra work in the winter. Many began traveling to cities—Bergen, Amsterdam, Christiania, Copenhagen, Hamburg, Bremen, Antwerp, Vienna, or Prague—to

TABLE I

IMMIGRATION FROM WESTERN EUROPE, 1820–1900

	1820s	1830s	1840s	1850s	1860s	1870s	1880s	1890s	Total
England	14,055	7,611	32,092	247,125	222,277	437,706	644,680	216,726	1,822,272
Scotland	2,912	2,667	3,712	38,331	38,769	87,564	149,869	44,188	368,012
Wales	170	185	1,261	6,319	4,313	6,631	12,640	10,557	42,076
Ireland	50,724	207,381	780,719	914,119	435,778	436,871	655,482	388,416	3,869,490
Canada	2,277	13,624	41,723	59,309	153,878	383,640	393,304	3,311	1,051,066
France	8,497	45,575	77,262	76,358	35,986	72,206	50,464	30,770	397,118
Germany	6,761	152,454	434,626	951,667	787,468	718,182	1,452,970	505,152	5,009,280
Belgium	27	22	5,074	4,738	6,734	7,221	20,177	18,167	62,160
Netherlands	1,078	1,412	8,251	10,789	9,102	16,541	53,701	26,758	127,632
Switzerland	3,226	4,821	4,644	25,011	23,286	28,293	81,988	31,179	202,448
Denmark	169	1,063	539	3,749	17,094	31,771	88,132	50,231	192,748
Sweden	91	1,201	13,903	20,931	37,667	115,922	391,776	226,266	794,665
Norway					71,631	95,323	176,586	95,015	451,647
TOTAL	89,987	438,016	1,403,806	2,358,446	1,843,983	2,437,871	4,171,769	1,646,736	14,390,614

SOURCE: *Annual Report*, U.S. Immigration and Naturalization Service, 1973.

look for jobs. Some became a migrant people long before they migrated to the United States.

Just as opportunities in agriculture were diminishing, changes in the industrial economy were eliminating other occupations. When cheap Canadian and American timber entered Europe in the nineteenth century, many jobs in the lumber industries of Sweden, Norway, Finland, and Germany disappeared. Shipbuilding in Canada and the United States eliminated more jobs in northern Europe. Factories gradually supplanted production of goods by independent artisans. Working longer hours for less money to compete with the mass-produced goods of American, English, and German factories, these independent artisans grew dissatisfied with the present and anxious about the future. After the 1870s millions of industrial workers immigrated to America looking for better jobs and higher wages in the Northeast and Midwest. Except for the Irish, immigrants were not generally the most impoverished people of Europe; chronically unemployed members of the proletariat and peasants working large estates usually did not emigrate. Both vision and resources were needed for such a drastic move. It was status-conscious workers and small farmers who traded Old World problems for New World opportunities.

Appetites whetted by the advertisements of railroads hungry for workers, steamship companies for passengers, and new states for settlers, they came from the British Isles, France, Germany, the Netherlands, Scandinavia, and China. The Irish left from Queenstown, in Cork Harbor, or crossed the Irish Sea on packet ships and departed from Liverpool; the Scots boarded immigrant vessels at Glasgow; the English and Welsh traveled by coach or rail to Liverpool and left from there; the Germans made their way to Antwerp, Bremen, or Hamburg; and the Scandinavians left first from Bergen, Christiania, or Göteborg for Liverpool, and from there sailed to America. Immigrant mortality rates in these sailing ships were extremely high. After weeks or months at sea in crowded holds, they landed in one of six places: the Maritime Provinces of Canada, Boston, New York, Philadelphia, Baltimore, or New Orleans. From Canada they traveled down the St. Lawrence to the Great Lakes or caught vessels to Boston; from the Atlantic ports most of them made rail, wagon, or steamboat connections to the interior; and from New Orleans they went up the Mississippi River and scattered out along its tributaries. The Chinese immigrants left from Canton, Hong Kong, and Macao, stopped over for a period in Hawaii, and sailed on to San Francisco.

Before 1890, most immigrants were white Protestants. Hardworking and literate, they scattered widely throughout the country, getting good jobs in the cities and building prosperous farms in the hinterland. Most

Americans welcomed them, and they in turn welcomed the religious toleration, political liberty, and economic opportunity they found in the United States. On the other hand, the immigration of Irish, German, and French-Canadian Catholics, as well as Chinese Buddhists, tested the American commitment to pluralism. Themselves affected by dislocations of industrialization and mobility—and without the traditional moorings of a powerful central government, a state church, or extended kinship systems—millions of Americans were afraid of the Catholic influx. Rumors of papal conspiracies and priestly orgies became common, as did discrimination against Catholics. Chinese immigrants ran into similar fears. Few Americans had any idea of how to incorporate these immigrants into the society.

While the Great Migration was generating cultural controversy, the westward movement was creating disputes involving Indians and Mexicans on the frontier. German, Scandinavian, English, and Scots-Irish farmers were moving into the Ohio Valley, the southeastern forests, and west of the Mississippi. In the Treaty of Paris ending the American Revolution, Britain ceded its land east of the Mississippi River, and in 1803 President Thomas Jefferson added the Louisiana Purchase. Spain sold Florida in 1819. Britain ceded all of Oregon below the forty-ninth parallel in 1846; and after the Mexican War the Treaty of Guadalupe Hidalgo gave Texas, New Mexico, Arizona, California, Nevada, Utah, and part of Colorado and Wyoming to the United States. The American empire now stretched from ocean to ocean. Native Americans pushed to the west and Mexicans whose ancestral homes were in the west had new difficulties. Both peoples faced the pressures of the immigration of tens of thousands of whites, and eventually both would lose their land. Their plight too would test the reality of freedom and equality in American life.

Finally, southern society confronted the natural rights philosophy. During the American Revolution the hypocrisy of fighting for freedom while ignoring slavery was clear, and first in New England and then throughout the North, slavery was attacked. Many southerners began defending it as a positive good that made possible an advanced stage of civilization for part of the population. There was little room for compromise, because the economic and social imperatives of slavery, the need to control a large black population, in order to make use of its involuntary labor, rendered natural rights irrelevant in most planters' minds. During the Missouri debates of 1819 and 1820, regarding the status of slavery in new states, the North and South became sharply divided over the question of slavery, and especially its expansion into the western territories. The Liberty party in 1840 and the Free-Soil party in 1848 campaigned to keep slavery out of the West, while southerners in the Democratic party wanted desperately to see slavery expand. The sectional crisis deepened in the 1850s and then exploded into civil war.

Meanwhile immigration was having significant effects in the northeast. One indication was the clandestine fraternities. In 1849 right-wing Protestants organized the Supreme Order of the Star Spangled Banner, a secret society complete with oaths, signs, and ceremonial garb. Described as Know-Nothings because of their refusal to talk about their activities, they called for immigration restriction, strict naturalization laws, discrimination against Catholics, and exclusion of Chinese. Renaming themselves the American party in 1854, they organized politically and did spectacularly well in areas where Irish Catholic immigrants were settling, taking control of the Massachusetts state government and winning local elections throughout the Northeast. Other shifts in political loyalty occurred. Throughout the nineteenth century, poor immigrants were drawn to the Democratic party—descended from Jefferson's Republican party—because of its cultural diversity and sympathy for working people. But because of the increasing numbers of Irish Catholics in the party during the 1850s, many immigrant Protestants, especially the British and Scandinavians, began looking for a new political vehicle.

They found it when the Republican party was formed in the 1850s. By supporting tariffs, a sound currency, a national bank, and internal improvements, the Republicans won the loyalty of conservative businessmen; by condemning slavery and opposing its expansion into the western territories, they were joined by abolitionists and Free-Soilers; by tacitly supporting stricter naturalization laws to keep new immigrants from voting, they gained the support of anti-Catholic nativists who feared foreigners; and by calling for free homesteads in the West, they won the support of English, Scandinavian, Dutch, and German farmers in the Midwest. The Republican party represented everything the South feared—abolition, free soil, a national bank, protective tariffs, and internal improvements, any or all of which might create an economic alliance between the North and the West. When the Republican candidate, Abraham Lincoln, won the election of 1860, the South panicked and seceded from the Union. The Civil War had begun.

For northerners the Civil War became a crusade against slavery, a reaffirmation of the American commitment to equality and toleration. The Emancipation Proclamation of 1863, the Thirteenth, Fourteenth, and Fifteenth amendments to the Constitution, and the Civil Rights Act of 1866 all extended political rights to black people. Cultural pluralism and the natural rights philosophy were sounding again, this time in a much broader context. Politics and society did not yet reflect those ideals: anti-Catholicism would rise again; native Americans and

Mexican-Americans were losing their land; the Chinese were about to be excluded permanently from the United States; and with the end of Reconstruction in 1876, Afro-Americans were consigned to a social and economic lower class for years to come. Still, American values had survived controversy and the most terrible war the world had seen. They were durable enough to remain a hope if not yet an all-embracing actuality.

Chapter Four

British Protestants and the Great Migration

During the Great Migration, the British Isles sent the largest number of immigrants to the United States; between 1783 and 1924 more than 8 million people emigrated from England, Scotland, Wales, and Ireland. More than 2 million British-Canadians crossed the border into America during the same period. These British Protestants made the most rapid adjustment to American society. Although the number of competing religious groups, the proud disdain for authority, the cult of the individual, and the national self-confidence bewildered many of them, they shared much with Americans.

Immigrants from the British Isles had, after all, peopled colonial America, and their religious values, cultural attitudes, and political institutions had become the ideological foundation of American society. Indeed, their beliefs in decentralized religious authority, individual liberty, hard work, and the dangers of concentrated power all had a place in the American political culture. Beyond that, those early colonists had generated the peculiarly American sense of mission and destiny that shaped United States history.

Anglo-America

By the nineteenth century a number of Anglo-American cultures had emerged out of the colonial migrations from England, Scotland, and northern Ireland. Most visible was the Yankee society of New England, an elitist group of people already proclaiming their special role in the religious, humanitarian, and cultural life of America. Central to the New England ethos was the idea of the chosen people which Puritan settlers had transplanted to America in the 1630s. Convinced of their own election by a transcendent God, they felt called to set an example of pure religion, good government, hard work, and a wholesome society for the rest of the world. This was their divine mission. Even in the eighteenth century, when the more rigid forms of Calvinism were deteriorating, that sense of mission still imbued New England religion.

Repudiating the notion of rigid predestination, the Congregationalist minister Jonathan Edwards set the stage for the Great Awakening in the 1730s; and in the 1740s, after George Whitfield's evangelical tour, the revivalist spirit spread throughout the American colonies. A Second Great Awakening occurred in the early nineteenth century, and these highly emotional religious experiences helped produce a host of nineteenth-century religious movements which emphasized the idea of the chosen people. Joseph Smith and Brigham Young, both born into New England Congregationalist families, led the Mormon Church in the 1830s and 1840s. William Miller, spiritual leader of Seventh Day Adventism, began his ministry in Portland, Maine, in 1840. Mary Baker Eddy, founder of Christian Science, was born to Congregationalist parents in New Hampshire in 1821. And Charles Taze Russell, early leader of the Jehovah's Witnesses, had left the Congregationalist Church in 1868. Although nineteenth-century Yankees were hardly tolerant of these new religions, New England had nevertheless given birth to them.

Yankee culture also initiated the major reform movements of the nineteenth century. William Ellery Channing helped transform Puritanism into Unitarianism, and by preaching the dignity and perfectibility of man, laid the foundation for the reform movements. George Ripley founded Brook Farm and John Humphrey Noyes the Oneida Community to demonstrate the virtues of utopian socialism; William Lloyd Garrison attacked the institution of slavery; Horace Mann started the public school movement in Massachusetts; Dorothea Dix campaigned for improvements in the treatment of the mentally ill. Susan B. Anthony and Elizabeth Cady Stanton led the movement for women's suffrage; Lyman Beecher and Justin Edwards worked tirelessly on behalf of prohibition; and William Ladd established the American Peace Society. In antebellum America, New England Yankees saw themselves as a moral aristocracy dedicated to equality and purity.

They also had a keen sense of their own history. Recalling the Sons of Liberty, the Boston Massacre, the Boston Tea Party, the battles of Lexington, Concord, and Bunker Hill, and the leadership of James Otis,

John Adams, Sam Adams, and John Hancock, the Yankees saw themselves as the cutting edge of the American Revolution, the real founders of the Republic. Groups like the Daughters of the American Revolution nurtured that vision. At the same time, Yankee prosperity justified the Puritan commitment to hard work and temporal success. Yankees put a premium on practicality and efficiency. In the technical ingenuity of men like Eli Whitney, Samuel Slater, and Paul Revere, and in the great commercial talents of the Amorys, Browns, Cabots, Lowells, and Russells, they saw proof of their election as leaders of the American destiny.

With that background of confidence and success, many New England Yankees devoted themselves to intellectual and cultural pursuits. Around an axis reaching from Yale in New Haven to Harvard in Cambridge, American literary culture produced the Transcendentalists Ralph Waldo Emerson, Henry David Thoreau, and Bronson Alcott; historians George Bancroft, Francis Parkman, Henry Adams, and Herbert Baxter Adams; novelists Harriet Beecher Stowe, Nathaniel Hawthorne, Herman Melville, and Henry James; and poets Henry Wadsworth Longfellow, John Greenleaf Whittier, and Emily Dickinson. In New England, Yankees believed, rested the center of American culture.

A completely different Anglo-American culture appeared in the planter aristocracy of the South. Resting on the labor of black slaves and poor whites, the planter class by the nineteenth century had constructed an elaborate collective ego. Deeply concerned about the drift of American development—industrialization, technological change, democratic egalitarianism, and business materialism—they chose to cultivate a different set of values based upon rural, aristocratic gentility. Planter society rested on two myths: that rich whites could trace their ethnic roots back to the "Cavalier" society of old England, and that they were somehow above the mercenary acquisitiveness of northern, Yankee businessmen. In reality they were usually neither patrician nor antibusiness; most of them came from the English and Scots lower and middle classes, and as planters they were businessmen who speculated in slaves, real estate, and commodity futures, seeking profits through commercial agriculture. The truth, of course, is hardly relevant, for these southerners came to believe in aristocratic origins and tradition, and their rhetoric expressed hostility to materialism, progress, cities, and social ambition. They looked down upon Yankee culture as crass and superficial, busy and unstable, hectic and unpredictable; on poor white southerners as a boorish lot of temperamental, uncivilized "trash"; and on black slaves as incompetent children unable to function on their own. Southern "Cavaliers" would consider marrying or mixing with none of these groups, and instead lived in a social world of their own, isolated and convinced of their moral superiority.

Closely related to planter society, though quite distinct from it, was the world of poor southern whites. Imbued with populistic resentments of concentrated wealth and power, they were nevertheless bound to the planter elite by shared convictions of white superiority, of the need for all whites, regardless of class, to maintain a solid front against blacks. Similar sentiments of white solidarity animated the southern middle class. Although Scots-Irish geographic mobility had made for a fluid society in the colonial South, the nineteenth century witnessed a settling down which created powerful localistic values—strong attachments to home and region. As a result of stable residential patterns in the rural and small-town South, extended family ties were more influential there than in other areas of Anglo-America. Finally, these white southerners shared the planter view of a society under siege, surrounded by a powerful and hostile Yankee culture. The abolition movement, the Civil War, and Reconstruction only reinforced that psychological posture during the nineteenth century.

A variant of this culture appeared in the southern Appalachian mountains by the nineteenth century. There, in the mountain hollows, thousands of people lived in isolation from the larger society. They nurtured a sense of individualism and family independence so profound that they could hardly conceive of membership in or loyalty to such corporate organizations as governments and schools. Respect and status revolved around economic and social autonomy. Mountain people were also highly traditionalist in their values; life was difficult and insecure, there was poverty and danger, and people developed a philosophical fatalism about the present and future, feeling little control over the course of their lives. They rarely complained or rebelled; their folk culture looked to the past rather than the future, and they were far removed from material progress and middle-class success.

The Search for a Better Life

Into this Anglo-American environment came the immigrants from England, Scotland, and Wales. The traditional lure of America survived in the British Isles, and glowing letters from other immigrants as well as American advertisements exaggerated the attraction. But unlike the colonial immigrants, these settlers were inspired less by social, political, and religious discontent than by economic motivations. Social and political conditions in Great Britain were better than during the tumultuous years of the seventeenth and eighteenth centuries. Some people, like the Mormon converts, left for religious reasons, but they were heading for the Utah Zion rather than escaping persecution in England;

In this cartoon, entitled "The Lure of American Wages," John Bull, symbolic of Great Britain, tries to restrain people from going to America while Uncle Sam, across the sea, invites them to immigrate. (The Granger Collection)

inspiration, not desperation, drove them to America. Except in Ireland, the religious atmosphere of nineteenth-century Britain was tolerant and calm; the sectarian controversies of the past had yielded to more worldly considerations. And because of the Reform Acts of 1832 and 1867, which had extended the franchise, democratic ideals were emerging. The English, Welsh, and Scots immigrants were not fleeing repression at home but were seeking their fortunes in America.

Nor were most coming to escape poverty. Some of the Welsh workers and Highland Scots farmers were poor, but most British Protestants had decided that opportunities for economic success were too limited at home. Most brought money with them to America; and because taxes, rents, and tithes were heavy in Britain, they expected the return on their capital to be higher in the United States. Writing home in 1818, one English immigrant said:

> I *own* here a far better estate than I *rented* in England, and am already more attached to the soil. . . . We are in a good country, are in no danger of perishing for want of society, and have abundant means of supplying every other want.*

* Quoted in Edith Abbott, *Historical Aspects of the Immigration Problem* (Chicago, 1926), p. 47.

By 1830 Great Britain was the most advanced industrial nation in the world, and perhaps half those immigrants were skilled workers. When the Industrial Revolution reached America, the traditional labor shortage became even more acute. The demand for skilled workers produced high wages, and skilled immigrants usually found work in their own crafts. Unlike most immigrants, whose residence determined occupation, British Protestants settled where their skills could best be employed. Theirs was a lateral, occupational move from one region in Britain to its economic counterpart in the United States. Cornish tin miners, for example, settled in New England not because it was the first place they landed but because hard-rock mining there resembled that at home.

For years textiles were the backbone of British industry. Processing cotton was mechanized by 1850, and huge mills replaced home and workshop production. Britain tried desperately to keep its industrial secrets, but the spread of technology to the United States was inevitable. In the 1790s textile factories appeared in New England, and soon hundreds of mills sprang up throughout the region. Because wages were much higher in America, tens of thousands of English and Scots mill hands, weavers, cloth printers, and spinners immigrated to New England, New York, and Philadelphia. So did woolen workers, carpet weavers, silk operatives, hosiery and linen workers, thread spinners, and lace-curtain workers. An English immigrant weaver wrote home in 1830:

> I hope brother William [and his family] will come all together, for they can get spinning here. I have just begun to work in a broad loom, and I think I shall get on with it. There is hundreds of factories here, both cotton and woollen, and some weavers wanted in the same shop with me. It is a very pleasant country. . . . Meat is very cheap, about two-pence half-penny per pound, and flour.*

By 1900 British textile workers had settled all along the East Coast.

Mining also supplied workers to the United States. British coal and iron ore miners came by the tens of thousands because their skills were in such demand. On both sides of the Atlantic the Industrial Revolution was based on coal because steamships, railroads, blast furnaces, forges, and factories needed energy. Colliers from South Wales poured into the anthracite fields of eastern Pennsylvania; Scots and English miners immigrated to the bituminous fields of western Pennsylvania, Maryland, West Virginia, and Ohio; and thousands of tin, copper, and iron ore miners from Cornwall went to various regions. In 1830 Cornish tin and copper mines were the most productive in the world, but wages were higher in the lead mines of Wisconsin and Colorado, the silver mines in

* Ibid., p. 77.

Nevada and Arizona, the tin mines in California and New Hampshire, the copper mines in Michigan and Utah, and the iron ore mines in Minnesota.

Heavy industry sent thousands more workers to America. As the furnaces and foundries of the United States boomed in the 1800s, demand for metal workers increased enormously; and iron and steel workers from Manchester and Sheffield, tin sheet-metal workers from South Wales, shipbuilders from southern England, machine-tool specialists from Birmingham, and skilled engineers from Yorkshire all immigrated in search of higher wages. Many ended up in the industrial towns of western New York, Pennsylvania, and Ohio.

Though not on the same scale as textiles, mining, and heavy industry, other British industries also contributed workers to America. Potters from Staffordshire moved to East Liverpool, Ohio, and Trenton, New Jersey, the two centers of pottery manufacturing. Skilled construction workers arrived. From the North Wales slate quarries came workers attracted to the slate quarries of eastern Pennsylvania. Scots granite workers moved to the New England granite deposits, and British masons, carpenters, and painters settled throughout the country. Life in America was good for them; they found good jobs and social acceptance.

Thousands of small leaseholders and farm laborers displaced by the rise of large-scale agriculture after the Napoleonic Wars joined the immigration to America. Most had gone into the cities to find factory jobs but had never lost the desire to become farmers again. The possibility of owning land in America was irresistible. Rural life in America came as a shock to them, however. There were often cold winters, hot summers, dust storms, droughts, and too many insects, as well as great distances and desperate loneliness. Nevertheless, they came by the thousands because property ownership made their hardships bearable.

More than seven hundred and fifty thousand British-Canadians immigrated between 1776 and 1900. Approximately ten thousand left Canada after the abortive rebellions of 1837 and 1838, when political radicals demanded popular sovereignty and the end of British rule. Nearly thirty thousand more left in the 1840s, when depression struck the timber and shipbuilding industries. Although thousands of skilled artisans left Canada for work in the factories and mines of America, most of the Canadian immigrants were farmers. When the Great Plains opened up after the Civil War, hundreds of thousands of farmers left Canada to take up land in the Dakotas, Iowa, Minnesota, and Nebraska. So great was the exodus that Canadian officials worried about depopulation, but they could not stop the flow. The border between the two countries was too long, too vague, and too unprotected. British-Canadian immigrants merged with the English Protestant community in the United States.

The English Immigrants

The English immigrants were readily accepted into American society, though the adjustment was not universally easy. Wages were high but so were prices, and many complained about the cost of living. Working conditions were more primitive than in England, and farming was different too. In England the land had long ago been cleared, but in America many of the English immigrants had to spend years clearing virgin land of trees, brush, and stumps. The work was tedious, backbreaking, and discouraging. Other complaints had to do with the loneliness of rural life in America, or the lack of stores, churches, schools, hospitals, banks, roads, and transportation. America was not an unmixed blessing.

But the advantages outweighed the disadvantages. The English were better off than other immigrants because they shared so much with the host society. In 1820 people of English descent were the largest group in the society, and most Americans felt comfortable with the English immigrants. Most of these immigrants were literate, and their command of the language enhanced acculturation. Yankee Americans respected their technical abilities, willingness to work hard, and commitment to success. Moreover, most of them joined Methodist, Baptist, Congregational, and Episcopalian churches. Not surprisingly, their absorption into the larger society was rapid. Language and industrial skills helped them get good jobs and supervisory positions while other immigrants often spent years at the bottom of the occupational ladder. English families were often smaller than those of other groups; and with fewer children to support parents were more likely to save money, enjoy material security, and promote education. Few stereotypes of English indigency ever developed. While often perceiving other immigrants as economic parasites, Americans looked upon the English as economic assets. Economically as well as socially, they moved directly into the mainstream of American life.

Their transition was made even easier by the fact that a transatlantic Anglo-American community existed in the minds of many Americans. People admired England, despite the bitter feelings aroused by the American Revolution and the War of 1812. Its industrial wealth was the envy of other nations and its Parliament a beacon for the oppressed. American liberals admired William Gladstone and the Liberal party, and conservatives held Benjamin Disraeli and the Conservatives in high regard. British literature and British universities were considered superior to their American counterparts; the children of wealthy Americans traveled to England for their educations; and Americans looked to England for models of municipal and industrial reform. In short, the United States functioned in a cultural framework that was largely British, and the English immigrants prospered because of that special relationship.

The English immigrants did not develop the ethnic culture so characteristic of other groups. There seemed no need. They were prosperous and socially accepted. They shared racial, religious, and cultural values with most Americans. British-American newspapers survived for a while, and British-Canadians held annual picnics to celebrate their origins, but these were tepid affairs when compared to those of the Welsh, Scots, Irish, Germans, and Scandinavians. The English settled widely throughout the country and were more evenly distributed than any other group. In the late nineteenth and early twentieth centuries nearly half the English immigrants married within their group, but only one in six of the second generation did. They were already at home with other Americans through their relationships at work and school. Assimilation through intermarriage completed the transition; intermarriage itself with other European Protestants did not immediately destroy ethnicity, but after several generations the vast majority of people of English descent came to define themselves as "Yankees," "Cavaliers," or "Old Americans."

The Welsh Immigrants

The Welsh shared a racial, religious, and national heritage with most Americans, but their language set them apart and led to a brief flowering of ethnic Welsh culture in the United States. Between 1820 and 1900, more than forty thousand people left Wales for America, and another fifty thousand Welsh came from England. Most were searching for good land or good jobs. More than 80 percent settled in Pennsylvania, Ohio, New York, Illinois, and Wisconsin, where they worked in slate quarries, coal mines, lead mines, and iron and steel mills, or took up land as farmers. Hardworking, literate Protestants, they too were readily accepted in America.

Unlike the English, however, the Welsh settled into ethnic enclaves. And wherever they settled, Protestant churches appeared offering services in Welsh. The Welsh Baptist Church, the Welsh Congregational Church, and the Welsh Presbyterian Church were all active, but the Welsh Methodist Church commanded the loyalties of most immigrants. The rise of Methodism had been a significant development in eighteenth-century England. Dissatisfied with Anglican formalism yet uncomfortable with the Calvinist emphasis on human depravity and predestination, John Wesley began preaching a different gospel to English and Welsh workers. He was convinced that neither Anglicanism nor Puritanism was meeting the spiritual needs of the lower classes, so he preached a salvation requiring only personal acceptance of a loving grace which Christ offered to everyone. Mankind was not depraved, everyone could be saved, and people in a state of grace could achieve spiritual perfection in this life. Wesley preached all over England and Wales and generated revivalist atmosphere wherever he went. He also established local societies in which people could discuss the Bible and "bear testimony."

Methodism spread rapidly throughout the working classes of England and Wales just as a series of economic crises were devastating the woolen industry south of Bristol, the industrial villages of Yorkshire, Lancashire, and the Midlands, and the mines of Cornwall and Wales. The evangelical emphasis on "sweet redemption" and disdain for theological disputes, clerical orders, and formal rites appealed to the working classes; Wesleyan societies which invited the participation of working people in church government gave them a stake in society; evangelistic revivalism provided poor people an outlet for the frustrations of toil and poverty; and the Wesleyan emphasis on achieving spiritual perfection inspired the working classes to labor constantly at improving their lives. Methodism conquered Wales and helped prevent social unrest in the British Isles. It was a conservative force that helped to abort the revolutionary pressures growing out of the Industrial Revolution. English and Welsh workers who came to America imbued with a sense of evangelical perfectionism blended well into the revivalistic atmosphere of nineteenth-century Protestant America.

Living together and worshiping in their own churches, the Welsh were a tight community and established other ethnic organizations to preserve Old World values. Founded in 1843, the Welsh Society of America was dedicated to preserving the Welsh language and culture, and the Ancient Britons Benevolent Society and Cambrian Mutual Aid Society assisted incoming immigrants. Throughout the Welsh communities the immigrants established the ubiquitous *Eisteddfod* to promote singing and choral competition as well as literary and cultural activities. A Welsh farmer in Kansas proudly wrote home in 1871:

> [It] is surprising to the Welsh in this country that so many of our nation stay at home rather than come here. I have now moved here to live and can describe the place better. I have not changed my opinion of this wonderful place. We expect to have an *eisteddfod* on 5 August, the subjects for competition being prose, poetry, etc. The choir is practicing for the occasion.*

* Alan Conway, ed., *The Welsh in America* (Minneapolis, 1961), p. 136.

Welsh America enjoyed a separate community spirit in the United States, but acculturation was rapid. With the second generation the Welsh church services began switching to English, and the Welsh language press, led by Y Drych in Milwaukee, gradually lost readers. In 1850 there were 29,868 people claiming Welsh heritage in the United States, and the number grew to 250,000 in 1920 when it began to decline. Although more than 50 percent of first-generation Welsh married within their group, the second and third generation began to move away from their home communities and intermarry with other ethnic groups—usually other white Protestants and more often than not the English. Small in number and generally conservative, they did not threaten American society; indeed, they flowed easily into the Anglo-Protestant mainstream. By the fourth generation Welsh culture was rapidly disappearing.

The Scots Immigrants

Similar forces worked on the Scots immigrants, but because they were divided into three separate peoples, acculturation and assimilation occurred at different rates. In the colonial period the Scots-Irish had far outnumbered other Scots, but between 1830 and 1924 the number of Scots immigrants increased dramatically. During the Great Migration more than seven hundred thousand came from the Lowlands and the Highlands, half before 1900 and half between 1900 and 1924. The Scots-Irish immigration continued as it had in the eighteenth century, with large numbers of the immigrants pouring into the South and West, mingling with the Scots-Irish and English communities, and then disappearing into the larger society.

Over the centuries Scotland was divided into the Lowlands and the Highlands. The Lowlands was south of a line running from Glasgow to Edinburgh and included a strip of land along the entire northeastern coast of the country. Scotland was first settled by Gaelic-speaking Celts from Ireland, but later, when Anglo-Saxons from southern England moved there, the Celts retreated north into the Highlands. By the eighteenth century the Lowlanders were largely English-speaking descendants of Anglo-Saxons while Highlanders were Gaelic-speaking descendants of Irish Celts. Most of the Scots immigrants of the nineteenth century settled in New York, Massachusetts, and Pennsylvania, but there were other concentrations in Ohio, Illinois, Michigan, and California.

Although both Lowlanders and Highlanders adjusted quickly to American life, there were differences in the pace of acculturation. As English-speaking Anglo-Saxon Protestants, the Lowlanders scattered throughout the Northeast, and after a few years it was difficult to locate many Lowland-Scot communities. Next to the English, they were the most readily accepted immigrant group in the United States. The Scots wanted to be accepted. One immigrant complained in 1866 that his brethren tried

> to smooth down the rough Doric of their northern tongue, and to lisp or sniffle out the natural speech with which the Creator has endowed them. They would just as soon have people believe that they had been born on this side of the Atlantic and that their grandfather had signed the Declaration of Independence as that they came direct from Drumclog with the parish minister's certificate that their luckie-daddy was ruling elder for forty years.*

They did organize charitable and literary societies, usually called St. Andrew's clubs, and tried to support a Scots-American press, but neither endeavor attracted more than a few. Scots sports such as curling and golf were transplanted. John Reid, a native of Dunfermline, founded the St. Andrew's Golf Club of New York in 1888, and the Grand National Curling Club introduced that sport to America. To be sure, they were proud to be Scots, and immigrants married Scots more than 40 percent of the time. Their children and grandchildren, however, did not, and by the third generation Lowlanders were disappearing into Anglo-American society.

Assimilation was more retarded for Highlanders. While the Lowlanders shared an Anglo-Saxon heritage with England and America, the Highlanders were descendants of Irish Celts, and many still spoke Gaelic. Nor was there any love between the Highlanders and the English, and some of that antipathy accompanied them to America. Highlands society had revolved for centuries around the power of isolated feudal clans. The clan chieftan was a tribal leader who leased land to blood-relative warriors in return for rent payments and military loyalty. Although the English conquest of Scotland had broken the political power of the clan chieftans by the eighteenth century, the social pull of clan loyalty and family obligation survived. Clan leaders, of course, lost their authority in America, but loyalty to the Highlander family was strong. Highlanders settled among other Highlanders, where Presbyterian churches could be established. They formed clan societies like the Clan Donald Society of America; they joined Caledonian clubs, the Sons of St. George, piper bands, Gaelic clubs, and in 1878 established the Order of Scottish Clans; they played bagpipes, wore kilts, celebrated Halloween and Hogmanay (New Year's Eve), enjoyed curling, and sponsored Highland games athletic contests.

* *Scottish-American Journal*, September 15, 1886.

But like the Welsh they soon filtered into the larger society through relationships at school and work and then intermarriage. Their white skin and Presbyterianism opened the society to them; they learned English and were caught up in the mass education and mass mobility of America; and, particularly after the fourth generation, they married outside the clan and merged into the Anglo-American culture.

Like the Scots-Irish, the Scots made a major contribution to American life. A dualism existed in Scottish culture. On the one hand there was the Calvinist asceticism of early Presbyterianism. The Scots clergyman John Knox, after visiting John Calvin in Geneva, returned to Scotland in 1559 and converted the nation to a belief in an awful, majestic God, the predestined election or damnation of every soul, and the presbyterian form of church government in which power flowed up from the congregation to the hierarchy. Because of English attempts to impose first Catholicism and then Anglicanism on the Scots, Presbyterianism became the national faith of Scotland, almost a test of citizenship. Being Presbyterian and being a Scot were almost synonymous. But equally embedded in the Scots mentality was the metaphysical tradition of the universities of Glasgow and Edinburgh, the spiritual homes of people such as the historian Thomas Carlyle, the economist Adam Smith, and the philosophers James Mill, Francis Hutcheson, and David Hume. Here was an analytical idealism which rejected dogma and tradition. Apparently contradictory, the dualism between religious loyalty and metaphysical intuition created the Presbyterian commitment to equity, individuality, intellectual virility, hard work, and success. The Scots immigrants carried those values to the United States in the nineteenth century and found ready acceptance for them by Anglo-Americans.

On another level Presbyterianism failed to hold the Scots-American community together. The Presbyterian Church was prone to schism because of its commitment to individualism and congregational independence. Since authority flowed from the bottom up, the Scots argued constantly over religion. In the colonial period the Scots-Irish had insisted that the American church was independent of the Church of Scotland, but Lowlanders disagreed. In the nineteenth century the "MacDonaldites" of Canada and Massachusetts claimed to be the true church; Alexander Campbell left the church and started the Disciples of Christ; and John Davie founded the Christian Catholic Apostolic Church in 1896. Constant schism and the fact that Highlanders, Lowlanders, and English settlers attended the Presbyterian Church prevented Presbyterianism from integrating Scots ethnic life.

Of all the immigrants to America the English, Scots, and Welsh made the most complete transition from Old World attitudes to the American value system revolving around competing loyalties to family, church, occupation, and income group. All of them enjoyed the color status conferred on whites and denied to blacks, Indians, Mexicans, and Asians. The English and Lowlanders spoke English, and the Welsh and Highlanders knew it as a second language. They had an Anglo-Saxon concern for fairness, success, and individuality. The English and Lowlanders benefited from the thinking of such men as Herbert Baxter Adams and William Graham Sumner, who were then attributing American success to the Anglo-Saxon heritage. Most of the British immigrants were also skilled workers, who were welcomed by the upper classes. And the immigrants were mostly Protestants; whether it was the Presbyterianism of the Scots, the Methodism of the English and Welsh, or the Anglicanism and Congregationalism of the English, their faiths were not alien to older Americans.

British-Americans went to college in record numbers, dominated membership in such professional groups as the American Bar Association and the American Medical Association, and disproportionately served in state legislatures, Congress, and the federal courts. In 1870 nearly 90 percent of corporate executives were of British descent, a number that would decline only to 65 percent in 1950. There were, to be sure, "swamp" Yankees—poor rural southerners of English descent— and an English blue-collar class of urban workers and miners who did not become rich or well-to-do, but in terms of political influence and occupational status, most British-Americans succeeded in their new homeland.

SUGGESTED READINGS

Amory, Cleveland. *The Proper Bostonians*. New York: 1947.

Anderson, Charles. *White Protestant Americans: From National Origins to Religious Groups*. Englewood Cliffs, N.J.: 1970.

Berthoff, Rowland. *British Immigrants in Industrial America, 1839–1900*. Totowa, N.J.: 1971.

Bushman, Richard. *From Puritan to Yankee: Character and Social Order in Connecticut, 1690–1765*. Cambridge, Mass.: 1967.

Conway, Alan. *The Welsh in America*. Minneapolis, Minn.: 1961.

Davis, Lawrence B. *Immigrants, Baptists, and the Protestant Mind in America*. Urbana, Ill.: 1973.

Dowie, J. Iverne, and Tredway, J. Thomas. *The Immigration of Ideas: Studies in the North Atlantic Community*. Rock Island, Ill.: 1968.

Eighmy, John Lee. *Churches in Cultural Captivity: A History of the Social Attitudes of Southern Baptists*. Knoxville, Tenn.: 1972.

Erickson, Charlotte. *Invisible Immigrants: The Adaptation of English and Scottish Immigrants in the Nineteenth Century.* Coral Gables, Fla.: 1972.

Esslinger, Dean R. *Immigrants and the City: Ethnicity and Mobility in a Nineteenth Century Midwestern Community.* New York: 1971.

Foster, Stephen. *Their Solitary Way: The Puritan Social Ethic in the First Century of Settlement in New England.* New Haven, Conn.: 1971.

Hansen, Marcus Lee. *The Mingling of the Canadian and American Peoples.* New York: 1940.

Hartmann, Edward George. *Americans from Wales.* Boston: 1967.

Hudson, Winthrop. *American Protestantism.* Chicago: 1961.

Huggins, Nathan I. *Protestants Against Poverty: Boston's Charities, 1870–1900.* Westport, Conn.: 1971.

Kelley, Robert. *The Transatlantic Persuasion: The Liberal-Democratic Mind in the Age of Gladstone.* New York: 1969.

Knights, Peter. *The Plain People of Boston.* Boston: 1971.

Lehmann, William C. *Scottish and Scotch-Irish Contributions to Early American Life and Culture.* Port Washington, N.Y.: 1978.

Marty, Martin. *Righteous Empire: The Protestant Experience in America.* New York: 1970.

Rowe, John. *The Hard Rock Men: Cornish Immigrants and the North American Mining Frontier.* New York: 1974.

Sennett, Richard. *Families Against the City: Middle Class Homes of Industrial Chicago, 1872–1890.* Chicago: 1970.

Shepperson, Wilbur S. *Emigration and Disenchantment: Portraits of Englishmen Repatriated from the United States.* Norman, Oklahoma: 1965.

Solomon, Barbara. *Ancestors and Immigrants: A Changing New England Tradition.* Cambridge, Mass.: 1956.

Taylor, A. M. *Expectations Westward: The Mormons and the Emigration of their British Converts in the Nineteenth Century.* Ithaca, N.Y.: 1966.

Thernstrom, Stephen. *Poverty and Progress. Social Mobility in a Nineteenth Century City.* Cambridge, Mass.: 1964.

Tindall, George B. *The Ethnic Southerners.* Baton Rouge, La.: 1975.

Tomisch, John. *A Genteel Endeavor: American Culture and Politics in the Gilded Age.* Stanford, Cal.: 1971.

Weller, Jack E. *Yesterday's People: Life in Contemporary Appalachia.* Lexington, Kentucky: 1965.

Woodward, C. Vann "The Southern Ethic in a Puritan World." *William and Mary Quarterly*, 25 (July 1968), 343–370.

Chapter Five

The Irish Catholics in America

Thousands of years ago Nordic hunters crossed the land marshes of what is now the North Sea, reached England, and from there settled in Ireland. In the sixth century B.C. Celtic tribes swept out of western Europe and became the dominant culture in Brittany, Wales, the Scottish Highlands, and Ireland. British-born St. Patrick brought Christianity from Rome to Ireland in the fifth century A.D. (in legend he also drove all the snakes from the island); Bishop Palladius headed the first Irish bishopric in 431; and Roman Catholicism became a cultural foundation of Irish society. But an accident of geography directed the course of Irish history after 1169, when the Norman supporters of King Henry II of England invaded the island. Though culturally united by Celtic customs, the Gaelic language, and Roman Catholicism, Ireland before the Anglo invasions was politically decentralized into clan societies in which tribal chieftans controlled regional areas. Gaelic Ireland was divided into four general areas: Leinster, Munster, Connaught, and Ulster. The rich soil of Leinster made it especially attractive; and since Leinster also faced England across the Channel, the English settled there in Dublin, Meath, Louth, Westmeath, and Kildare counties. Known as the Pale, the area extended about forty miles inland from the coast, and English influence was pervasive. But it was only a bridgehead, and control of the Pale never implied control of Ireland.

From the Pale the English moved west and southwest into Connaught and Munster, but their control was not as strong there. Treacherous terrain isolated them from the Pale, and, outnumbered by native Irish,

they often married into local families. In 1366 England passed the
Statutes of Kilkenny, which forbade English settlers to adopt Irish
customs, but it was a losing proposition. Gaelic Ireland thrived in the
rural areas, and Anglo-Norman society had its only real foothold in the
larger towns. In Ulster, English influence hardly existed until the seventeenth century, when English landlords and Scots settlers took the land
from the Irish natives.

During the sixteenth century English monarchs extended their authority over Ireland, but beyond the Pale the island remained overwhelmingly Gaelic. After the English Reformation royal officials insisted that the Irish repudiate Catholicism as a test of loyalty. This
cultural imperialism succeeded in the Pale, where thousands of Catho-

lics reluctantly swore allegiance, but in Connaught and Munster the natives refused and in Ulster they resisted violently. What had once been a political struggle now became a religious and ethnic civil war between Anglo-Protestants and Irish Catholics.

Under such pressures Roman Catholicism became indelibly imprinted on Irish culture. It had always been a nationalistic faith, deeply mixed with older Celtic rites. Irish pilgrims walked barefoot up the rocky Croagh Patrick in County Mayo each July to celebrate St. Patrick's vanquishing of the snakes, but in July each year at that same rocky hill the ancient Celts had celebrated Lugnas, a festival in which the sun god Lug promised a bounteous harvest. On the eve of St. Martin's Day, Irish Catholics would kill a sheep or cock, sprinkle blood around their home, and trace out a bloody cross on the forehead of each family member to ward off evil spirits. Halloween was a mystical religious occasion for the Irish, the eve of the Samhain festival on November 1 that marked the end of the growing season and the beginning of the Celtic winter. It was a night of dread and ominous terror, for in the darkness the ghosts and spirits of the dead were thought to return to the real world; indeed, it was a night when the barriers between this world and the next broke down. Masks and costumes, acts of mischief, and jack-o'-lanterns distracted people from the fear of death. On March 17 they celebrated St. Patrick's Day and wore the green shamrock, national flower of Ireland, supposedly used by St. Patrick to explain the Holy Trinity to unbelievers. The three leaves and one stalk of the plant signified the three personages—Father, Son, and Holy Ghost—of the one God.

In Ireland, under centuries of Anglo-Protestant persecution, religion and nationality fused. Indeed, the Gaelic word *Sassenach* meant both "Protestant" and "English." England's attempt to Anglicize Ireland created an ideological dualism in Irish life: a deep, personal reverence for Roman Catholicism and a proud consciousness of Irish nationality. The Irish Catholic clergy were without vested interests or property to protect; like most of their parishioners they were poor, landless, and politically impotent. A siege mentality possessed both priests and peasants, and the Irish identified with the church as the central institution of their lives.

But the more Catholic Ireland became, the more England worried about it. Faced with a rival in Catholic Spain in the sixteenth century, and worried about Catholic Ireland on its western flank, England decided to Anglicize the entire island, not just the Pale. Queen Elizabeth awarded large plantations in Ireland to English landlords, who in turn invited Scots to settle there. The Scots fought ferociously against Catholic guerrillas, and between 1580 and 1690 Catholic ownership of the land declined from 95 to less than 15 percent. In the process the Catholic upper and middle classes were almost destroyed.

In England the fear of Catholicism as well as the new support for natural rights led to the Glorious Revolution; Catholic King James II was exiled to France, and Protestant William of Orange assumed the throne. Immediately after his flight from England, James II turned to Ireland, collected an army of French sympathizers and Irish Catholics, and summoned an anti-Protestant Irish Parliament. But in July 1690 William of Orange invaded Ireland and defeated the Catholic army at the Battle of the Boyne. He then dissolved the Parliament and chased James II back to France. Celebration of that victory, known as Orange Day, became a national holiday for the Anglo-Irish, a time when they chanted:

> To the Glorious, Pious and Immortal Memory of the great and good King William, who freed us from Pope and Popery, Knavery and Slavery, Brass Money and Wooden Shoes, and he who refuses this toast may be damned, crammed, and rammed down the Great Gun of Athlone.*

For Irish Catholics it was a call to battle.

Parliament magnified the crisis in the 1690s by abolishing civil rights for Catholics. Bishops were exiled, monastic orders prohibited, and foreign priests no longer permitted in Ireland. Catholics could not vote, hold public office or government jobs, teach school, own property, or carry weapons. England even prohibited the use of the Gaelic language throughout Ireland. Court proceedings had to be conducted in English; road and shop signs were in English; and school instruction had to be in English. English landlords controlled Ireland, and Catholics were a helpless lower caste. Hating all things Protestant and all things English, the Irish became united, and a strong Irish-Catholic identity emerged. An eighteenth-century Irish revolutionary song, "The Wearing of the Green," symbolized the discontent:

> O Patrick dear! and did you hear the news that's going round?
> The shamrock is by law forbid to grow on Irish ground.
> No more St. Patrick's day we'll keep—his color can't be seen,
> For there's a bloody law agen the wearing of the Green.
>   . . .
> I met with Napper Tandy, and he took me by the hand,
> Saying, "How is old Ireland and how does she stand?"
> She's the most distressful country that ever yet was seen
> They are hanging men and women for the wearing of the green.†

---

* Quoted in Edward M. Levine, *The Irish and Irish Politicians* (Notre Dame, Ind., 1966), p.29.
† Quoted in Andrew M. Greeley, *That Most Distressful Nation: The Taming of the American Irish* (Chicago, 1972), p. xxv.

Savage economic problems also afflicted Ireland and precipitated the migration of 4 million Irish to the United States in the nineteenth century. During the Napoleonic Wars, European wheat production declined and prices rose, so Irish landlords put more land into wheat production and raised the rents of Catholic tenants. But when peace returned and European farming revived, prices collapsed and peasants were hard-pressed to pay the higher rents. With grain prices plummeting, landlords turned most acreage back to pasture in hope of recouping their losses by raising sheep. They evicted Catholic peasants by the thousands, and between 1815 and 1825 more than a hundred thousand of them came to America.

Nor did Ireland escape the enormous population increases that affected the rest of Europe. As a result, more and more people were crowded onto fewer and fewer leaseholds. Perhaps half the Irish lived on the edge of existence, in hovels and lean-tos, subsisting on milk and potatoes. Then came the Great Famine. Potatoes had become the staple because they flourished in poor soil, required little attention, and yielded enough per acre to feed a family. But they were also a risky crop because yield fluctuations could mean life or death for millions. Crop failures occurred in 1817, 1822, and the 1830s, but a fungus destroyed the entire crop in 1845. The blight continued in 1846 and 1847, bringing starvation to nearly a million people. In 1848 one of the largest of the perennial rebel movements, the Young Irelanders, was thoroughly defeated, and the cause of Irish separatism seemed doomed. For starving people evicted from the land that was their only hope of life, the future seemed across the Atlantic in America.

In a number of ways the typical Irish immigrants were a unique people. Most of them had little money and few skills to take to America, and even the more prosperous among them had only enough money to sustain them for a matter of weeks. Few Irish day laborers made the migration, so the movement was confined to small peasant farmers whose only economic skills consisted of primitive methods of raising potatoes and oats. Economic desperation characterized much of Irish life. But despite this poverty, the Irish possessed an ethnic culture which would serve them well in the United States. Theirs was a communal, "chain" migration to America in which whole families uprooted themselves; this transplanting of Irish villages from the Old World to the New made for an ethnic solidarity unknown among most other immigrants.

Immigration from the most Protestant and anglicized regions of Ulster and Leinster was quite limited, so most of the immigrants were Roman Catholics from Munster and Connaught, and their religion would bind them together in America. Because of the English elementary school program, probably half of the immigrants were literate and

This 1851 engraving shows the village priest blessing Irish emigrants who are leaving for America. (The Granger Collection)

most of them spoke English; and because of their political struggles against England, they were conditioned to Anglo politics and direct action. These immigrants heading for the United States were a highly politicized people.

Refugees of Disaster

Between 1820 and 1900 4 million Irish immigrants entered the United States—1,694,838 during the Great Famine years of the 1840s and 1850s. Ireland lost 3 million people to the famine and the famine migration in 1847-1855, and by the end of the century more Irish would be living in the United States than in Ireland. Poverty and the Atlantic trade routes left them along the Eastern Seaboard. Ireland had for years imported Canadian timber, and British shippers completed the round trip profitably by carrying immigrants back to the Maritime Provinces of Canada. Preferring the climate and economic opportunities in New England, they moved when they could to Massachusetts, Rhode Island, and Connecticut. Because Ireland also purchased cotton, wheat, flaxseed, potash, and naval stores from American producers, ships brought other immigrants to New York, Philadelphia, Baltimore, Charleston, and New Orleans.

The Irish were America's first ghetto people, the first to occupy large ethnic enclaves in the cities. Despite an agrarian background, they were ill suited for rural life in America. Farming in Ireland had been a primitive affair based on the potato, nothing like the large-scale, capital-intensive agriculture of the Midwest. After centuries of misery in Ireland, land had come to mean high rents, short leases, and capricious landlords. And in Ireland they had been a gregarious, close-knit people. Ireland was agrarian, to be sure, but far from sparsely populated. In 1830 8 million people were living on 26,000 square miles. There were more than three hundred people per square mile, compared to only around sixty-five in the United States today and around three hundred in India. People lived in sight of each other's houses, visited frequently, and watched their children play together. It was a village existence in even the most rural areas, with Catholic churches within walking distance, priests in every village, and religious holidays frequent. The Irish immigrants preferred cities because crowds meant friends, families, neighbors, and churches.

Urban life was also an emotional defense, security in a strange world. And it was especially important to those who came to the United States knowing little English. The Irish retained Old World loyalties to town, county, village, clan, and nation. Like that of the Germans, Italians, and Russian Jews, theirs was a "chain migration" of kinship and village systems which, under other circumstances, might have divided them into centrifugal subcommunities. But centuries of struggle with English Protestantism had imbued them with an intense sense of ethnic nationality. One immigrant wrote that his nationality was

> perhaps less of love . . . than of hate—less of filial affection to my country than of scornful impatience at the thought I had the misfortune . . . to be born in a country which suffered itself to be oppressed and humiliated by another. . . . And hatred being the thing I chiefly cherished and cultivated . . . I . . . hated . . . the British system . . . *

In many ways American Protestants intensified those feelings. American culture had a distinctly Anglo-Protestant flavor. To be sure, there were no tax-supported Protestant churches in the country by the 1840s, but Yankees controlled wealth and power in the United States. In New England especially, many Americans thought the Irish threatened Anglo-Saxon civilization. Irish immigration coincided with the democratic, antiauthoritarian worship of the common man popular during the era of President Andrew Jackson, and Roman Catholicism seemed contradictory because it gave authoritarian power to the pope. Some Yankees questioned Irish allegiance, doubting that they could become "true Americans" because dual loyalty to a religious monarchy and a liberal democracy seemed impossible.

Also present in most northeastern cities was a small but vocal minority

---

* Quoted in Lawrence McCaffrey, *The Irish Diaspora in America* (Bloomington, Ind.), p.110.

of Anglo-Irish Protestant immigrants, descendants of the English settlers who had colonized Ireland in the sixteenth and seventeenth centuries. Known as Orangemen (after William of Orange's victory over Irish Catholics at the Battle of the Boyne), they were usually Episcopalians and Methodists after settling in America. Militantly anti-Catholic and anti-Democratic, they identified closely with Anglo-American Protestants. The immigrants transplanted their Old World rivalries to America. Conflicts between Anglo-Irish and Irish Catholic volunteer fire companies were frequent in Boston, New York, and Philadelphia, and in 1870 and 1871 ethnic competition erupted into open violence after Irish Protestants paraded through New York City on July 12 celebrating the Battle of the Boyne. Considering it an open affront to their history, Irish Catholics lined the parade route and taunted the marchers until a riot broke out and thirty-three people died.

Anti-Catholicism became a dominant social theme at mid-century. Newspapers, books, and pamphlets ridiculing Catholics became best sellers, and frightened Protestants avidly consumed the most sensational propaganda. *The Awful Disclosures of Maria Monk* (1836)— allegedly the confessions of a former nun, who described depraved priests, licentious nuns, and monastic orgies—was a piece of religious pornography that sold more than three hundred thousand copies before the Civil War. Many Americans were convinced that Irish Catholics were sexually irresponsible alcoholics subject to the dictates of Rome. Occasionally the anti-Catholicism turned violent. On Christmas Day, 1806, mobs in New York City disrupted Catholic religious services, and in August 1834 arsonists set fire to the Ursuline convent in Charlestown, Massachusetts. During the 1840s, when Catholics protested sectarian instruction in public schools and requested tax support for church schools, the parochial school issue caused considerable debate and exploded into the Philadelphia Riots of 1844, when priests and nuns were attacked, homes burned, and Catholic churches vandalized. In 1854 a mob destroyed the Irish ghetto in Lawrence, Massachusetts.

American Protestants also worried about Irish community organizations and the distinct ethnic culture represented in such newspapers as the *Gaelic-American*, the *Irish World*, and the *Irish Nation*. To assist incoming immigrants, the Irish formed the Irish Emigrant Society; and in every eastern city a number of volunteer firemen's groups, militia companies, and benevolent associations served the Irish community. The Irish also made enormous financial sacrifices to build Catholic parishes and parochial schools in their neighborhoods. With their devotion to the liberation of the old country, their religion, and their communities, they defied Anglo-American conformity. Many Americans resented such pride.

Poverty, crime, and unemployment in the Irish ghettos convinced some Americans that the Irish were an illiterate, brutish people incapable of improving themselves. Except for the most menial, low-paying jobs, many Americans preferred not to hire Irish workers at all. As always, much of the social prejudice had economic roots: the newest immigrants would work for the lowest pay, and were seen as a threat by other workers as well as by middle-class businessmen. Newspaper advertisements in New York and Boston during the 1840s and 1850s commonly asked for Protestant workers or stated flatly that "Irish need not apply."

Irish children were mistreated in public schools; but when their parents established parochial schools, some Americans were enraged. The Irish were poor but they could not get good jobs; they were illiterate but Americans did not want them educated in church schools.

For all these reasons large metropolitan areas like Boston, New York, Philadelphia, Cleveland, and Baltimore, as well as smaller cities like Springfield, Massachusetts, and Trenton, New Jersey, developed substantial Irish communities. In 1877 more than 80 percent of Irish workers were personal and domestic servants, porters, street cleaners, chimney sweeps, stevedores, longshoremen, hod carriers, ditch diggers, or highway and railroad builders. They could be found working the lead mines of Illinois; cleaning streets in Boston, New York, and Philadelphia; loading freight in port cities; digging the Erie and Chesapeake and Ohio canals; laying track on the transcontinental railroads; building houses in Chicago; working the rolling mills in Cleveland; breaking up rock quarries in New Hampshire; building ships in the Brooklyn and Philadelphia navy yards; or toiling in the New England textile mills. Some were farmers and businessmen, but most were poor workers in the cities.

From Poverty to Power

Still, the Irish eventually made a good life for themselves in the United States and came to enjoy a standard of living and influence that would have been unthinkable in the Old World. A fighting disposition was part of the Celtic heritage, and centuries of English rule had bred a spirit of resistance. The Irish who made it to America raised their children to have a sense of personal strength and encouraged participation in sports. The Irish game of hurling, a violent sport resembling field hockey, was one avenue for expressing strength and aggression, and Irish children easily made the transition to football in the United States. Because the squalor, disease, and poverty of the early ghettos in America engendered crime, Irish-American fathers taught their sons how to defend themselves. Indeed, being a good fighter was a measure of status in the Irish-American community, and it is no surprise that the first heavyweight boxing champions were Irish.

Occasionally the American Irish struck back at discrimination. During the Civil War the famous Draft Riots were provoked by conscription laws discriminating against poor people by allowing the rich to buy a replacement for $300. Although most of the Irish supported the Union during the war, there was opposition to the draft throughout the North, especially among the New York Irish, some of whom even termed the Civil War a "Protestant Republican war for black slaves." On July 11, 1863, when Republican officials and New York marshals began drawing the names of draftees, that hostility burst into violence. For nearly five days Irish mobs attacked blacks, Republicans, and rich "$300 boys," and set fire to dozens of buildings. More than a hundred people died before United States troops quelled the uprising. Later, in the anthracite coal fields of Pennsylvania, the Irish "Molly Maguires" allegedly killed nine people after being laid off by coal operators in the 1870s.

Such resistance was infrequent, however, and the Irish journey out of poverty was based on the strength of the family, urban politics, hard work, and a powerful sense of group identity. These sustained them in the first dreadful ghetto years. Poor, illiterate, and unaccustomed to urban life, the Irish suffered in the ghettos. Old mansions, stores, and warehouses were often converted into crowded tenements, and many Irish lived in lean-tos and shacks made of tar paper or wooden crates. In some urban areas, raw sewage flowed down the streets, there was a constant battle against rats and lice, and cholera and tuberculosis were common. Most jobs paid poorly, and many of the poor turned to crime and prostitution for surival. Yet the Irish family survived. In Ireland the father was always the head of the family, and he kept his role as the provider and decision maker in America. But mothers were emotionally dominant in the family because they were more often at home to influence and discipline the children and because the Irish believed strongly in the virtues of motherhood. The spirit of the Irish home was moralistic; children were expected to be respectful and obedient to church and family. Given the scarce resources of Irish families, emphasis on family cohesion and mutual cooperation was strong. In Ireland women had not been expected to work outside the home and farm, but in America it was acceptable. Children too could be called on to contribute to family resources. And kinship ties extended all the way through the father's relationships. Although a family's independence was a matter of great pride, people in need could call on paternal relatives for help and were expected to assist others when asked. Family ties were an important asset in coping with the American environment.

The political talents of the Irish also served them well. Arriving during the Jackson era, when property barriers to voting were collapsing, the Irish became a powerful voting bloc. Although they lacked industrial skills, they were equipped with centuries of experience in life-or-death political battles with the English. In Ireland mass and direct action politics had gone on for years; and slowly, between 1820 and 1880, the Irish constructed their famous American political machines, epitomized by Tammany Hall in the New York of the 1880s and the Richard Daley machine in twentieth-century Chicago. Working with ethnic and religious unity through local parishes and saloons, Irish politicians first became street captains, and later district and precinct leaders, aldermen, and state and national legislators. Using police, fire department, sanitation, and public-works jobs as patronage, they attracted the loyalty of voters economically dependent upon the political success of the machine. And by championing the workingman and the need to end poverty, Irish Catholic politicians became very influential in the Democratic party. In New York, Boston, Cleveland, Chicago, Pittsburgh, Baltimore, St. Louis, and New Orleans, Irish political machines were powerful, and power is easily translated into respectability.

Although often graft-ridden, Irish machine politics contradicted laissez-faire individualism by distributing food, fuel, and jobs to poor people in the cities. Skeptical about human nature, concerned with improvement rather than perfection, the Irish became the cornerstone of Democratic politics, which eventually became the New Deal of Franklin D. Roosevelt, the Fair Deal of Harry Truman, the New Frontier of John Kennedy, and the Great Society of Lyndon Johnson.

Through hard work and struggle the Irish soon defied stereotypes that tied them to poor ghettos. Second-generation Irish found skilled jobs in the construction industry and in factories; and although unskilled Irish workers had more difficulty finding skilled and white-collar jobs than Protestant workers, enough succeeded to make the possibility real. A small business and professional elite of grocers, dry goods dealers, real estate brokers, attorneys, physicians, and commission merchants also appeared and became the "lace-curtain" Irish, a socially respectable class in Victorian America. And all classes of Irish-Americans were highly mobile in the nineteenth century. They had an intense drive for property ownership, and they established ethnic savings and loan associations—with such names as Flanagan, Hibernia, Emerald, Erin, Shamrock, and St. Patrick—to help them buy or build homes. They were prudent and thrifty, put their savings into the banks, sent wives and children to work, and finally bought their own homes in more respectable neighborhoods. The ghetto survived, but a constant stream of new immigrants—many of them also Irish—filled the vacancies left by departing Irish workers and businessmen.

The new Irish immigrants were different from the old ones. During the Great Famine nearly half were illiterate; but after England introduced elementary education throughout Ireland, literacy rates increased rapidly. By 1900 more than 85 percent of the Irish immigrants could read and write English, and virtually all could speak it. And although the Irish economy was still retarded, the rural standard of living had improved somewhat since 1850. Death and emigration had reduced the population from 8 to less than 5 million people, the pressure on the land eased, and farms expanded in acreage. Though still poverty-stricken and unskilled technologically, these immigrants were better equipped to succeed in the United States. By 1900 the Irish were scattered throughout urban America.

The Irish succeeded in part because of the strengths they brought with them from the Old World, and they held on to their Old World identity. Throughout the nineteenth century they provided money and weapons to Irish revolutionaries fighting England, and just as frequently tried to use their leverage in the Democratic party to influence American foreign policy against England. Their nostalgia was strong. During the controversy with England over the Oregon territory in 1844–1846, the Irish clamored for war. American Fenians, a group of Irish-Americans dedicated to the liberation of Ireland, invaded Canada in 1866 hoping to weaken English power. Between 1914 and 1917 the Irish would lobby intensely to keep the United States out of World War I, and they would bitterly condemn President Woodrow Wilson when the United States finally joined England against Germany. And as late as the 1970s pacifists in Northern Ireland would be begging Irish-Americans to stop sending money to finance the violence between Catholics and Protestants. Old World politics were powerful ingredients in the New World ethnic nationalism of Irish America.

The Catholic Church solidified Irish-Americans, and when success came they did not desert it. By sheer force of numbers the Irish clergy controlled the Catholic hierarchy in America, and the bond between the Irish clergy and parishioners was very strong. The local parish church, in the center of the community, was surrounded by homes, apartments, taverns, stores, and shops. The priests knew all the families, directed their church activity, and comforted them. For a son to enter the priesthood was a great honor to an Irish-American family. People were active in the parish, attending weekly mass, parochial schools, catechism classes, and frequent confessions; serving as altar boys and abstaining from meat on Fridays and other worldly pleasures during

Lent; and faithfully contributing money for the construction and maintenance of parish institutions. A compact, relatively close community, the parish was the emotional heart of Irish-American life.

Catholicism in Ireland changed during the nineteenth century, and these changes were reflected in Irish Catholic life in the United States. Until the 1840s the Irish church was highly independent, more nationalist than worldly, more a function of Irish needs than of Roman demands. But after the famine the antinationalist Paul Cullen, appointed archbishop of Dublin in 1852, transformed the church by making parish priests loyal to their bishops and the bishops loyal to Rome. Authoritarian and legalistic, Irish Catholicism produced a morally austere people, while the effects of Anglo-Protestantism, especially its evangelical puritanism, were echoed in an emphasis on celibacy, chastity, and sexual morality, and on the evils of masturbation, homosexuality, birth control, and fornication. Thus post-1870 immigrants were more disciplined and morally conservative than their brethren of the famine years. Irish Catholicism would eventually have enormous consequences for the other Catholic immigrants who poured into America during the twentieth century. Militant, authoritarian, and puritanical, the American Catholic Church would have trouble absorbing the richly diverse, nationalistic traditions of eastern Europe. But for the Irish-Americans the new discipline had the virtue of helping to reassure many Americans that the Irish were not an unruly mob.

At the same time, patriotic enthusiasm swept through some American Catholic circles during and after the Civil War. Led by John Ireland, a chaplain in the Union army and then archbishop of St. Paul, Minnesota, Catholic patriotism extolled the virtues of an American democracy blessed by God. Ireland praised freedom of religion, began a modest dialogue with eastern Protestants, and even celebrated the public school system as the backbone of democracy. It became difficult for most Protestants to condemn the Catholic patriots, especially when they praised the American government and applauded the melting pot.

By 1924, when the National Origins Act finally restricted immigration from Ireland, Irish-Americans had become a powerful ethnic minority. Politically, they were—and still are—deeply ensconced in the urban machines of the Democratic party. Some of the most colorful figures in American politics have been Irish Catholics: "Honest" John Kelley, who took over Tammany Hall in the 1870s and 1880s; James Michael Curley, mayor of Boston in the 1920s; John, Robert, and Edward Kennedy; Mike Mansfield, Senate majority leader in the 1960s and 1970s; and even into the late 1970s, with Tip O'Neill, speaker of the House of Representatives; Hugh Carey, governor of New York; and Jerry Brown, governor of California. American Catholicism has seen men like John Ireland,

James Cardinal Gibbons, Richard Cardinal Cushing, James Cardinal McIntyre, and Dennis Cardinal Dougherty; American letters, such men as Eugene O'Neill, James Farrell, and F. Scott Fitzgerald. Paddy Ryan, John L. Sullivan, "Gentleman" Jim Corbett, and Jim Jeffries stand out in boxing; and Michael Kelly, John McGraw, Charles Comiskey, Mickey Cochrane, and John Doyle in baseball. Women too have made their contributions: New York City Police Commissioner Ellen O'Grady, social workers Margaret Gaffney and Mary Frances Clarke, labor organizer Mary Harris Jones, and authors Mary Deasy and Margaret Marchard. These were the Irish Catholics—a separate community with a powerful ethnic nationalism based on their Gaelic heritage, their resistance to the British Empire, their New World experiences, and their Roman Catholicism.

SUGGESTED READINGS

Abramson, Harold J. *Ethnic Diversity in Catholic America*. New York: 1973.

Adams, William F. *Ireland and Irish Emigration to the New World, from 1815 to the Famine*. New Haven, Conn.: 1932.

Alba, Richard D. "Social Assimilation Among American Catholic National Origins Groups." *American Sociological Review*, 41 (December 1976), 1030–1046.

Allswang, John M. *A House for All Peoples: Ethnic Politics in Chicago, 1890–1936*. Lexington, Kentucky: 1971.

Brown, Thomas B. *Irish-American Nationalism, 1870–1900*. Philadelphia: 1966.

Clark, Dennis. *The Irish in Philadelphia*. Philadelphia: 1973.

Cook, Adrian. *The Armies of the Streets: The New York City Draft Riots of 1863*. Lexington, Kentucky: 1974.

Dolan, Jay P. *The Immigrant Church: New York Irish and German Catholics, 1815–1865*. Baltimore: 1975.

Esslinger, Dean R. *Immigrants and the City: Ethnicity and Mobility in a Nineteenth Century Midwestern Community*. New York: 1975.

Farrell, James T. *Studs Lonigan*. New York: 1938.

Feldberg, Michael. *The Philadelphia Riots of 1844: A Study of Ethnic Conflict*. Westport, Conn.: 1975.

Glazer, Nathan, and Moynihan, Daniel P. *Beyond the Melting Pot: The Negroes, Puerto Ricans, Jews, Italians, and Irish of New York City*. Cambridge, Mass.: 1963.

Greeley, Andrew M. *The American Catholic: A Social Portrait*. New York: 1977.

————. *That Most Distressful Nation: The Taming of the American Irish*. Chicago: 1972.

Gutman, Herbert. *Work, Culture, and Society in Industrializing America*. New York: 1976.

Handlin, Oscar. *Boston's Immigrants, 1790–1865: A Study in Acculturation*. Cambridge, Mass.: 1941.

Kennedy, Robert E., Jr. *The Irish: Emigration, Marriage, and Fertility*. Berkeley, Cal.: 1973.

Knights, Peter R. *The Plain People of Boston*. Boston: 1971.

Levine, Edward M. *The Irish and Irish Politicians*. Notre Dame, Ind.: 1966.

MacDonagh, Oliver. "The Irish Famine Emigration to the United States." *Perspectives in American History*, 10 (1976), 357–446.

McCaffrey, Lawrence. *The Irish Diaspora in America*. Bloomington, Ind.: 1976.

Merwick, Donna. *Boston Priests, 1848–1910: A Study of Social and Intellectual Change*. Cambridge, Mass.: 1973.

Niehaus, Earl F. *The Irish in New Orleans, 1800–1860*. Baton Rouge, La.: 1965.

O'Connor, Richard. *The Irish: A Portrait of a People*. New York: 1971.

O'Grady, Joseph P. *How the Irish Became American*. New York: 1973.

Osofsky, Gilbert. "Abolitonists, Irish Immigrants, and the Dilemmas of Romantic Nationalism." *American Historical Review*, 80 (October 1975), 889–912.

Pessen, Edward. *Riches, Class and Power Before the Civil War*. New York: 1973.

Potter, George. *To the Golden Door: The Story of the Irish in Ireland and America*. Boston: 1960.

Quinn, David B. *The Elizabethans and the Irish*. New York: 1966.

Shannon, William V. *The American Irish*. New York: 1963.

Thernstrom, Stephen. *The Other Bostonians: Poverty and Progress in the American Metropolis, 1880–1970*. Cambridge, Mass.: 1973.

Wakin, Edward. *Enter the Irish-American*. New York: 1976.

Warner, Sam Bass. *Streetcar Suburbs: The Process of Growth in Boston, 1870–1900*. Cambridge, Mass.: 1962.

Wittke, Carl. *The Irish in America*. Baton Rouge, La.: 1956.

Chapter Six

Dutch and Deutsch: Immigration from Holland and Germany

From central Europe came a large bloc of immigrants in the nineteenth century. Although the Dutch and Germans shared a Teutonic heritage and similar languages, their national histories had led them in different political and religious directions. But as economic changes swept through central Europe in the 1800s, both the Dutch and German people experienced serious difficulties in supporting themselves, and millions turned to the United States for solutions to their problems.

The Dutch Immigrants

In the seventeenth century the Dutch empire stretched across the globe, from Newfoundland to West Africa to the East Indies, and in 1624 the Dutch West India Company planted a colony in North America. They purchased Manhattan Island from the Indians, named the settlement New Netherland, and extended the colony up the Hudson River in what is now New York State, down the Delaware River in New Jersey and Pennsylvania, and across the East River to Breuckelen (Brooklyn). Within forty years nearly ten thousand people lived in New Netherland.

But New Netherland never attracted enough settlers to remain independent of the surrounding English colonies. By 1664 more than fifty thousand Puritans were in New England and thousands of Anglicans were in Maryland and Virginia. Feudal Dutch patroonships along the

Hudson River discouraged immigrants from coming because few wanted to cross the Atlantic and become serfs in the New World. Conflict with the Indians also deterred settlement. Surrounded by English settlers interested in the port at New Amsterdam (New York City) and the rich estates on the Hudson, the colony was a ripe plum that fell to an English fleet in 1664. New Netherland became New York.

Thousands of Dutch still came to America. Some Dutch Quakers and Mennonites moved to Pennsylvania in the 1680s; Dutch Labadists, members of a utopian sect, settled in Maryland in the 1680s; and thousands of Dutch farmers came in the 1700s. By 1776 there were nearly a hundred thousand people of Dutch descent living in America, and from their original nucleus along the Hudson and Delaware rivers they settled throughout the Hudson Valley, the Mohawk Valley in upstate New York, the Passaic and Hackensack valleys of New Jersey, and in York, Bucks, and Adams counties in Pennsylvania. From there they moved out to western Pennsylvania and Kentucky.

They were a highly visible group in colonial America. Compact rural communities and poor communications kept Dutch culture intact. Virtually every Dutch community had its Dutch Reformed Church and parochial schools offering services and education in the native language. Most of the Dutch Reformed clergy serving in the United States were foreign-born, and they too helped preserve Dutch culture. Old World values were strong. In many parts of New Jersey and upstate New York, the Dutch often absorbed the English, Germans, or French Huguenots settling near them. Describing Bergen County, New Jersey, on the eve of the Revolution, an observer said:

> The men and women . . . spoke Jersey Dutch most of the time and English when they had to, just as many New Yorkers did. They listened to Dutch sermons on Sunday and gave their children Dutch names, and the women and children wore clothes having more than a hint of Holland in their style. Certainly no one could have confused the Dutch country in and around Hackensack with English settlements in middle Jersey or the Pennsylvania German settlements in the neighboring province to the south.*

The Great Migration sent nearly 250,000 Dutch immigrants to America, 128,000 between 1820 and 1900 and another 120,000 between 1900 and 1924. By 1840 King William I controlled the Dutch Reformed Church and closely supervised church meetings and the training of ministers. When "Seceders" protested, the government broke up their meetings, jailed ministers, and arrested parishioners. Whole congregations fled to America. Reverend Albertus van Raalte and fifty followers

---

* Quoted in Gerald F. DeJong, *The Dutch in America* (New York, 1975), p. 55.

settled near Grand Rapids, Michigan, in 1846, and in 1847 Reverend Pieter Zonne moved his congregation to Sheboygan County, Wisconsin, north of Milwaukee. Henry P. Scholte led another group to Iowa in 1847. During the 1840s thousands of Dutch dissenters came to the United States hoping to practice their religion without interference. But even more Dutch immigrants came because economic opportunities at home could not match those of the New World.

They followed the colonial Dutch to New York City and the Hudson Valley, and also settled in Michigan, Illinois, Wisconsin, and Iowa. Farms were small in Michigan, usually forty to eighty acres, and Dutch farmers raised hay, wheat, oats, corn, hogs, cattle, chickens, and truck crops. Adept at draining swamp land, they purchased "poor" land at low prices and were able to accumulate equity in a short period of time. They were also a careful, sober people uninterested in speculation, so they tended to remain in settled areas, not moving on to new farms every few years. The largest Dutch communities developed in Kalamazoo and Grand Rapids, Michigan, and after the Civil War the Dutch pushed out to southwestern Minnesota, the Dakotas, western Iowa, eastern Nebraska, Montana, and Washington because of the availability of cheap land.

Eventually a split developed between the descendants of New Netherland and the immigrants of the Great Migration. More liberal and relaxed after two centuries in America, the old Dutch and the Dutch Reformed Church seemed strange to the new immigrants. Offering Holy Communion to nonmembers, sending children to public schools, permitting members to join secret societies, and giving up Dutch language services, the Dutch Reformed Church seemed to have lost touch with its Calvinist roots. In 1857 some of the new immigrants founded the Christian Reformed Church. Conservative and strict in the Calvinist tradition, it insisted on services in the Dutch language and on Dutch parochial schools, and condemned worldly amusements, the participation of women in church services, membership in secret lodges, and any trace of an ecumenical spirit.

By 1900 there were two Dutch communities in the United States. In the East the descendants of New Netherland were in a state of advanced assimilation. English was their mother tongue; public schools educated their children; the Dutch Reformed Church attracted a wide variety of Protestants; and marriages to English and German Protestants were the rule. Across the whole range of social relationships they were mixing with other Americans.

But in the West the Christian Reformed Dutch held tenaciously to the Old World faith, speaking Dutch, attending church schools from kindergarten through Calvin College in Grand Rapids, and taking Dutch

Immigration to America could be a wrenching and frightening experience, as the faces of these Dutch immigrant children suggest. (Brown Brothers)

spouses more than 80 percent of the time. As Calvinists they were hardworking and ambitious, modest about their abilities, extremely pious, thrifty, and family oriented. Families prayed, read the scriptures, and attended church together. In 1912 Jacob Van der Zee argued that the Dutch immigrant

> prefers to throw in his lot with . . . fellow-countrymen, he conforms to a . . . social order based on Dutch stability . . . his Dutch neighbors have lived and worked within the confines of their settlement . . . nearly all are engaged and interested in the same occupations . . . their whole life is centered about their church. . . . Dutch national traits [are] intensified by constant accessions of fresh blood from the Netherlands . . . the Hollanders of Iowa . . . are still for the most part [an] unassimilated, clannish, though not entirely isolated, mass of foreigners who have necessarily acquired an American veneer from the environment created by the political and social ideas of America.*

They were also proud to be Dutch. The Netherlands had fought hard for its independence over the centuries, and most of the immigrants were literate and knew their Dutch history. In 1899, when the Boer War broke

* Jacob Van der Zee, *The Hollanders of Iowa* (Iowa City, 1912), p. 219.

out in South Africa, Dutch-Americans rallied to the support of the Dutch Afrikaners fighting to remain independent of the British Empire. Representatives of the Boer Republics traveled on speaking engagements throughout the Midwest, receiving money and even volunteers to fight the British.

The Dutch would contribute much to American history, not only in terms of the ambitiousness, cleanliness, and stability of their communities, but in people like presidents Martin Van Buren, Theodore Roosevelt, and Franklin D. Roosevelt; writers Herman Melville and Van Wyck Brooks; the inventor of the famous Norden bomb site during World War II, Carl Norden; and businessmen John Van Heusen and Cornelius Vanderbilt. The flavor of Dutch culture would survive in parts of New York City, in Sayville, Long Island, in Bergen County, New Jersey, and in Grand Rapids and Kalamazoo. The Dutch character was such that Dutch immigrants flowed naturally into an ideological mainstream prepared by English Puritans and Scots-Irish Presbyterians.

The German Immigrants

By 1820 colonial German society was rapidly acculturating in America, breaking out of the Old World patterns which had dominated it earlier. As late as 1790 German was the daily language of immigrant communities, and Germans married Germans nearly 90 percent of the time. But after 1800 church registers were frequently written in English, and regular English services were introduced. In 1820, at the Lutheran Church in Hagerstown, Maryland, 214 people attended the German service and 189 the English service. But by 1840 only 90 were attending the German services while 206 were going to the English meetings. Old-timers objected, but soon it became difficult to find a minister who could preach in both languages. The triumph of English was inevitable. And as English took over, the Lutheran and Reformed churches ceased to be purely German institutions and opened their doors to English, Welsh, Scots, and Scots-Irish settlers. But just as colonial German society seemed to be making the transition from acculturation to assimilation, the Great Migration began. Between 1820 and 1924 more than 5,700,000 people immigrated from Germany, perhaps 500,000 from Austria, 200,000 Germans from Alsace and Lorraine, 120,000 Russian-Germans from the Volga River and Black Sea coast, and more than 270,000 people from Switzerland. German culture revived immediately.

Before the 1880s the German community in the United States consisted primarily of religious dissenters, political refugees, and farmers. In 1805 Father George Rapp established a communist colony at Harmony,

Pennsylvania, just outside Pittsburgh, and in 1815 they moved to New Harmony, Indiana. In 1817 Joseph Baummler led 300 Germans to Zoar, Ohio, where their tiny community survived until 1898. After the Napoleonic Wars, several thousand German Mennonites settled in the Midwest. South of Cedar Rapids, Iowa, Christian Metz established the Amana colonies in 1842 for 800 German pietists; they held property in common, thrived economically, and founded the Amana Refrigeration Company, a successful manufacturer of electrical appliances. These colonies lasted well into the twentieth century.

In the early 1870s Germany—unified at last under Prussian dominance—began the *Kulturkampf*, "culture battle," annulling papal authority and abolishing Catholic orders and Catholic education. Some German Catholics emigrated to America. And after 1874 thousands of German Hutterites, an Anabaptist sect that had fled to Russia to escape persecution, came to the Dakotas, where even today they still speak German.

Political problems had inspired immigration even earlier. The Vienna Revolution of 1848 against the Hapsburg regime brought peasant and burgher uprisings which broke out in the states of Württemberg and Baden, engulfed the Rhineland Province, and spread into Prussia. Most of the radicals demanded popular sovereignty and liberal reform. On May 18, 1848, liberals and radicals convened the Frankfurt Parliament to draft a constitution for a united, democratic Germany, but bitter disagreements between the liberal bourgeoisie and radical intellectuals hurt the assembly. While they argued about the pace of change, whether to have a republic or a limited monarchy, and whether to create a unitary or federal government, the conservatives regained the initiative and suppressed the rebellion. Disappointed and in danger, perhaps five thousand of the rebellious "Forty-Eighters" came to the United States. Democratic, anticlerical, and intensely nationalistic, men like Carl Schurz, Edward Salomon, Jacob Muller, Gottlieb Kellman, Lorenz Brentano, Joseph Weydemeyer, and Heinrich Bornstein stimulated the revival of German ethnicity in America.

None was more illustrious than Carl Schurz. Born in 1829 at Liblar, Germany, he became active in liberal politics at the University of Bonn, and after the revolutions of 1848 he fled to London and then to Wisconsin. He joined the antislavery movement and played a major role in building the Republican party in Wisconsin. Appointed minister to Spain in 1860, he returned in 1862 as a brigadier general in the Union Army and served with distinction at Chancellorsville and Gettysburg. After the Civil War he was a United States Senator from Missouri, a leader of the liberal Republican uprising against President Ulysses S. Grant in 1872, Secretary of the Interior under Rutherford B. Hayes, president of the National Civil Service Reform League, and editor of several newspapers. He was perhaps the most influential German immigrant in American history.

Later in the century the unification of Germany sent more political dissidents to America. King William I of Prussia began universal military conscription in 1861, and to avoid the draft thousands of Prussian youths came to America. The king eventually summoned Otto von Bismarck, a political conservative dedicated to a united, Prussian-dominated Germany, and named him Minister-President of Prussia. Between 1862 and 1870 Bismarck created a North German Federation, annexed Bavaria and Württemberg, and in the Franco-Prussian War acquired most of Alsace and Lorraine. Thousands of Germans emigrated because of boundary instability and wars.

But for every German who immigrated to America for religious or political reasons, a hundred came for economic reasons. Like the rest of Europe, Germany experienced economic changes just when rumors about the United States were attracting interest all over the Continent. Population increases made life difficult for peasant families; American wheat depressed grain prices; periodic potato famines left thousands on the verge of starvation; factories centralized production and destroyed

GERMANY ON THE EVE OF WORLD WAR I

PROVINCES OF GERMANY
1 ANHALT
2 BRUNSWICK
3 HANOVER
4 LIPPE
5 MECKLENBURG-STRELITZ
6 OLDENBURG
7 PALATINATE
8 SCHLESWIG-HOLSTEIN
9 THURINGIAN STATES
10 WALDECK
11 WÜRTTEMBERG

jobs for many artisans; and skilled workers left country villages and crowded into Vienna, Berlin, Hamburg, Breslau, Munich, and Dresden. Food and labor riots erupted in Silesia, Saxony, Ulm, Bohemia, Berlin, and Stuttgart in the 1840s. From all over Germany workers headed for America: coal miners and heavy-metal workers left the Ruhr Valley; textile workers abandoned Saxony, Bavaria, Alsace, Lorraine, and Silesia; and glassworkers, cobblers, construction workers, leather workers, and cabinetmakers set out from Westphalia and Prussia. Describing Bavaria in the 1840s, a French journalist wrote:

> It is a lamentable sight when you are traveling on the Strasburg road, to see the long files of carts that you meet every mile, carrying poor wretches, who are about to cross the Atlantic. . . . There they go slowly along; their miserable tumbrils—drawn by such starved, drooping beasts, that your only wonder is, how can they possibly hope to reach Havre alive—piled with scanty boxes containing their few effects. . . . One might take it for a convoy of wounded, the relics of a battlefield, but for the rows of little white heads peeping from beneath the ragged hood.*

Not everyone was in such desperate circumstances, but for all of them the uprooting was a difficult experience.

Closely related to the Germans were the 270,000 Swiss who immigrated between 1820 and 1924. Although some were French- and Italian-Swiss, most were German-Swiss who, except for Mormons and Quakers, came to the United States for economic reasons. Industrialization was eliminating the jobs of rural craftsmen, and small farmers were leaving the land because they could not support their families on it. Most of the Swiss headed for Ohio, Illinois, Missouri, Wisconsin, New York, and Pennsylvania. After 1890, largely because of the immigration of the Italian-Swiss, California had the largest Swiss colony in the country. The German-Swiss maintained a distinct identity throughout the nineteenth century, but powerful forces linked them to the larger German-American community.

Finally, 120,000 Russian-Germans immigrated. After 1763 the tsars had invited German colonists to settle in Russia, promising them free land, free churches, and military exemptions. By 1860 there were more than 1.7 million Germans living along the Volga River and Black Sea coast, with other colonies in the Ukraine, Bessarabia, and Transcaucasia. In 1871, when the government decided to Russianize the Germans and force them into the Russian army, they headed for the United States. Accustomed to the vast wheat steppes of western Russia, they settled in North Dakota, South Dakota, Kansas, and Nebraska,

---

* Quoted in Richard O' Connor, *The German Americans* (Boston, 1968), p. 100.

bringing with them the hard Turkish red wheat they had planted in the Old World. Clannishly loyal to Lutheran, Reformed, Catholic, or pietistic churches and used to cultural isolation in a strange society, the Russian-Germans settled in more than sixteen hundred colonies across the northern plains and tenaciously resisted assimilation. Well into the 1940s their newspaper *Dakota Freie Presse* circulated throughout the Midwest, and their children married other Russian-Germans.

By the late nineteenth century, then, there was a German belt extending from northern Massachusetts to Maryland, through the Ohio River basin to the Great Lakes, and then on out to the northern plains. New York, Philadelphia, Boston, Charleston, Cleveland, and Chicago had large German communities, and the German immigrants landing in New Orleans sailed up the Mississippi River to Memphis, St. Louis, and Minneapolis, and up the Ohio River to Louisville, Cincinnati, and Pittsburgh. Most settled in Ohio, Illinois, Wisconsin, and Missouri, the great "German triangle" lying between Milwaukee, Cincinnati, and St. Louis. Smaller German communities could be found in virtually every other state, but especially in Minnesota, Iowa, North Dakota, South Dakota, Kansas, Nebraska, Texas, Colorado, California, Oregon, and Washington.

The German Culture

German culture at first revolved around religion, language, and agrarian folkways. The German immigrants were a spiritual-minded people whose faith in an omnipotent God was strong; their churches institutionalized that faith, controlled behavior, and ordered community life in rural areas. This was *Kirchendeutschen* —churches promoting German culture and tradition. Indeed, there was little need for other ethnic organizations because the churches played such a central role in community affairs. Life was hard in rural America, troubled by Indians, the vagaries of nature, and general privation. Making a living consumed most of the immigrants' energies, and whatever time or resources remained went to the churches.

The German immigrants were also united in their conviction that the German language and religion were inextricable, believing that German was the best vehicle for expressing spirituality. Language was the underpinning of German culture in America. When the public school movement began in the nineteenth century, German farmers resented the intrusion of the state into their lives, feeling that the responsibility for educating children rested with parents. They associated value with production, the making of concrete goods, and many looked upon higher learning and the professions as parasitic and wasteful. To them,

Yankee commercialism was rude speculation, making money not from genuine labor but from the gullibility or misfortune of others. Through Lutheran, Reformed, or pietistic church schools, parents made sure their children were not "Anglicized" into a life outside the community. Founded to teach reading, writing, and arithmetic, church schools preserved the German language and taught Biblical truth, safeguarding German faith and culture from the influence of public schools committed to Anglo-American industrial values.

Finally, German culture in the early nineteenth century rested on Old World agrarian folkways, on a belief in ruralism as a way of life, not just as a way of making a living. Less restless than the English and Scots-Irish, the German immigrants had always looked for the best soil, for places where they could establish self-reliant, permanent communities. In general, they were not inclined to purchase virgin land, clear it, and then sell it and move on. They placed great emphasis on having large patriarchal families and their grown children living close to home. Children would usually accept spouses selected for them by their parents. It was common for parents to help young couples acquire farms of their own in the community; and because of the prevailing social stability, money was often lent interest free on the security of a handshake. And as in the colonial period, Germans prefered family-size farms over plantations, intensive subsistence agriculture over commercialism, and free labor over slave labor. Roots, stability, and productivity were the values of rural German communities.

Even their farming methods reflected a conscious cultural style. They did not use slash-and-burn techniques to clear land, nor did they belt trees until they decayed and fell down. Instead, they cut the trees down and removed the stumps and underbrush to make the land fully productive right away. German farmers loved the land and introduced scientific improvements very early: to condition the soil they grew clovers and grasses and rotated crops on a four-year basis; and huge barns and grain feeding kept livestock healthy and strong. They also planted fruit orchards and flower gardens, and they insisted on well-constructed fences, straight furrows, enclosed storage areas for hay and harvested crops, and clean, well-kept yards. They were obsessed with almanacs because they believed successful farming was intimately associated with the behavior of heavenly bodies. To guarantee high yields, they planted grains with the waxing of the moon, beans when the horns of the moon were down, and onions when the horns were up; they picked apples only in the dark to prevent rotting and used cider for vinegar only during the astrological sign of the Lion. Both superstitious and scientific, generally stable and productive, these were the German farmers.

By the middle of the nineteenth century, however, rural folkways began to give way to the more secular interests of the immigrants who came exclusively for economic reasons and settled in dense rural areas or cities. *Kirchendeutschen* gave way to *Vereinsdeutschen*, German societies. New organizations fostering German traditions were formed: singing societies (*Sangerfeste*), militia companies, sharpshooting clubs, fraternal associations (Sons of Hermann, Order of the Harugari, Masons, and Oddfellows), social clubs, literary clubs, mutual aid societies, theaters, beer halls, orchestras, and debating groups. Mid-century Lutheran and Reformed immigrants no longer had their identities inextricably linked with the church. Community life for the German Catholics, of course, still revolved around the parish, but all the German immigrants were acquiring an identity as Germans that transcended older religious visions.

But the existence of a German culture did not preclude the appearance of a number of German subcultures in the United States. Indeed, of all the nineteenth-century immigrants, the German-speaking people were probably the least homogenous. Linguistic, ideological, ethnic, regional, and finally religious differences set them apart from one another as well as from other Americans. Although they spoke German, for example, there were differences of idiom and dialect. For a thousand years each separate German duchy or state had enjoyed its own dialect, and not until the Reformation did some language unity begin to emerge; even then there were dozens of dialects which were idiomatically distinct. The most fundamental difference was between such Low German dialects as Dutch, Flemish, Friesian, and Prussian prevailing from Belgium and the Netherlands through Westphalia and Hanover to Prussia, and the High German dialects of Alsace, Bavaria, Austria, and Switzerland. So while the Germans shared a linguistic heritage, it was by no means a monolithic one.

There were also major regional differences based upon ancient tribal origins and historical development. Swabian tribesmen had originally settled throughout southwest Germany in Alsace, Baden, Wurttemberg, and Switzerland. Bavarian tribesmen migrated to Bavaria, Austria, and Bohemia, and Franconians ended up in Austria. Upper Saxons made their way into Hanover and Brunswick; Lower Saxons into Saxony, Silesia, and Bohemia; and Thuringians into central Germany. Upper Saxons and Borussian Slavs mixed to become Prussians. When the Great Migration from Germany began, the immigrants came from Alsace, Lorraine, Baden, Bavaria, Wurttemberg, Switzerland, Austria, Westphalia, the Palatinate, Hanover, Hesse, Holstein, Schleswig, Saxony, Thuringia, Silesia, Prussia, Pomerania, Posen, Brandenburg, and Brunswick, all of which had been independent kingdoms or duchies with their own political and tribal histories. If the immigrants had been asked their nationality, they would probably have called themselves by their origins in one of the German states, not by the name of Germany, especially before 1871.

In addition to these linguistic, tribal, and regional differences, the German immigrants were distinct from one another in terms of ideology and worldview. The Forty-Eighters, for example, were liberal nationalists, deeply concerned with political philosophies and bitterly anticlerical; they blamed organized religion, Protestant but especially Roman Catholic, for the historic inability of Germany to unite. More devout Germans, of course, resented the Forty-Eighter hostility. On another ideological level, the northern Germans by the mid-nineteenth century had accepted a lifestyle known as *Gesellschaft*, an accommodation to the more formal, anonymous values of an industrial, corporate world, while south Germans still lived in a world of *Gemeinschaft*, of such traditional, preindustrial values as village ruralism, familialism, and personalism. So while north Germans viewed southerners as a hopelessly backward people, the south Germans viewed northerners as stiff and formal, too materialistic and out of touch with life's more important qualities.

But the most profound differences were religious. Ever since the Protestant Reformation, Germany had been the scene of *Kleinstaaterei*, of religious wars and dissension between Protestants, Catholics, and pietists. Between 1830 and 1865 most of the immigrants were Protestants, but after the Civil War more and more Catholics immigrated from southern and southwestern Germany until in the 1880s they constituted half of the incoming Germans. By contrast, most English, Scots, Welsh, and Scandinavian immigrants were Protestants and practically all the Irish were Catholics. Religion and nationality were closely integrated for them. But for the Germans, religious loyalties divided the community and retarded any sense of pan-German ethnicity.

German Protestants all shared certain basic values by linking the secular and the sacred, arguing that worldly institutions like the family, government, and business were ordained by God to promote the heavenly kingdom. The concept of the calling or vocation to serve in the world rather than make a monastic withdrawal imbued the mentality of the German Protestants, as did their belief that mere obedience to church law was not necessarily a measure of genuine spirituality. And virtually all of them believed that Roman Catholicism was evil and corrupt, and that the hand of God had orchestrated the Reformation in the sixteenth century.

But despite some similarities, German Protestantism evolved into a number of subcultures in the United States. German Reformed, Baptists, and Presbyterians, for example, adhered to John Calvin's decree of human depravity and predestination, believing that an omnipotent and inscrutable God determined the salvation of the elect. As long as German remained their mother tongue in America, the German Calvinists maintained a cultural isolation, but as the second and third generations adopted English, they acculturated religiously, closely collaborating with Anglo-American Baptists, Methodists, Congregationalists, and Presbyterians in the work of the Lord.

Perhaps the most visible German subcultures in the United States were those of the communitarian reformers and the Protestant pietists. George Rapp's colony at New Harmony, Indiana, and Joseph Baummler's settlement at Zoar, Ohio, for example, both cultivated an isolationist spirit as a means of creating their experimental, communitarian societies. The pietistic sects rejected all forms of religious authority and emphasized the "inner light" between God and man. Convinced the world was corrupt and sinful, the German pietists—such as the Hutterites in the Dakotas, the Amish in Pennsylvania, members of the Amana colonies in Iowa, or the Mennonites in their scattered settlements—deliberately separated themselves from other people, hoping that in the cultural isolation of tightly-knit communities they could preserve their language and faith. They too emerged as distinct ethnic communities in the United States.

Though less intense than the isolationism of the pietists, the ethnicity of the German Lutherans was strong and revolved around theology and cultural nationalism. They had replaced the authority of the pope with the immutable authority of the Bible and, especially the Missouri Synod Lutherans, believed that the Lutheran Church embodied the only true church on earth. Ecumenical movements were condemned as compromises with heresy, and parochial schools were used to transmit language and the faith to children. Reinforcing their theological isolation was a heightened sense of nationalism, especially among German Lutherans emigrating after 1871. As part of the German unification movement, the Prussian *Kulturkampf*, by repressing German Catholicism, had enabled many to equate Lutheranism with German nationalism, and they brought these feelings with them to the United States.

Finally, there was the separate world of the German Catholics. Many came from southern and southwestern Germany where High German was spoken and where the *Gemeinschaft* world of traditional family and personal values prevailed. That set them apart from northern and northwestern Germans, but religious differences were even more important. Generations of religious wars had created a profound cultural gap between Protestants and Catholics. In the nineteenth century

German Catholicism had enjoyed a spiritual renaissance in which the number of parishes as well as attendance at mass had increased, membership in religious confraternities had multiplied, and pride in Catholic culture had intensified. In the German Catholic parishes of America the renaissance continued.

The German Catholics' love of pageantry and ceremony contrasted with the Irish devotion to ascetic simplicity, and was expressed in elaborate and colorful processions, bands, choirs, orchestras, vocalists, and parades. In addition, the German Catholics enjoyed a number of parish societies. Some, like the Archconfraternity of the Holy Rosary, were devoted to the Virgin Mary or particular saints; others, like St. Raphael's, assisted incoming immigrants. The Jaegers and Henry Henning Guards were military societies originally established during the Know-Nothing era of the 1850s to protect parish property from mobs of nativists. The *Unterstutzung-Verein* were mutual aid societies formed in the parishes to help the sick and the poor, and in 1855 all the German Catholic mutual aid societies in the United States established the Central Verein. By the early twentieth century the Central Verein had become committed to social reform and was providing English language schools, settlement houses, health and life insurance, day care centers, employment agencies, and welfare programs for German Catholics. Like the Calvinists, pietists, and Lutherans, the German Catholics formed a distinct subculture in nineteenth century America.

The Rise of German Ethnic Nationalism

Still, despite all that divided them, the immigrants from Germany were able to acquire a proud ethnic nationalism in the nineteenth and early twentieth centuries. The hostility of Anglo-Americans helped create that ethnicity, but most incoming Germans were not thrust into a completely alien, hostile world. Most of the first German immigrants of the Great Migration settled in the Mohawk Valley of upstate New York, eastern Pennsylvania, or Maryland, where remnants of colonial German society still thrived. And after 1840 most went to the German belt and the German triangle. German-language newspapers, more than a hundred of them, were circulating by 1850; German clubs and societies had been founded; and German churches were available. German workers immigrating later in the century left German cities only to enter German-American communities where German culture flourished. Immigration was traumatic, but most Germans did not experience the total psychological disruption characteristic of culture shock.

Still, nativism helped define their ethnicity, if only because other Americans looked upon them as Germans, not as Prussians, Bavarians, or Swabians. Their exclusiveness and cultural peculiarities worried many Americans, who considered the Germans less frightening than the Irish but far more threatening than the English or Scandinavians. Many Germans were Catholics, and some Americans conjured up sinister German conspiracies to transform America into a papal outpost. Upper-class Whigs considered the Forty-Eighters a revolutionary underground, and others worried about the German attachment to Old World values.

Many cities outlawed German militia companies, gymnasiums, and shooting clubs, while others refused to charter German social and mutual aid societies. The Irish bore the brunt of Know-Nothing venom, but Germans and particularly German Catholics suffered as well. Anti-German disturbances erupted in St. Louis, New Orleans, Philadelphia, Cincinnati, Columbus, and Louisville in the 1850s, and in some cases homes, churches, schools, and businesses were vandalized. This anti-German paranoia would rise again during World War I. All this helped create a sense of unity among German immigrants.

But German-American values were even more important in building an ethnic nationalism. Some German immigrants possessed a keen national pride. Though few in number, the Forty-Eighters profoundly influenced the German masses entering America in the nineteenth century. They worshiped Germany, believing in the superiority of the German people, German education, and German destiny. To promote German patriotism, they transplanted "Turner" organizations to the United States. Founded by Friedrich Jahn in 1811, the Turner groups represented an incipient form of German nationalism, dedicated to patriotism, physical fitness, preparedness, and a free, united Germany. The Forty-Eighters supported the *Turnvereine* ("tournament" or "gymnastic") ideal, and Turner societies developed throughout German America. Even more important, the Forty-Eighters controlled the German-American press before the Civil War and constantly editorialized on the German destiny. During the Franco-Prussian War of 1870 those sentiments escalated into a chauvinistic support for the fatherland. Incoming Germans after 1850 rapidly acquired a sense of German nationalism because the Forty-Eighters—along with their Turner groups and newspapers—bombarded them with news of home and the preached future of a unified Germany. After Bismarck united Germany in the 1870s, more and more immigrants arrived with an awareness of their German nationality.

Language strengthened their sense of being German. A German Lutheran immigrant would have felt uncomfortable worshiping at a Norwegian Lutheran church or with an Anglican congregation, as would a Bavarian Catholic in an Irish parish. Like the colonial Germans, they believed their faith was best expressed in the language of the Old World. The Reverend Anton H. Walburg of Cincinnati decided that a

> foreigner who loses his nationality is in danger of losing his faith and character. When the German immigrant . . . seeks to throw aside his nationality . . . the first word he learns is generally a curse, and . . . like as the Indians . . . [he adopts] the vices rather than the virtues . . .*

In the Old World they had defined themselves only as Reformed, Lutheran, Catholic, or pietist, but in the United States they became German Reformed, German Lutherans, German pietists, or German Catholics. German-language services and German-speaking clergymen, both taken for granted in the Old World, became precious values in the New World, and they helped impose on the immigrants a special sense of being German. Although the transition to English was inevitable, the cultural struggle between the immigrant and native-born generations embedded into both personalities a pervasive sense of the German heritage.

Irish domination of the American church posed a special challenge for German Catholics. In Protestantism, authority was decentralized, and it was relatively simple to establish churches and recruit ministers. Religious initiative usually implied no theological disloyalty. But for Roman Catholics the "keys of the priesthood" rested in a hierarchy. Power flowed from the pope down through archbishops and bishops to parish priests and congregations. Hence in America Irish priests helped strengthen German Catholic ethnicity. Catholic dioceses quickly spread throughout the German triangle as hundreds of thousands of German Catholics settled in towns and cities where other German Catholics already lived. John Henni became the unofficial leader of German Catholicism when he became bishop of Milwaukee in 1844. After becoming archbishop of the German triangle, he insisted on having only German-speaking priests in the archdiocese, a policy that enraged the Irish clergy. In 1891 Cardinal Gibbons of Baltimore, an Irishman, preached:

> Woe to him who would breed dissention among the leaders of Israel by introducing the spirit of nationalism into the camps of the Lord! Brothers we are, whatever may be our nationality, and brothers we shall remain. . . . Let us glory in the title of American citizen. We owe all our allegiance to one country, and that country is America.†

---

* Quoted in La Vern J. Rippley, *The German Americans* (New York, 1976), p. 111.
† Ibid., p. 113.

Ethnic parishes were critically important to the German Catholics; for although these German immigrants came from diverse regional, class, and occupational backgrounds, they shared language and religion. The refrain "language saves the faith" became the watchword of German Catholics in the United States. English-speaking Catholic parishes were as dangerous to these immigrants as any of the American Protestant churches, because loss of the language implied loss of the faith. German Catholics did join some ethnic clubs and societies although the church specifically warned them to avoid contact with the fraternal lodges and the Turner groups, but the parish was the center of their social and spiritual lives, and its schools and societies protected them from the larger Protestant culture.

German Catholics thus established many ethnic parishes. Holy Trinity Parish, St. Peter's Parish, and St. Alphonsus Parish were serving German Catholics in Philadelphia by 1853, and in northern Ohio there were St. Stephen's and St. Vincent de Paul Parishes in Cleveland, St. Bernard Parish in Akron, and St. Joseph Parish in Lorain. Many Irish priests argued that language was irrelevant in a "world church." German Catholics claimed that the church hierarchy ought to reflect the nationality of parish members. The Irish then argued that although they had lost the use of the Gaelic language, it had not retarded their commitment to the Kingdom of God. Eventually the struggle went all the way to Rome, and the Irish retained control of the church hierarchy in the United States. Nonetheless, the Germans secured a powerful foothold. By 1910 there were more than two thousand parishes using German-language services, more than twenty-six hundred German-speaking priests, and twenty dioceses with more than fifty German-speaking priests each; and more than 95 percent of German Catholic parishes had parochial schools where German was taught. The language controversy played a major role in making the Catholic immigrants conscious of their German origins.

The language issue continued to agitate German Protestants and Catholics; by the 1880s and 1890s, as more and more German children attended public schools, states in the German triangle passed laws permitting academic subjects to be taught in German wherever there were heavy concentrations of German-Americans. After the unification of Germany in the 1870s and years of an increasing sense of ethnicity in the United States, the German-American community was proud of its origins, and the use of German in public schools no longer had only religious motives but was intended to preserve the whole range of German culture. Immigrants and their children were more aware of being German than they had ever been before emigrating.

This is not to say, of course, that German America was monolithically united. Old distinctions died slowly. The ethnocentric pride of being Prussian still survived in 1900; condescension of northern Germans to southern Germans persisted; and the anticlericalism of the Forty-Eighters had alienated them from German Catholics. Nor had the Swiss or Volga Germans melted into the larger German-American community. Still, they were more of an ethnic community after coming to the United States than before. Immigration was so large and so continuous, feeding hundreds of thousands of new immigrants into the German triangle, that it constantly reinforced German culture. The immigration of nearly one million Germans after 1945 would continue to inject new life into German-American culture. In Milwaukee, Cincinnati, St. Louis, or along East Eighty-sixth Street in New York City, as well as in places like Omaha, Nebraska, and Fredericksburg, Texas, one would be able to hear German spoken, purchase a newspaper and books in German, eat at a Hindenburg or Hofbrau cafe, or attend a Steuben parade, a Sangerfest, or a bock beer festival.

From Germans to German-Americans

The emergence of ethnicity and ethnic nationalism was a step toward assimilation, for as they transcended the parochial loyalties of the Old World the Germans' sense of interrelationships expanded considerably. A German melting pot operated in America. Lutherans from the Rhineland married Lutherans from Bavaria, or Catholics from Silesia married Catholics from Westphalia. The children and grandchildren of these mixed marriages saw themselves as German Lutherans or German Catholics, losing in one or two generations the old vision of being Bavarian or Prussian or Silesian. Russian-Germans, Swiss-Germans, Alsatians, and Germans frequently intermarried, and their German-speaking children melted into the larger German-American community. It brought Germans one step closer to a sense of an American national identity.

Because of the fluidity of the social structure, geographical mobility, and toleration of religious diversity in the United States, as well as the economic success of German-Americans, the immigrants could not help gradually becoming part of the larger society. With the arrival of each new generation the sense of being American became more pronounced. By 1900 the Prussian immigrant of 1880 and his children still felt intensely German, but descendants of colonial Germans who had emigrated out of western Maryland in 1790 possessed much weaker loyalties to German culture. Those same forces would work on the nineteenth-century immigrants as well.

Still, Germans remained loyal to one another. Among people of German descent living in Wisconsin in 1908, nearly 80 percent were marrying Germans, and the same was true for Nebraska Germans and Texas Germans. Assimilation and even acculturation remained retarded during the nineteenth century. Even then, however, subtle changes were occurring which would prepare the descendants of these immigrants for assimilation in the twentieth century. Just as the first generation acquired an ethnic nationalism, succeeding generations developed new role definitions based on residence, religion, politics, occupation, and income which would compete with nationality. By 1900 most German-Americans were living in cities. At first they congregated in ghettos, but they moved to the suburbs as soon as income permitted. New immigrants then replaced them in their downtown ghettos of Philadelphia or St. Louis or New York. In the suburbs upwardly mobile Germans lived near other Germans but were also surrounded by people of English, Irish, Welsh, Scots, or Scandinavian background. Their sense of community among suburban Germans broadened to include middle-class residents of their neighborhoods. Complete assimilation was still not common, for in most of those areas the Germans married among themselves more than 60 percent of the time. But acculturation was certainly underway.

When German Lutherans married Scandinavian Lutherans, their children—or at least their grandchildren or great-grandchildren—often reverted to an Old World tradition, considering themselves simply Lutherans again or perhaps white Lutherans. Political loyalties in the charged atmosphere of the nineteenth century were also important, and German-Americans, whether Republicans or Democrats, often identified themselves with a party. Occupational patterns were important too. A fourth-generation machine-tool specialist from Milwaukee would look upon his membership in the American Federation of Labor as an important part of his identity, perhaps as important as the fact that his great-grandfather had emigrated from the Rhineland in 1820. German culture was certainly intact in 1900, but the stage was set for important changes in the twentieth century.

The size of the German immigration and their economic success gave German-Americans a special place in United States history. In science the German luminaries include Charles Steinmetz, inventor of electric generators; and George Westinghouse, inventor of railroad air brakes. In big business John Jacob Astor controlled the fur trade in the early nineteenth century; Frederick Weyerhaeuser became the famous timber magnate; John D. Rockefeller founded the Standard Oil Company; Henry Villard was a famous financier; and Adolph Busch and

Adolph Coors were beer magnates. German-Americans have become influential politicians, from socialists like Eugene V. Debs, founder of the Socialist party; to liberals like Carl Schurz, John Peter Altgeld, governor of Illinois in the 1890s, and New York Senator Robert Wagner; to conservatives like former Senator Everett Dirksen of Illinois and anarchists like Johann Most. In virtually every area of human endeavor German-Americans have made important contributions. In other fields the list includes baseball players Honus Wagner, Babe Ruth, and Lou Gehrig; journalists Walter Lippmann and H.L. Mencken; author Clara Berens; cartoonist Thomas Nast; philosophers Paul Tillich, Eric Hoffer, and Reinhold and Richard Niebuhr; opera star Ernestine Rossler; entertainers Jack Parr, Lawrence Welk, Rod Steiger, and Oscar Hammerstein; and scholars Hans Rosenberg, Felix Gilbert, and Hajo Holborn.

SUGGESTED READINGS

Arndt, Karl J. R., and Olson, May E. *The German Language Press of the Americas, 1732–1968*. Pullach, Germany: 1973.

Billigmeier, Robert. *Americans from Germany: A Study in Cultural Diversity*. Belmont, Cal.: 1974.

Boxer, Charles R. *The Dutch Seaborne Empire*. New York: 1965.

Child, Clifton J. *The German Americans in Politics, 1914–1917*. Madison, Wisconsin: 1939.

Cole, Cyrenus. *I Remember, I Remember*. Iowa City, Iowa: 1936.

Colman, Barry. *The Catholic Church and German Americans*. Milwaukee, Wisconsin: 1953.

Condon, Thomas J. *New York Beginnings: The Commercial Origins of New Netherland*. New York: 1968.

Conzen, Kathleen. *Immigrant Milwaukee, 1836–1860*. Cambridge, Mass.: 1976.

Cunz, Dieter. *The Maryland Germans*. Princeton, N.J.: 1948.

DeJong, Gerald F. *The Dutch in America, 1609–1974*. New York: 1975.

Ellis, David M. *Landlords and Farmers in the Hudson-Mohawk Region, 1790–1850*. New York: 1967.

Faust, Albert. *The German Element in the United States*. New York: 1927.

Fleming, Donald, and Bailyn, Bernard, eds. *The Intellectual Migration, Europe and America, 1930–1960*. Cambridge, Mass.: 1969.

Frye, Alton. *Nazi Germany and the American Hemisphere, 1933–1941*. New Haven, Conn.: 1967.

Gilbert, Glenn, ed. *The German Language in America*. Austin, Texas: 1971.

Gleason, Philip. *The Conservative Reformers: German-American Catholics and the Social Order*. Notre Dame, Ind.: 1968.

Graebner, Alan. *Uncertain Saints: The Laity in the Lutheran Church–Missouri Synod, 1900–1970.* Westport, Conn.: 1975.

Hawgood, John A. *The Tragedy of German-America.* New York: 1970.

Hostetler, John. *Hutterite Society.* Baltimore: 1974.

Hyma, Albert. *Albertus C. Van Raalte and His Dutch Settlements in the United States.* Grand Rapids, Mich.: 1947.

Johnson, Hildegard. "Intermarriages Between German Pioneers and Other Nationalities in Minnesota in 1860 and 1870." *American Journal of Sociology,* 51 (January 1946), 299–304.

Johnston, William M. *The Austrian Mind: An Intellectual and Social History 1848–1938.* Berkeley, Cal.: 1972.

Jordan, Terry G. *German Seed in Texas Soil: Immigrant Farmers in Nineteenth-Century Texas.* Austin, Texas: 1966.

Kent, Donald P. *The Refugee Intellectual: The Americanization of the Immigrants of 1933–1941.* New York: 1953.

Korman, Gerd. *Industrialization, Immigrants, and Americanizers: The View from Milwaukee, 1866–1921.* Madison, Wisconsin: 1967.

Kromminga, D. H. *The Christian Reformed Tradition.* Grand Rapids, Mich.: 1943.

Lucas, Henry S. *Netherlands in America: Dutch Immigration to the United States and Canada, 1789–1950.* Ann Arbor, Mich.: 1955.

Luebke, Frederick C. *Bonds of Loyalty: German Americans and World War I.* Dekalb, Ill.: 1974.

———. *Immigrants and Politics: The Germans of Nebraska, 1880–1900.* Lincoln, Neb.: 1969.

Mulder, Arnold. *Americans from Holland.* Philadelphia: 1947.

Nelson, E. Clifford. *Lutheranism in North America, 1914–1970.* Minneapolis: 1972.

O'Connor, Richard. *The German-Americans.* New York: 1968.

O'Grady, Joseph P. *The Immigrants' Influence on Wilson's Peace Policies.* Lexington, Kentucky: 1967.

Peters, Victor. *All Things Common: The Hutterian Way of Life.* Minneapolis: 1965.

Raesly, Ellis. *Portrait of New Netherland.* New York: 1945.

Rothan, Emmet. *The German Catholic Immigrant in the United States, 1830–1860.* Washington, D.C.: 1946.

Sallet, Richard. *The Russian-German Settlements in the United States.* Fargo, N.D.: 1974.

Schelburt, Leo, ed. *New Glarus, 1845–1970: The Making of a Swiss American Town.* Glarus, Switzerland: 1970.

Singmaster, Elsie. *The Magic Mirror.* New York: 1934.

Walker, Mack. *Germany and the Emigration, 1816–1885.* Cambridge, Mass.: 1964.

Wittke, Carl. *The German Language Press in America.* Lexington, Kentucky: 1957.

———. *Refugees of Revolution: The German Forty-Eighters in America.* Philadelphia: 1952.

Wood, Ralph, ed. *The Pennsylvania Germans*. Princeton, N.J.: 1942.
Wust, Klaus. *The Virginia Germans*. Charlottesville, Virginia: 1969.
Zucker, A. E., ed. *The Forty-Eighters: Political Refugees of the German Revolution of 1848*. New York: 1950.
Zwaanstra, Henry. *Reformed Thought in a New World*. Kampen, New Netherlands: 1973.

Chapter Seven

The Scandinavian Presence in America

Next to the British and the Germans, the Scandinavians were the largest group of "old immigrants" coming to the United States. Between 1820 and 1924 more than 750,000 Norwegians came to America, 580,000 of them after 1880. The Swedish migration was larger: more than 1.2 million Swedes settled in America. Perhaps 320,000 Danes immigrated, as did 300,000 Finns. Together they developed the upper Mississippi Valley and made significant contributions to American culture.

There were important differences among the Scandinavians in terms of culture, language, and history, but in a number of ways they had a similar perspective on life, one born of circumstance as well as history. After centuries of scraping a living out of rocky soil in a cold climate, they possessed a stoicism about life and determination to hold out against its capriciousness. Theirs was a bittersweet attachment to their homeland. If stubborn is too harsh a word, the Scandinavians were dogged and tenacious, somewhat inflexible on moral questions and incredibly persevering on economic ones. Central to the Scandinavian character was a profound sense of honor. Above all else Scandinavians respected a contract or promise as a covenant and felt morally bound, not because of guilt but because of a highly developed conscience, to fulfill personal obligations. Honesty and reliability were the measure of personal worth, and this showed in Scandinavian attitudes toward work, dependability, thoroughness, and efficiency. Anything less than working at the peak of one's ability, and finishing a job satisfactorily and on time, brought dishonor. Thus the Scandinavians became some of the most reliable workers in America. The Scandinavians loved freedom, thrilled to the libertarian stories of ancient Viking warriors, and constantly preached the superiority of democracy over aristocracy. In America they would be most impressed with the lack of class distinctions.

The Scandinavians also tended to be a private people, careful about expressing their feelings, almost introverted and even morose in their dealings with others. Self-control was expected of men and women. For the Swedes, Danes, Norwegians, and Finns it was more important to be trusted than to be loved. Because they placed such value on dependability, emotional control, and predictability in personal behavior, they were also a conservative people deeply concerned with preserving traditional folkways. Out of all this came their vision of loyalty and trust, a clannishness based not so much on need as on fidelity.

The Scandinavian presence in America reaches back to Leif Ericson and the Vikings who explored "Vinland" in the eleventh century. In 1638 the Swedish West India Company placed five hundred Swedes and Finns on the banks of the Delaware River. Swedish Lutheran churches, Swedish-born ministers, and parochial schools tried to preserve tradition in New Sweden; but the colony was sparsely populated, new immigrants were too few, and the surrounding non-Swedish population was too large. New Netherland took over the colony in 1655; and when England conquered New Netherland in 1664, the Swedes and Finns lost their independence. On the eve of the Revolution there were nearly twenty thousand Swedes in America; but because they were vastly outnumbered by other Protestants, they were already learning English as their primary language, intermarrying widely into the general population, and disappearing as a self-conscious ethnic group.

Scandinavians and the Lutheran Church

Scandinavian culture revived with the Great Migration. During the first half of the nineteenth century, religious unrest swept through Scandinavia and inspired thousands of people to come to the United States. Since the Protestant Reformation Lutheranism had been the national faith in Norway, Sweden, Denmark, and Finland; and the Scandinavians were a profoundly religious people with strong pietistic inclinations. Family prayer, Bible and sermon reading, and hymn singing were as much the routine of the home as working, eating, and sleeping; and attendance at church provided a respite from the constant toil of farm life. In towns and villages throughout Scandinavia the Lutheran church was the largest, most prominent building; people gathered there for socials and services, to visit and gossip with friends and relatives as well as to commune with heaven. Children were taught obedience and fear of God, and parental admonitions to hold to their religious training helped build a sense of reverent respect for the church. When children were baptized on the first warm Sunday of spring, the whole community gathered in anticipation; similar feelings prevailed on Confirmation Sunday, when children renewed their baptismal covenants and took Holy Communion. In the church cemetery rested the bodies of family ancestors; some of the gravestones reached back six centuries. Religion and the church served as the psychological center of Scandinavian life in the nineteenth century.

Martin Luther had emphasized the belief that man's relationship with God was a personal responsibility and that salvation depended on a willingness to accept heavenly grace. Bureaucracies, ordinances, and religious authorities were all subordinated to that overwhelming personal responsibility. So the Scandinavians had faith in private judgments and a conviction that all people were equal before God. Consequently they felt no guilt in questioning a minister's decisions or even in debating the theological merits of confession, infant baptism, determinism, and freedom of choice. Characteristic of the Protestant spirit, the church as an institution of authority was less important than its role in bringing people closer to God.

But after three centuries state Lutheranism seemed to contradict the pietistic inclinations of Scandinavian spirituality. To many people the church seemed formalistic and conservative, more worried about protecting its position in the society than in truly building the kingdom of God. Local churches appeared too willing to acquiesce in the wishes of the wealthy and not concerned enough about the lives of humble people. Restlessness swept through the church. Quaker congregations began to grow and Mormon missionaries began having some success, especially in Denmark and Norway. But even more influential were the pietistic reform movements which appeared in the early nineteenth century. In Norway Hans Nielsen Hauge initiated a pietistic movement to purify the church of its formalistic overtones and bring it into the reach of common farming and working people, and Eric Janssen started a similar movement in the Swedish Lutheran Church. N. F. S. Grundtvig began the pietistic reform of the Danish Lutheran Church, and Lars L. Lastadius did the same in Finland. In each country tens of thousands of people were caught up in the movement to make religion more personal. The state churches felt threatened and began to harass the new converts.

In 1825 fifty Haugenists sailed in the ship *Restauration* from

Stavanger, Norway, and settled near Rochester, New York. After being tried and convicted of heresy, Eric Janssen led some of his followers to Bishop Hill, Michigan, in 1846. One Janssenist wrote home in 1847:

> And from this it follows that the light God has brought forth through Eric Janssen cannot be dimmed . . . we have opportunity here to edify each other in the most sacred faith . . . this country's laws are different from those of our fatherland. We are protected here by both the secular law and the secular power, and thus have the rights of citizenship which a true Christian could not enjoy in our fatherland.*

Thousands of other dissenters fled Scandinavia in the 1840s and 1850s to trade the oppressive atmosphere of state Lutheranism for the freer environment of the United States.

Immigration for Economic Gain

After the Civil War, however, most people immigrated for economic reasons. The Scandinavian soil was either too moist or too rocky; farmers were perpetually draining the land or removing the stones. The growing season was short, the winters bitterly cold and dark, and less than one acre in ten was arable. As the population grew and land became more difficult to acquire, many people wearied of life in rural mud homes, subsisting on potatoes and some meat in good times and rye bark or moss bread in bad times, and paying heavy mortgages. Later in the century, as American wheat, Canadian timber, and English and American manufactured goods flooded Scandinavian markets, and as the world shifted to steam-driven ships, Scandinavian peasants, lumberjacks, and shipbuilders in search of work moved to Christiania, Stockholm, Copenhagen, and Helsinki, and some then went on to America. Finland was not integrated into the Atlantic economy until the 1880s, but Finns began to emigrate then too. Finally, the Industrial Revolution, which reached Scandinavia in the 1870s, upset traditional systems of production and cut thousands of artisans loose from their moorings.

As steamship companies, railroads, and other immigrants littered Scandinavia with propaganda about America, the Great Migration began. When one emigrant returned home for a visit a Norwegian remarked:

---

*H. Arnold Barton, ed., *Letters from the Promised Land: Swedes in America, 1840–1914* (Minneapolis, 1973), pp. 40–41.

Whatever may have been the results of his visit . . . personally, they were of far-reaching importance to the emigration movement in western Norway. From near and far . . . people came . . . to talk with this experienced . . . man about life in New York or Illinois. . . . The "America fever" contracted in conference with Slogvig . . . was hard to shake off . . . when he prepared to go back to the United States in 1836 a large party was ready to go with him.*

Most of the Scandinavians were not destitute; but when the immigration fever caught hold of them, they became determined to find in America the security that was disappearing in Europe.

Until the 1880s most of the Scandinavian immigrants were farmers who settled in Michigan, Wisconsin, Illinois, Iowa, Minnesota, and the Dakotas. They carved out new lives on the great wheat fields of the northern prairies and forests where icy winters reminded them of home. Southern Wisconsin and northern Illinois contained more than 70 percent of the Norwegians in 1860, and from there they pressed into Minnesota, Iowa, and the Dakotas after the Civil War. During those first years they lived in sod houses or crude lean-tos, and braved blizzards, dust storms, humid summers, and locusts, but the rough shelters soon gave way to log cabins and then to more substantial wood-frame homes. One immigrant from Sweden warned that an immigrant would

have to suffer much in the beginning . . . and sacrifice much of what he is accustomed to in Europe. Without work, often with work that is hard and painful, he cannot hope to achieve success. I caution against all exaggerated hopes and golden air castles; cold reality will otherwise lame your arm and crush your courage; both must be fresh and alive . . . we do not regret our undertaking. We are living a free and independent life in one of the most beautiful valleys the world can offer . . .†

After 1880, when the best land was taken and most immigrants were workers, the Scandinavians increasingly settled in the cities. Large Scandinavian colonies appeared in New York, Buffalo, Cleveland, Chicago, Duluth, Minneapolis, Des Moines, and in dozens of smaller cities in the North. Along the Great Lakes Norwegian sailors were in great demand because of their maritime skills. Swedish painters, masons, machinists, carpenters, miners, and iron and steel workers filled the waiting industrial jobs, and next to the British they supplied more skilled workers to the American economy than any other immigrant

---

* Andreas Ueland, *Recollections of an Immigrant* (New York, 1929), p. 137.
† Barton, *Letters from the Promised Land*, p. 24.

This 1851 wood engraving depicts a party of Swedish immigrants heading west. (The Granger Collection)

group. Because of their unusually high educational level, the Danes secured white-collar positions as clerks and sales personnel. The Finns had few industrial skills and took the hardest jobs as miners, lumberjacks, stevedores, and laborers clearing farms. The largest Finnish settlement developed around the huge copper mines in Hancock, Michigan, and other Finns worked in the iron mountains of the Mesabi range in Minnesota and in the western gold, silver, and coal mines. In the Great Lakes port cities they loaded freight, and large Finnish settlements appeared in the New England mill towns, especially Worcester and Fitchburg, Massachusetts. By 1900 the Scandinavian community in the United States had both an urban and rural base.

Like so many other immigrants, the Scandinavians reconstructed Old World values in the New World setting. The rural pioneers arriving in the Midwest during the 1840s and 1850s were awed by the availability and fertility of land. In Scandinavia a farm of six acres had been a respectable holding, but in America the immigrants often acquired eighty to several hundred acres. Through pride, hard work, thrift, and fear of debt, they increased the values of their farms instead of trying to increase their size. Scandinavian farmers loved the land and believed that rural life preserved ethical values as well as family independence.

Scandinavian Ethnicity in America

At first Scandinavian ethnicity was centered in the Lutheran Church. The immigrants tried desperately to reconstitute the church just as it had been in the Old World. Church buildings were constructed at the highest point in the community so they could be seen from far away, if possible near the first graveyard so the dead could rest "in the shadow of the Lord's house." Meeting houses had a tower and bell and an altar facing east, covered with an altar cloth, candles, and a huge Bible. Ministers, often circuit riders in the early days, preached from a raised podium, and men and women sat on opposite sides of the chapel. The congregation sang the same hymns, repeated the same prayers, offered up the same confessions, and observed the same communion, baptism, confirmation, marriage, and burial rites as before.

But it was impossible for the Lutheran Church to play the same role in America that it had in Europe. The theological tensions inherent in Protestantism, contained in Scandinavia by the political power of the Lutheran Church, brought factionalism in the United States. Language was a major stumbling block; there was simply no way the Swedes, Norwegians, Danes, and Finns could worship together. Like the Germans, all four groups believed that language saves the faith. The Augustana Synod, for example, was formed in 1860; but in 1870 a Danish-Norwegian faction defected, and a few years later the Danes and Norwegians split into different synods. Soon there were Norwegian, Swedish, Danish, and Finnish Lutheran churches in the United States.

And just as frequently Norwegians fought Norwegians or Swedes fought Swedes over religion. The pietistic movement in Scandinavia had rejected rational formalism for a warmer, more personal faith that gave full reign to individual emotions. Immigrants naturally carried those feelings to America, and, free of the control of state Lutheranism, the Scandinavian churches disintegrated into many different units. In Scandinavia the state church had started all congregations, financed them, and appointed ministers. But in the United States the people of the community carried the major responsibility for incorporating a new church, supporting it financially, and recruiting a minister. With more control over the church, they were free to quarrel with policies or doctrines they disliked and always ready to bolt the congregation or the synod to create their own church.

Because of the strong pietistic tradition in Scandinavia and the puritanical overtones of American culture, immigrant congregations often struggled with issues of personal morality. A consensus condemned divorce because it dissolved a union sanctioned by God, and premarital sex was likewise forbidden. Old peasant mores had permitted premarital sexual unions between a betrothed couple because economic considerations often forced postponement of marriage. Few stigmas were attached to illegitimate pregnancy as long as the parents married later on. But in the New World the pietists, who triumphed in America, condemned premarital sex and ostracized those who engaged in it, especially the women. In the Old World consumption of alcohol had been common, but poverty usually confined it to special occasions and holidays. In America, where liquor was as plentiful as the money to purchase it, the custom became a vice. In the Scandinavian communities the pietists called for temperance, while other Lutherans defended the right to drink. The pietists also condemned dancing, social games, card playing, Sabbath breaking, and joining secret societies.

Such were the debates, and they led to fissures in the Scandinavian churches. The Augustana Synod represented Swedish Lutheranism, but it lost many groups, including the Evangelical Mission Covenant Church. Norwegian Lutheranism ranged from the pietist Haugenists to high church formalists, with many groups in between. Danish Lutheranism was divided between high church formalism and the Danish Evangelical Lutheranism. The Finns had the Finnish Lutheran Church, the Finnish Apostolic Lutheran Church, and the National Evangelical Lutheran Church. The individualistic, congregational autonomy so central to Protestantism prevented Scandinavian Lutheranism from consolidating immigrant ethnicity as Roman Catholicism did for the Irish and the French Canadians.

As a result, Scandinavian ethnicity in the United States soon expanded beyond the church. Home and family were basic values, and the immigrants appreciated America because the abundant land and non-rigid social structure permitted them to provide adequately for their families. Immigrant workers considered America superior to the Old World because they enjoyed a higher standard of living, manual labor was respected, there was a real possibility of moving into the middle and upper class without being stigmatized by lower-class origins, and families could be independent. In those families, the authority of the father went unquestioned; Scandinavian wives rarely defied his power, and children were expected to be obedient. Beyond the nuclear family, kinship loyalties were strong and required an older resident to board arriving relatives and help them find jobs. Repayment was not usually expected.

A number of ethnic organizations promoted group solidarity and Old World values. Like other groups Scandinavians established fraternal societies and mutual aid associations to provide a social outlet and help members through hard times. The Swedes had the Vasa Order, the Order of Vikings, the Order of Runeberg, and the International Order of Good Templars; the Norwegians formed the Sons of Norway; the Danes had the Danish Brotherhood; and the Finns established the Knights of Kaleva. Tens of thousands of Norwegians had immigrated in village chains, and once in the United States they revived those relationships in *bygdelag* societies, in which groups of immigrants were united by regional origins. Finns had the Finnish American Society, Finnish Halls, and the Finlandia Foundation. Swedish-Americans founded Augustana College, Kendall College, Adolphus College, and Bethany College; Norwegians had Concordia College, Luther College, and St. Olaf's College; and the Finns had Suomi College. During the Great Migration there were more than a thousand Swedish-American newspapers, more than three hundred Norwegian, three hundred Finnish, and one hundred Danish papers. All these institutions contained and expressed Scandinavian ethnicity in the United States.

Four Different Heritages

The Swedes, Norwegians, Danes, and Finns, however, had different levels of ethnicity and ethnic nationalism. Generally the Finns and Norwegians were more concerned about preserving Old World traditions, more dedicated to their own communities, and married compatriots more often than the Danes and Swedes. Those differences stemmed from their different cultures. In Denmark and southern Sweden small farms were mixed with large estates, all scattered around clustered village markets where peasants sold their produce and purchased goods from village artisans. These Scandinavians were commercial farmers functioning in a money economy. Because news, travelers, and goods from the outside world reached them through rail, steamship, and highway connections, the Danes and Swedes were more open and adaptable to social change, strangers, and new ideas.

But in Norway and Finland a rural society prevailed that enjoyed no central village existence. In the heavily wooded forests and mountains each valley had a separate identity complete with variations in food, dialect, clothing, and customs. Homesteads had to be largely self-sufficient, and the commercial production of surpluses was virtually nonexistent. From the nearby woods peasant farmers took the wood for building houses and warming them, carving shoes, and fashioning farm implements; from crude iron ore they made metal tools; from hides they cured their own leather; and from grain crops they distilled their own liquor. Extended families were close and so were neighbors throughout the valley; everyone knew everyone else. Less cosmopolitan than the Danish and Swedish peasants, as well as more isolated, they were suspicious of strangers, self-reliant, and more conservative about social change. In the United States the Norwegians and Finns held closely to people who spoke their language, worshiped in their churches, and joined their associations.

History contributed to immigrant ethnicity. Denmark had enjoyed a national history since the Middle Ages, and the Danish immigrants accepted nationality as a fact of life. And since 1523, when Sweden withdrew from the Kalmar Union with Denmark and Norway, Swedes too had had national independence. Consequently these people felt no need to defend their national identity in America.

It was markedly different, however, for the Norwegians and Finns. Sweden had lost Finland to Russia in 1809, and in the Treaty of Kiel of 1814 Denmark, which had sided with Napoleon in the European conflict, was forced to cede Norway to Sweden. Trapped in a semicolonial relationship with Sweden, nineteenth-century Norwegians had a strong national consciousness, and immigrants carried that consciousness to the New World. In 1849 a Norwegian immigrant wrote home:

> As American citizens who have tasted the joys of being free . . . and having in common with you the Norwegian temper, love of liberty, and warmth of heart, we would say to you who swell amid Norway's mountains: Show yourselves worthy sons of the north. Stand as a man for your liberties. Let freedom and equality be your demands, truth and the right your reliance, and the God of justice will give you victory.*

When Norway peacefully achieved independence from Sweden in 1905, Norwegian-Americans celebrated by forming the Nordmanns-Forbundet, to strengthen Norwegian freedom.

Finland had been part of Sweden from the twelfth through the eighteenth century, and the language of the state bureaucracy was Swedish. Swedes controlled politics and looked down upon the Finns as narrow-minded provincials. But Sweden ceded Finland to Russia during the Napoleonic Wars, and by the end of the nineteenth century the tsar was abolishing the Finnish army, drafting Finns into the Russian army, and trying to make Russian the official language of Finland. As a result of years of domination, nationalism pervaded Finland in the nineteenth century. Thus both the Norwegian and the Finnish immigrants arrived in the United States imbued with a sense of ethnic nationalism.

The Danes and to a lesser extent the Swedes did not resist acculturation and assimilation. In 1890, for example, when only 8 percent of the Danish population and 22 percent of the Swedish population could be considered the dominant group in certain upper midwest counties, nearly 60 percent of the Norwegians and 70 percent of the Finns were dominant in certain areas. The Norwegians and Finns showed a far stronger inclination to settle among their compatriots. While the Danes and Swedes enthusiastically supported the public school movement in Minnesota, Michigan, Iowa, and Wisconsin, the Norwegians and Finns

---

* Quoted in Theodore C. Blegen, *Land of their Choice* (Minneapolis, 1955), p. 203.

were more inclined to start parochial schools in conjunction with their Lutheran churches. And while half the male Danish immigrants and perhaps 30 percent of the Swedes married outside their nationality, only 20 percent of the Norwegians and less than 10 percent of the Finns did. In many counties in Minnesota, Wisconsin, Iowa, and the Dakotas, Norwegians held to the old ways, and well into the 1920s Norwegian was the spoken language in many public and parochial schools, churches, homes, and businesses, as Finnish was in many mining and textile towns.

Of all the Scandinavians, the Finns were the most exclusive and group oriented. The American environment interacted with Finnish clannishness to create a cultural tenacity unknown among other Scandinavians. Despite their Protestant traditions, many Americans—including some Scandinavian-Americans—were critical of the Finnish immigrants. Part of the problem was economic. Because Finnish industrialization and the integration of Finland into the Atlantic economy did not begin until late in the century, most Finns were unskilled workers and peasant farmers just when more and more German, Norwegian, Danish, Swedish, English, Scots, and Welsh immigrants were arriving with industrial skills. Many Americans considered the Finns a backward people and grouped them with the immigrants from southern and eastern Europe. And in the Midwest, other Scandinavians looked down on the Finns. The Swedes, Norwegians, and Danes were all descendants of ancient Nordic tribes and took pride in the legendary history of the Vikings. They were also able to understand one another's language. The Finns were descendants of ancient Magyar tribes which had emigrated out of central Asia, some to the Pannonian Plains of Hungary and others to Finland, and the Finnish language bore no resemblance to Swedish, Norwegian, or Danish. To other Scandinavians in America, the Finns were a rather primitive, culturally retarded people.

But even if older Americans and Scandinavian immigrants had welcomed the Finns, Finnish ethnicity would still have led to group isolation and solidarity. Language and cultural barriers, as well as an intense sense of nationalism, helped drive them together in the United States, but Finnish ethnicity also revolved around a strong impulse toward group integrity. Suspicious of others, Finns relied on Finns for help and security. Society was defined in terms of moral absolutes, usually on a class basis. For the Finns the economic world was divided between the *meikalainen* ("good working people") and the *herrat* ("bad aristocrats"), and the *herrat* would risk annihilation rather than surrender prerogatives to the *meikalainen*. Concluding that real mobility was impossible to achieve anywhere, some Finns withdrew to a rural environment, hoping there to work out their lives in peace. Others joined movements of American workers protesting capitalism. By 1912 they were the largest foreign-language group in the Socialist party (about 12 percent of its membership), and for a time in the 1920s the Finns made up nearly 40 percent of the American Communist party.

By 1900 there were four Scandinavian "islands" in the United States, and because immigration from Sweden, Norway, Denmark, and Finland was just reaching its peak, the forces of assimilation were still weak. Like the British and German Protestants, the Scandinavians—except for the Finns—were generally well received in America. They were literate, white, Protestant, and socially conservative, and older Americans did not fear Scandinavian culture. Nativistic criticisms focused much less on Swedes, Norwegians, and Danes than on the Irish and German immigrants. But the prevailing hospitality did little to destroy Scandinavian self-reliance and clannishness, and large-scale assimilation would not occur until well into the twentieth century.

SUGGESTED READINGS

Ahlstrom, Sydney. *A Religious History of America*. New Haven, Conn.: 1972.

Allswang, John M. *A House for All Peoples: Ethnic Politics in Chicago, 1890–1936*. Lexington, Kentucky: 1971.

Anderson, Arlow W. *The Norwegian Americans*. New York: 1975.

Anderson, Charles. *White Protestant Americans: From National Origins to Religious Groups*. Englewood Cliffs, N.J.: 1970.

Barton, H. Arnold, ed. *Letters from the Promised Land: Swedes in America, 1840–1914*. Minneapolis, Minn.: 1973.

Benson, Adolph B., and Hedin, Naboth. *Americans from Sweden*. Philadelphia: 1950.

Blegen, Theodore. *Land of Their Choice*. Minneapolis, Minn.: 1955.

———. *Norwegian Migration to America, 1825–1860*. Northfield, Minn.: 1931.

Capps, Finis Herbert. *From Isolationism to Involvement: The Swedish Immigrant Press in America, 1914–1945*. Chicago: 1966.

Choresman, Noel J. *Ethnic Influence on Urban Groups: The Danish Americans*. New York: 1973.

Dowie, J. Iverne, and Espelie, Ernest M. *The Swedish Immigrant Community in Transition*. Rock Island, Ill.: 1963.

Esslinger, Dean R. *Immigrants and the City: Ethnicity and Mobility in a Nineteenth-Century Midwestern Community*. New York: 1975.

Friis, Erik J., ed. *The Scandinavian Presence in North America*. New York: 1976.

Graebner, Alan. *Uncertain Saints: The Laity in the Lutheran Church–Missouri Synod, 1900–1970*. Westport, Conn.: 1975.

Hoglund, Arthur. *Finnish Immigrants in America, 1880–1920*. Madison, Wisc.: 1960.

Hvidt, Kristian. *Flight to America: The Social Background of 300,000 Danish Immigrants*. Copenhagen, Denmark: 1975.

Jalkanen, Ralph J. *The Finns in North America*. Lansing, Mich.: 1969.

Karni, Michael G., Kaups, Matti E., and Ollila, Douglas J., Jr. *The Finnish Experience in the Western Great Lakes Region*. Turku, Finland: 1975.

Knaplund, Paul. *Moorings Old and New*. Madison, Wisconsin: 1963.

Knudsen, Johanne. *The Danish-American Immigrant*. Des Moines, Iowa: 1950.

Kolehmainen, John I., and Hill, George. *Haven in the Woods: The Story of the Finns in Wisconsin*. Madison, Wisconsin: 1965.

Larson, Laurence M. *The Log Book of a Young Immigrant*. Northfield, Minn.: 1939.

Lindmark, Sture. *Swedish America, 1914–1932*. Uppsala, Sweden: 1971.

Lovoll, Odd Sverre. *A Folk Epic: The Bygdelag in America*. Boston: 1975.

Marty, Martin E. *Righteous Empire: The Protestant Experience in America*. New York: 1970.

Nelson, E. Clifford. *Lutheranism in North America*. Minneapolis, Minn.: 1972.

Nelson, Helge. *The Swedes and Swedish Settlements in North America*. Lund, Sweden: 1943.

Nyholm, Paul C. *The Americanization of the Danish Lutheran Churches in America*. Copenhagen, Denmark: 1963.

Riis, Jacob A. *The Making of an American*. New York: 1947.

Rolvaag, Ole E. *Giants in the Earth*. New York: 1927.

Runblom, Harald, and Norman, Hans, eds. *From Sweden to America: A History of the Migration*. Minneapolis, Minn.: 1976.

Skardal, Dorothy. *The Divided Heart: Scandinavian Immigrant Experience Through Literary Sources*. Lincoln, Neb.: 1974.

Stephen, George M. *The Religious Aspects of Swedish Immigration*. Minneapolis, Minn.: 1932.

Strandvold, Georg. *Danes Who Helped Build America*. New York: 1960.

Wefald, Jon. *A Voice of Protest: Norwegians in American Politics, 1890–1917*. Northfield, Minn.: 1971.

Chapter Eight

The French in America

In the seventeenth century France and England were competing ferociously for supremacy in North America. In 1534 Jacques Cartier had set out in search of Indian treasure and a water route to the Pacific Ocean, and after exploring the gulf of the St. Lawrence River he had established the French claim to Canada. For the next seventy years French fishermen worked the Grand Banks off Newfoundland catching codfish and seals, and French companies established temporary trading posts in what were to become the Maritime Provinces of Canada to purchase furs from the Indians. Then, at the beginning of the seventeenth century, both England and France established permanent colonies in the New World. Between 1603 and 1608 Samuel de Champlain placed several fur trading colonies in Acadia (Nova Scotia and New Brunswick) and along the St. Lawrence River in Quebec, and between 1607 and 1629 England was setting up permanent colonies in New England and near Chesapeake Bay. Both nations expanded their empires throughout the seventeenth century—the English moving down the Atlantic coast and the French toward the Great Lakes. After the voyages of Robert LaSalle down the Mississippi River in the 1680s, New France was a great colonial arc running from Newfoundland in the northeast, west along the St. Lawrence River to Lake Superior, and down the Mississippi River to the Gulf of Mexico.

But as the English colonies and New France expanded, the Ohio River Valley became a point of geopolitical contention. From the opening salvos of King William's War in 1689 to Napoleon's defeat at Water-loo in 1815, France and England struggled for world supremacy, and in North America hostilities revolved around the land and furs of the Ohio River watershed. They fought four colonial wars over it—King William's War, 1689–1697; Queen Anne's War, 1702–1713; King George's War, 1740–1748; and the French and Indian War, 1754–1763. England finally prevailed in 1763 when war-weary France ceded Canada in the Treaty of Paris. Caught in a financial squeeze and weary of administering his New World territories, Napoleon completed the work of the Treaty of Paris by selling Louisiana to the United States for $15 million in 1803. After nearly two centuries the Franco-American empire was gone.

That was not, however, the end of French culture in America. Over the centuries four separate waves of French immigrants came to the New World. Several thousand French Huguenots, fleeing religious per-secution in France, relocated in America in the 1690s; more than seven thousand French Acadians were driven from Canada after 1755 and nearly two thousand of them settled in Louisiana; between 1820 and 1924 more than five hundred thousand people emigrated from France, although most of them were German-speaking immigrants from eastern France, Alsace, and Lorraine; and finally, perhaps four hundred thousand French-Canadians crossed the border to America before 1924. They became the nucleus of the Franco-American community.

The Huguenots

The Huguenots were Calvinist reformers, a tiny Protestant colony in Roman Catholic France. Like the Puritans in England, Presbyterians in Scotland, Walloons in Belgium, and Reformed congregations in Hol-land and Germany, they were mostly successful merchants and skilled artisans who found in Calvinism freedom from the restrictions of medieval life. The new spirit of the Reformation liberated them from the static, organic conservatism of medieval Catholicism; Huguenots enjoyed success without misgivings, prosperity without guilt. They were the most productive segment of the French population, an elite group responsible for much of the growth in the national economy. Out of personal sympathy for them as well as a sense of their importance to France, King Henry IV had granted them religious toleration in 1598 with the Edict of Nantes. They were, in effect, a "state within the state," with Huguenot military groups protecting Huguenot cities in southern and western France. They were a unique people, republicans in the age of absolutism, dissenters in a bastion of religious despotism.

Life became difficult for them in the seventeenth century. When Cardinal Richelieu took over the French bureaucracy in 1624, he was obsessed with centralizing the power of the monarchy. Huguenot independence bothered him, and although he still respected their religious freedom, he worked against their special status in France. Harassment and restrictive legislation continued throughout the century, and on October 18, 1685, King Louis XIV revoked the Edict of Nantes, setting off anti-Huguenot persecutions in much of the country. Protestant services were prohibited, Protestant books and Bibles burned, and Protestant chapels closed. Restrictions were placed on Huguenots becoming doctors, lawyers, teachers, or civil servants. Their property was confiscated, their ministers harassed, and their civil rights impaired. Remembering the terrors they had endured before the edict—especially the Massacre of St. Bartholomew in 1572—the Huguenots were enraged, and more than four hundred thousand left France in the 1690s. Most of them settled in Holland and England, but several thousand came to America.

They settled widely in colonial America, but especially in Massachusetts, New York, Pennsylvania, and South Carolina. Indeed, South Carolina was a center of Huguenot culture. Huguenot communities sprouted in Boston and New Oxford, Massachusetts; near Providence, Rhode Island; New York City, New Rochelle, and New Paltz in New York; Philadelphia, Pennsylvania; and Charleston, St. Thomas, St. Denis, and St. John, South Carolina. Although no more than fifteen thousand Huguenots ever lived in America during the seventeenth century, some of the most famous families in United States history—the Bayards, Marions, Du Ponts, Delanceys, Delanos, and Reveres—were of Huguenot descent.

There were reasons for such success. The Huguenots were Calvinists and adapted easily to the individualistic, success-oriented society developing in the British colonies. Like the New England Puritans, they prospered in commerce and craftsmanship. They also possessed a powerful sense of their own rights. The Edict of Nantes had granted them religious freedom and property rights; and when Louis XIV revoked those privileges, the Huguenots lost something they had enjoyed for nearly a century. With their strong convictions about rights, toleration, and property, the Huguenots found an ideological home in British North America. Americans welcomed the Huguenots, and some colonies actively recruited them.

Of all the non-English ethnic groups in early America, the Huguenots assimilated the most quickly and completely. As white Protestants who were successful and widely dispersed, they soon lost a separate identity.

Highly educated, ambitious, and skilled entrepreneurs, they appreciated the social climate of America, the economic opportunity, and the
religious freedom. And Anglo-Americans appreciated them not only for
their economic skills but as a Protestant people fleeing Roman Catholicism. Open acceptance encouraged assimilation. Learning English
quickly, their children married Puritans in New England, Anglicans in
New York and South Carolina, and Scots-Irish Presbyterians in the
South and West. They did not, of course, disappear in a generation;
their sense of self-esteem and personal worth was too well developed for
that, and as late as the American Revolution recognizable Huguenot
settlements still existed. But by the early nineteenth century French
Huguenots hardly functioned as a self-conscious ethnic group.

The Acadians

The Acadians were the second wave of French-speaking immigrants.
With roots in the beginning of New France, they are one of the oldest
ethnic groups in North America. In 1603 King Henry IV of France had
issued a large proprietary land grant to Pierre du Guast, who promptly
established a fur trading post, commanded by Samuel de Chaplain, on
the Bay of Fundy. The new colony of Acadia expanded around the main
settlement of Port Royal. Acadians supported themselves by fishing, fur
trading, and farming; but the cold, humid, and windy winters and
mosquito-infested summers made life difficult and austere. Because
immigration from Europe was small and population growth slow, at least
when compared to the growth of the English colonies, strong village
kinship systems developed throughout Acadia. The original families of
the early seventeenth century became the Acadian clans of the
eighteenth century. Roman Catholic in religion, Gallic in culture, and
bound together in strong extended families, they were a distinct community in North America, imbued by a powerful emotional insularity.
    Anglo-French rivalry eventually disrupted Acadian society. After
Queen Anne's War ended in 1713, England acquired Acadia from
France, and for the next forty years the Acadians preserved their culture
in an Anglo-Protestant polity. It was an untenable position, living under
English protection in an English colony but culturally loyal to France.
England perceived the Acadians as potential traitors ready to rise and
strike back in the name of French patriotism. When the Acadians
refused to take a blanket loyalty oath to England at the outset of the
French and Indian War, English politicians expelled them.
    The exile began in 1755, when there were probably ten thousand

An artist's conception of the embarkation of the Acadians, who were herded onto ships with only the possessions they could carry. (Brown Brothers)

Acadians in Nova Scotia and another five thousand on Prince Edward and Cape Breton islands. To this day Cajuns (Acadians who settled in Louisiana) call the exile *Le Grand Dérangement*, the "Big Upheaval." Cramped into the dark holds of transport vessels, they were shipped out of Nova Scotia on a moment's notice with only the possessions they could carry. Men left for work one day only to return at dusk and find their families gone. Henry Wadsworth Longfellow's famous poem "Evangeline," itself now part of the Acadian heritage, was based on the life of Emmeline Labiche, an Acadian woman betrothed to Louis Arcenaux. They were separated during *Le Grand Dérangement*, but years later they found each other in St. Martinville, Louisiana. According to the story, he was already married and she lived out her life heartbroken.

For all the Acadians the voyages were terrifying. Passengers suffered from smallpox, scurvy, and starvation, as well as the loss of their families. More than 700 Acadians shipped to Philadelphia had to wait six weeks on board ship while the colonial assembly decided whether to let them land, and more than 230 died of smallpox during the delay. On December 10, 1755, two rickety ships, the *Violet* and the *Duke William*, sank off the Atlantic coast with 650 Acadian refugees. The *Cornwallis* left Nova Scotia with 450 Acadians, but only 210 survived the voyage to Charleston. The Acadians were dispersed throughout the Old and New Worlds, wherever anyone would take them in, with the largest colonies in Boston, New York, Philadelphia, and Charleston in America; Liverpool, Southampton, Falmouth, and Bristol in England; and Normandy, Brittany, Aunis, and Guienne in France.

Thirty years after the expulsion of the Acadians and more than twenty years after Spain had acquired Louisiana from France, the Spanish government recruited some sixteen hundred Acadians living in France to return to America, colonize the territory, and develop it economically. Seven expeditions deposited them in New Orleans in 1785, and from there they moved west to the bayous, rivers, swamps, and lakes of southern Louisiana. Loyal to their heritage, the Acadians became fishermen, fur trappers, and cattle, cane, and cotton farmers. (Earlier French colonists, in contrast, had tended to settle in New Orleans and along the Mississippi River as commercial farmers, merchants, craftsmen, and shop-owners.) In 1803, when President Thomas Jefferson completed the Louisiana Purchase, this was French Louisiana: the urban commercial elite in New Orleans and up the Mississippi River, and the rural Cajuns, as the Acadians came to be called, of the southwestern parishes. To this day, as the Cajuns trap the nutria and muskrat, gather shrimp, raise cattle, and grow rice, cotton, and cane, links to early Louisiana and Acadia remain strong.

Cajun society evolved on its own. The influx of English merchants, bankers, planters, and small farmers in the nineteenth century gradually overwhelmed the French-speaking people of northern and eastern Louisiana and New Orleans. And as they succumbed to English culture, retaining Catholicism but losing the French language and identity, the Cajuns became a linguistic and cultural island in southwestern Louisiana. From their early origins in France they had nurtured an independent spirit, and the powerful family clans of Acadia that were reinstituted in Louisiana helped reinforce their autonomy. Wronged historically and conscious of it, poor but independent, knitted into strong family networks, and isolated culturally and physically from the rest of the country, the Cajuns were deeply suspicious of outsiders, a separate people in nineteenth-century America.

By the 1970s there would be hundreds of thousands of Cajuns in Louisiana. When intermarriage occurred, the non-Cajun spouse would usually blend into Cajun society. Sugar cane, rice, shrimp, and fur festivals celebrating the benevolence of nature would still occur, and Cajun music and dancing would still thrive. The Council for the Development of French in Louisiana would promote the use of French in the state; all public schools would offer French at all grade levels; bilingual teachers would work in all Cajun schools; *Télévision-Louisiane* would broadcast in French to the Cajun community; Quebec would distribute French newspapers, magazines, and radio and television programs throughout southern Louisiana; and France would maintain a French Educational Mission there to teach French in the schools. Edwin Edwards would become the first Cajun governor in Louisiana history.

Suspicious and proud, still Gallic and intensely Roman Catholic, Cajun-America would continue to defy the melting pot, preferring instead the isolation of rural Louisiana.

The Great Migration from France

Between 1820 and 1924 more than 550,000 people immigrated from France; but until the Franco-Prussian War of 1870, when France ceded Alsace and Lorraine to Germany, most were German-speaking people leaving northeastern France for economic reasons. Perhaps only 200,000 French-speaking immigrants settled in America. Given the total population of France, that was a small number. Because of the French Revolution, France was more open socially and politically than the rest of Europe, and there was a maturity to French culture; people were more satisfied with their environment. The population of rural France remained relatively stable and the pressures for land that were so strong elsewhere did not cause serious trouble—in part because peasants divided and redivided their land through inheritance and did not practice primogeniture. Not even the Industrial Revolution could displace cottage industry and settled rural family life in nineteenth-century France.

In the years of the French Revolution and the Napolenic Wars, a few scattered French colonies developed in the United States. Royalists fleeing the French Revolution in 1794 founded Asylum, Pennsylvania, and other refugees settled in New York, Boston, and Philadelphia. Hoping to build wine and olive industries in the South, French immigrants organized the French Agricultural and Manufacturing Society in 1816 and built the town of Demopolis, Alabama. After the Revolution of 1848, perhaps twenty thousand French refugees came to America, and both royalists and radicals made their living teaching French, editing newspapers, and giving art, music, and dance lessons. Most of the nineteenth-century French immigrants, however, were neither royalists nor refugees but skilled workers and professionals. Settling into the major cities, they established ethnic cultural institutions similar to those of other immigrants. Fraternal and social organizations—like French benevolent societies, the Cercle Français, and the Societie Française de L'Amatie—appeared, as did French Catholic churches, military companies, political clubs, and cultural groups. French newspapers were common, such as New York *Franco Americaine* or *Courrier des Etats Unis*, the Philadelphia *Le Courrier de l'Amerique*, and the Charleston *Moniteur Français*.

In one sense French immigration was unique, for despite their Roman Catholicism the French encountered little hostility in America. It was partly demographic. French immigration averaged less than three thousand people each year; compared to the migrations from Ireland and Germany, it was inconsequential. At the same time, most of the French immigrants were craftsmen and professionals; Americans perceived them as economic assets. And in addition many Americans admired French culture. France had helped the colonies during the Revolution, and although many upper-class Federalists in the United States feared the French Revolution and resented Thomas Jefferson's love for France, most Americans shared his feelings. There was an affinity of political philosophy.

Many Americans of the 1800s seemed obsessed with things French. Inns and taverns became hotels, lunchrooms and saloons soon were cafés and restaurants, and cooks became chefs. French art salons, theaters, operas, conservatories, and dance schools were popular, and French became the second language of the American upper class. French finishing schools and tours of France were requirements for "sophisticated young ladies," as were French fashions and toiletries. French wines, liqueurs, pastries, breads, entrées, and soups became standard fare for wealthy Americans. Indeed, the American upper class, new and parochial, aped French culture and welcomed its proponents.

The French-Canadians

When England took Canada in 1763, there were about seventy thousand French citizens living there, most of them in Quebec. The two Canadas coexisted independently until 1840, with English Upper Canada and French Lower Canada functioning as a dual federation. The French-Canadians were a close-knit community, bound together by strong kinship ties, language, religion, and pride in the history of France. Four colonial wars with England had left them with an Anglophobia rivaling that of the Irish. Great Britain united Upper and Lower Canada in 1840, and the French lost control over their internal affairs, becoming a religious and political minority. English rule only intensified French ethnicity. When Britain made English the national language, the French converted their own language into a cultural symbol; and when the English made known their preference for Protestantism, French-Canadian Catholicism became a badge of faith and community. Quebec separatism today is only the latest episode in a long struggle for independence. This was French Canada: a conquered people devoted to the French language, Roman Catholicism, and ethnic nationalism.

But they too felt the same push-and-pull forces that influenced Europeans in the nineteenth century. Until industrialization began in the 1890s, economic life in Quebec was desperate. The land had become unable to sustain a growing population. Outmoded farming techniques were depleting the soil; and the old French inheritance system, which required subdivision of land among all children—and which was still working well in France—was reducing farms to small parcels unable to support a family. Speculators held the best land, and it was too expensive for small farmers. Other land was held by the British government and was unavailable for settlement. In upper Quebec, where some good land was still available there were few roads for shipment of goods to urban markets. Land in western Canada was open to settlement, but French-Canadians were reluctant to pioneer where Anglo-Protestants were too many and Catholic churches too few. Instead they looked southward.

The demand for labor in lumber yards, canals, railroads, mines, quarries, harbors, mills, and factories of the United States was enormous, and manufacturers sent recruiters to Quebec, Toronto, Montreal, and Ottawa looking for new workers. Before the Civil War most French-Canadian immigrants were itinerant workers intending to earn good wages, save money, and return home to rebuild the family farm and pay off debts. They formed few ethnic organizations, churches, or societies. But only 10 percent ever returned permanently to Canada; economic security south of the border made the exodus permanent. Whole villages were transplanted. Most French-Canadians settled in the mill towns of New England and replaced or displaced some of the Irish as unskilled workers. Others found work in the mines and steel mills of New York, Pennsylvania, and Ohio; the copper and lead mines of Upper Michigan; the automobile factories of Detroit; the mines and farms of Minnesota; and railroad labor gangs throughout the upper Midwest. By 1900 there were more than 500,000 French-Canadians in New England alone. That number would eventually grow to 1.25 million by 1945, out of a total New England population of 8 million. In upper New England they constituted more than 40 percent of the population. Another 400,000 French-Canadians would live in Michigan, 350,000 in New York, 300,000 in Illinois, and 125,000 in Minnesota—making them one of the more visible ethnic groups in the Northeast.

Like the Cajuns, the French-Canadians resisted assimilation. Nearly 180 years of conflict with English Protestants had sharply defined Gallic culture and Roman Catholicism, and supplied them with a strong sense of ethnic nationalism. What had happened in Quebec was the historical fusion of religion, language, and nationality. French was not simply the medium of culture to the French-Canadians; it was a mystical badge of ethnicity and the "defender of the faith." French-Canadians believed that the loss of their language implied loss of Catholicism. The center of cultural life had thus been the French-speaking parish and parochial schools; they were bastions of Gallicism and Catholicism where religion, society, and politics mixed. The French-Canadians made few distinctions between political citizenship in the state and religious citizenship in the church. The immigrants carried these feelings with them to the United States, and the proximity of Quebec, with its family ties and traditions, permitted them to return home frequently and maintain their culture.

Family life and religion were similarly inseparable in Quebec. French-Canadian families were always large, not only to encourage economic development but to fulfill procreation roles expected by the church. Elder males were ruling patriarchs, and extended families included those of married sons. Women and children played subservient roles. But even so the patriarch was subject to the rule of the parish priest. Since the parish was the center of social, religious, and political life and the priest had full authority there, French-Canadian fathers always consulted him about births, marriages, deaths, schools, and taxes. Higher education or migration from the local community was discouraged because either could create loyalties independent of parish life. Only economic desperation made migration to the United States acceptable, and even then the immigrants were expected to maintain a cultural separation.

The social climate of the United States further defined French-Canadian values. Americans welcomed craftsmen and professionals from France but worried about the French-Canadians. Poor and unskilled, ignorant of English, and concentrated into "Little Canadas," the French-Canadians were a conspicuous and growing minority in the nineteenth century. Their loyalty to Roman Catholicism and suspicion of public schools generated even more uneasiness. The nineteenth-century immigrants from France were often worldly and even rather secular about religion. But this was not true of the French-Canadians, and they encountered the wrath of Know-Nothing activists in the 1850s and the Yankee sensitivities of other antiforeign groups in the 1890s. As they competed with the Irish for jobs in the mills, businessmen frequently used them as strikebreakers. Irish workers resented them and fights were common.

There was religious competition as well. Like other immigrants, the French-Canadians wanted to worship in their own language, and the Irish Catholic hierarchy opposed them. French-Canadians resented Irish domination of the church, while the Irish clergy viewed French-Canadian priests as threats to their own power. Caught between the hostility of Anglo-Protestants and Irish Catholics, the French-Canadians established a separate ghetto culture in New England. Carrying their religious case to the Vatican, they gained their first ethnic parish in 1850, and by 1890 there were 86 French-Canadian parishes and 53 French-Canadian parochial schools, such as Notre-Dame des Canadiens, Saint Jean Baptiste, and Sacre-Coeur de Marie, and Précieux Sang. By 1945 there would be 320 Franco-American parishes, more than 250 parochial schools, and 30 hospitals and orphanages. Nearly a thousand French-speaking priests would minister to the pastoral needs of the French-Canadian population.

French-Candians would eventually establish more than 200 newspapers, such as *Le Messager* of Lewiston, Maine, and *L'Indépendent* of Fall River, Massachusetts, and such mutual aid societies and fraternal organizations as l'Union Saint-Jean-Baptiste d'Amerique, l'Association Canada-Americaine, l'Order des Chevaliers de Jacques Cartier, and les Francs-Tireurs. Separate and distinct, proud and hopeful, the French-Canadians were another cultural island in America, their children attending French-Canadian parishes and parochial schools and marrying one another, their loyalties to the language as powerful as ever, and their love for Quebec undiminished.

All this was Franco-America in the nineteenth century. The Huguenots had largely disappeared by the mid-1800s, victims of their Protestantism, urbanity, and economic prosperity. And the new immigrants arriving directly from France were readily accepted by an American society starved for French culture. The two main centers of French culture were in New England and Louisiana, where French-Canadians and the Cajun descendants of French-Canadians lived separate lives in homogeneous communities. Both were close-knit people bound together by an ethnic culture which fused language, religion, family, and politics.

SUGGESTED READINGS

Avery, Elizabeth H. *The Influence of French Immigration on the Political History of the United States*. New York: 1972.

Blumenthal, Henry. *American and French Culture, 1800–1900*. Baton Rouge, La.: 1975.

Byrne, William D. *History of the Catholic Church in the New England States*. Boston: 1899.

Chase, John. *Frenchmen, Desire, Good Children*. New Orleans: 1949.

Chopin, Kate. *Bayou Folk*. New York: 1894.

———. *A Night in Acadie*. New York: 1897.

Conrad, Glenn R., ed. *The Cajuns: Essays on Their History and Culture*. Lafayette, La.: 1978.

Dumarche, Jacques. *The Delusson Family*. New York: 1939.

———. *The Shadows of the Trees: The Story of the French Canadians in New*

England. Boston: 1943.

Dumont, Fernand. "The Systematic Study of the French-Canadian Total Society." In Marcel Rioux and Yves Martin, eds. *French-Canadian Society*. Vol. I. Toronto, Canada: 1965.

Eccles, W. J. *France in America*. New York: 1972.

Evans, Oliver. "Melting Pot in the Bayous." *American Heritage*, 15 (December 1963), 30–42.

Gilman, Malcolm B. *The Huguenot Migration in Europe and America: Its Cause and Effect*. Red Bank, N.J.: 1962.

Grayson, L. M., and Bliss, Michael, eds. *The Wretched of Canada*. Toronto, Canada: 1971.

Griffiths, Naomi. *The Acadians: Creation of a People*. New York: 1973.

Hirsch, Arthur H. *The Huguenots of Colonial South Carolina*. New York: 1928.

Hughes, Everett. *French Canada in Transition*. Chicago: 1943.

Jaenen, Cornelius J. *Friend and Foe: Aspects of French-American Cultural Conflict in the Sixteenth and Seventeenth Centuries*. New York: 1976.

John, Elizabeth A. H. *Storms Brewed in Other Men's Worlds: The Confrontation of the Indians, Spanish, and French in the Southwest, 1540–1795*. College Station, Texas: 1975.

Kane, Harnett. *The Bayous of Louisiana*. New York: 1943.

Lemaire, Herve-B. "Franco-American Efforts on Behalf of the French Language in New England." In Joshua A. Fishman et al., *Language Loyalty in the United States*. The Hague, Netherlands: 1966.

Lieberson, Stanley. *Language and Ethnic Relations in Canada*. New York: 1970.

McDermitt, John. *Frenchmen and French Ways in the Mississippi Valley*. Urbana, Ill.: 1969.

McInnis, Edgar. *Canada*. New York: 1947.

Miner, Horace. *St. Denis: A French-Canadian Parish*. Chicago: 1967

Podea, Iris. "Quebec to 'Little Canada': The Coming of the French Canadians to New England in the Nineteenth Century." *New England Quarterly*, 23 (Fall 1950), 365–384.

Porter, John. *The Vertical Mosaic: An Analysis of Social Class and Power in Canada*. Toronto, Canada: 1965.

Post, Lauren C. *Cajun Sketches*. Baton Rouge, La.: 1962.

Ramsey, Carolyn. *Cajuns on the Bayou*. New York: 1957.

Read, William A. *Louisiana French*. Baton Rouge, La.: 1963.

Sorrell, Richard S. "Franco-Americans in New England." *The Journal of Ethnic Studies*, 5 (Spring 1977), 90–94.

Theriault, George F. "The Franco-Americans of New England." In Mason Wade, ed. *Canadian Dualism*. Toronto, Canada: 1960.

Violette, Maurice. *The Franco Americans*. New York: 1976.

Wade, Mason. "The French Parish and *Survivance* in Nineteenth Century New England." *Catholic Historical Review*, 36 (July 1950), 163–178.

Winzerling, Oscar. *Acadian Odyssey*. Baton Rouge, La.: 1955.

Chapter Nine

Manifest Destiny and Native Americans

Between 1776 and 1830 the United States reassessed its Indian policy, replacing militance with more cautious, deliberate programs recognizing that native Americans had some rights to the land. Concerned during the Revolution about fighting Indians in the West and the English in the East, the government wanted Indians to resist British enticements and remain neutral. There were a number of isolated but serious confrontations, especially when British military officials encouraged the Indians to fight. Except for the Oneidas, Iroquois tribes were loyal to England, and on several occasions between 1777 and 1779 American troops invaded Iroquois territory; the invasion of General John Sullivan into upstate New York was perhaps the most successful of such missions. But generally the relationship between whites and Indians was tranquil; in a few instances the government even nullified the land claims of speculators. In 1777 and 1779 government officials repudiated attempts by speculators and white pioneers to settle on Indian lands in the Ohio Valley. The war had slowed the westward movement, and with fewer people crossing the mountains there were fewer confrontations; the government's policies seemed to be working.

Immediately after the Revolution, the government continued to be cautious in its policies toward the Indian tribes. American leaders hoped to avoid conflict with Indians in the West because it might divide westerners and easterners and threaten the young republic with political disintegration, especially if Britain and Spain tried to detach the western territories. American leaders therefore tried to some extent to conciliate the Indians. It was, of course, only a temporary lull in the tension, for as soon as the mass migration of whites across the Appalachians began again in earnest, the conflict over land would appear once more.

The hunger for land among white farmers was as insatiable as ever, and the government would have to respond by making way for those pioneers. The "backwardness" of native America was still used to justify taking land. A Baptist missionary journal argued in 1849 that the Indians were

> deficient in intellectual and moral culture. . . . They do not furnish their share to the advancement of society, and the prosperity and wealth of the world . . . their priests are ignorant and overbearing; their rulers are narrow and prejudiced; they have no properly instructed physicians, no schools . . . no hospitals . . . nor mutual aid associations. . . . There is nothing in their religious rites . . . but . . . that which is degrading and polluting.*

Such attitudes led inevitably to confrontation on the frontier. But at the same time, Europeans believed in Christian humanitarianism and the natural rights philosophy; missionaries as well as Jeffersonian idealists had to rationalize the taking of Indian land with their faith in natural rights. To these people assimilation seemed an ideal solution. Transforming native Americans into settled farmers who could support a family on only a few dozen acres of land would liberate millions of acres for white settlement, while upholding the natural rights philosophy. Another missionary society predicted in 1823:

> You may look forward to the period when the savage shall be converted into the citizen; when the hunter shall be transformed into the mechanic; when the farm, the work shop, the School-House, and the Church shall adorn every Indian village; when the fruits of Industry, good order, and sound morals, shall bless every Indian dwelling . . . red man and the white man shall everywhere be found, mingling in the same benevolent and friendly feelings, fellow citizens of the same civil and religious community, and fellow-heirs to a glorious inheritance in the kingdom of Immanuel.†

But this too would prove destructive to the Indians. Assimilationists wanted them to abandon their religious beliefs, the hunter-warrior ideal, tribal government, and communal ownership of the land—to exchange their culture for that of white society. Well into the twentieth century whites would pursue that dream.

* *Baptist Missionary Magazine*, April 1849, pp. 101–105.
† Quoted in Robert Berkhofer, *Salvation and the Savage* (Lexington, Kentucky, 1965), pp. 8–9.

After the Revolution the Indian tribes along the frontier were powerful, and the British agents still in the Ohio Valley could create trouble. Many Americans, wanting to placate the Indians, argued that Indian land claims were sovereign and could be nullified only with their consent. In 1784 Congress negotiated the Treaty of Fort Stanwix, which reestablished peace with the Iroquois, and in 1785 the federal government concluded a treaty with the Cherokees guaranteeing their land claims and inviting them to send a representative to Congress. Two years later Congress promised in the Northwest Ordinance to respect Indian rights in the Ohio Valley.

But these measures could not cope with the postwar wave of white settlers pouring across the Appalachians. By 1790 there were more than 35,000 settlers in Kentucky and nearly 75,000 in the Ohio Territory, and it was then that sporadic attacks on white settlements began. Whites demanded immediate assistance from the federal government, and President Washington dispatched troops to the Ohio Valley. There, on November 4, 1791, the Shawnees surprised the expedition, and in a pitched battle more than six hundred soldiers died, the worst single defeat United States forces were ever to suffer at the hands of native Americans. People roared for retribution. After three more years of periodic violence a military expedition led by General "Mad" Anthony Wayne defeated a large Shawnee force at the Battle of Fallen Timbers; the subsequent Treaty of Greenville of 1795 forced most of the Shawnees out of Ohio and into Indiana.

The Treaty of Greenville initiated a recurrent cycle in which the Indians, after resistance and military defeat, would surrender their land for guaranteed ownership of territory farther west. By 1810 there were 230,000 whites in Ohio, 406,000 in Kentucky, 260,000 in Tennessee, 25,000 in Indiana, 12,000 in Illinois, and 20,000 in Missouri. As white farmers cleared the forests, native Americans were hard-pressed to maintain their traditional lifestyles, and some rebelled. Tecumseh, a Shawnee war chief, and his brother, a religious leader called the Prophet, tried to unite the Great Lakes, Ohio Valley, and Gulf Coast tribes into a single military coalition. But the Indians could not overcome centuries of tribal conflict; some would temporarily bolt the alliance to support the government or to fight each other, and some even sold their land. Between 1811 and 1813 troops under William Henry Harrison, governor of the Indiana Territory, relentlessly pursued Tecumseh and the Prophet, defeating their forces at the Battle of Tippecanoe in 1811 and killing Tecumseh in 1813 at the Battle of the Thames. The end of the War of 1812 forced British officials out of the United States and weakened the Indians by depriving them of English support. After that, the northern tribes gradually yielded all their land east of the Mississippi River.

White idealists continued their crusade to remake native American culture. Throughout the early nineteenth century War Department agents introduced European culture into Indian villages, as did Protestant missionary groups like the Society of United Brethren for Propagating the Gospel Among the Heathen and the American Board of Foreign Missions. People like Isaac McCoy, John Heckewelder, and Stephen Riggs wanted the Indians to accept the superiority of individualism over tribal communism, Christianity over native religions, commercial farming over hunting and subsistence agriculture, and English over their own tongues. Missionary boarding schools like the Foreign Missionary School in Connecticut and the Choctaw Academy taught English, Christianity, Protestant views of morality, and European views of society and economics. Missionaries preached the same message to friendly tribes on the frontier, and envisioned native American villages where Indians worked their own farms and worshiped each Sunday at a community church. They hoped to reform native American society, not only to save Indian souls but to end the violence that was threatening Indian survival as well as white expansion.

But most Indians refused to oblige, believing that the Great Spirit had established two separate ways of life for the two peoples—had ordained each race to its own customs, land, languages, foods, and religions— and if people deviated from their own ways, the Great Spirit would bring the apocalypse. Furthermore, some argued, if God had wanted the Indians to be Christians, he would have given them the Bible years ago or would have sent Christ himself. In that the Indians cared about immortality and honorable behavior, they shared a broad perspective with the missionaries, but they wanted nothing of institutional Christianity. They still looked upon their tribal customs as more useful and humane than American individualism and found in their own culture the most sensible way of interpreting their environment. Christianity and European culture were alien.

Some native Americans did convert to Christianity, shed native dress for European clothes, attended mission schools, and tried to farm their own land. But once converted they were often outcast from their own tribes. The Chippewas ridiculed the converts as "praying Indians," and Sioux warriors often physically abused them. And no matter how sincere or pious, Christian Indians were not accepted by whites. Caught between two cultures, facing double discrimination, many returned to their tribe rather than endure a life of social ostracism. When tribes adopted the whites' faith but not white customs, their religions often became synthesized tribal and Christian beliefs. Many simply added God to an existing pantheon of deities or, like the Spokanes, mixed their medicine cermonies with Christian prayers.

Whether the Indians adopted or repudiated white customs, missionaries were realizing by the early 1830s that native American culture was tenaciously resilient and that most Indians had no intention of passively accepting European culture. Yet to white idealists Anglo conformity seemed the only way to stop the seemingly endless violence on the frontier. Eventually the removal policies of Andrew Jackson, the reservation policies, and even the allottment policies would be concerned in part with changing Indian society, not just for the sake of change but to guarantee native American survival.

If noble, the sentiments of white idealists were naïve. Even if the Indians had submitted to conversion, whites would still have wanted their land. By 1820, for example, there were hundreds of thousands of whites in Georgia, Alabama, and Mississippi. Much of the game on which Indians relied had disappeared, and Indian ways were difficult to maintain. Hoping to keep their land, some of the tribes tried to accommodate themselves to white society. In 1808 Cherokee leaders had formulated a legal code, and by 1821 the brilliant Cherokee Sequoyah had developed written characters for eighty-six Cherokee syllables. Most Cherokees then became literate. In 1828 the tribe began publishing its own newspaper; and books, Bibles, hymnals, and tracts circulated widely throughout Cherokee society. Missionaries established new schools in Cherokee communities, and Protestant churches made more converts than ever before. The Cherokees fenced their farms, built comfortable homes, sold livestock commercially, and established a political system based on a written constitution, democratic elections, jury trials, and a bicameral legislature. But it was all in vain; most whites were more interested in their land than in cultural accommodation. With cotton production booming in the 1820s, tens of thousands of whites poured into the southeastern states and territories, and the Five Civilized Tribes, of which the Cherokees were one, were forced westward. Cultural accommodation could not counter economic expansion.

The Trail of Tears, 1830–1860

Since 1789 Americans as distinguished as Thomas Jefferson, George Washington, and John C. Calhoun had been suggesting that the eastern tribes be evicted to lands across the Mississippi River. At first the proposal met opposition; but as white farmers pushed west, it gained acceptance, both among land speculators and white idealists interested in protecting the Indians. Materialism and humanitarianism again made common cause. When Andrew Jackson entered the White House in 1829, the proposal gained a powerful advocate. He had made his reputation fighting Indians in the Southwest, trying to drive them across the Mississippi River. When informed of Indian attacks on white settle-

Robert Lindneux's painting of "The Trail of Tears" migration that followed passage of the Indian Removal Act of 1830. (The Granger Collection)

ments, he would fly into uncontrollable rages. At the same time he was concerned about Indian survival and realized that as long as they remained in their traditional homelands, white assaults would continue. To open southeastern land for white settlement and to protect native Americans, President Jackson signed the Indian Removal Act in 1830.

In what is remembered as "The Trail of Tears," one hundred thousand Indians were transported to Oklahoma. The peaceful Choctaws of the Deep South were first to go, marching in the winter of 1831. Many died of hunger and disease along the way. The Creeks were moved four years later after massive white attacks on them in Georgia and Alabama. The United States Army supervised the removal of the Chickasaws in 1837. The Cherokees had fought removal in the federal courts, and the Supreme Court upheld their claims in 1832. Jackson refused to abide by the court decision. The Cherokees held out for several years, but in 1838 soldiers evicted them; four thousand died on the way west. Only the Seminoles resisted violently. Under Chief Osceola they waged a guerrilla war in the Florida Everglades between 1835 and 1842 that cost the government two thousand soldiers and $55 million. But they too were finally defeated and removed to Oklahoma in 1843.

Removal was equally relentless in the Ohio Valley. The Iroquois managed to stay in upstate New York, but since the defeat of Tecumseh in 1813 the fate of the other northern tribes had been sealed. The Ottawas, Potawatomis, Wyandots, Shawnees, Miamis, Kickapoos, Winnebagos, Delawares, Peorias, and the Sauk and the Fox had to leave. Only the Sauk and the Fox resisted. Under Chief Black Hawk they had been removed to Iowa in 1831, but they turned back a few months later. United States troops chased them across Illinois and Wisconsin and finally defeated them at the Battle of Bad Axe. Black Hawk wrote in his autobiography:

> On our way down, I surveyed the country that had cost us so much trouble, anxiety and blood . . . I reflected on the ingratitute of the whites, when I saw their fine houses, rich harvests, and everything desirable around them; and recollected that all this land had been ours, for which we and my people never received a dollar, and that the whites were not satisfied until they took our village and our grave-yards from us, and removed us across the Mississippi. *

The removal treaties guaranteed perpetual ownership of the new land to the Indians, but only a permanent end to the westward movement could have preserved Indian land tenure. By the 1850s white farmers were fighting Indians for control of the Oregon Territory; the gold rush and other expeditions were bringing the California Indians to the brink of extinction; Mormons were settling the Great Basin; miners, traders, and ranchers had invaded the lands of the southwestern tribes in New Mexico; and white pioneers in Kansas and Nebraska were already clamoring for removal of the "removed" tribes.

Since the Lewis and Clark expedition of 1804–1806, the Indians of the Pacific Northwest had encountered a few white explorers, fur trappers, and missionaries and had responded with curiosity and disdain. With the acquisition of the Oregon Territory in 1846, however, thousands of American farmers poured in. When a long winter killed much of the game and a measles epidemic devastated several tribes in 1847 and 1848, Cayuse Indians attacked the Protestant mission of Marcus and Narcissa Whitman, killing them both. In 1853, when a new territorial governor began placing various tribes on reservations to clear the way for a transcontinental railroad, the Yakimas revolted, and government troops did not subdue them until 1858. The Yakimas, Cayuses, Wallawallas, Nez Percés, Spokanes, and Palouses were all moved to reservations.

The gold rush of 1849 brought disaster to the nomadic California tribes. Massacres, epidemic diseases, and forced slave labor almost destroyed them entirely. Their population declined from more than 100,000 people in 1849 to less than 15,000 in 1860.

When Mormon settlers entered the Great Basin in 1847, the lives of the Utes, Paiutes, and Shoshones changed immediately. Persecution at the hands of fanatical Protestants had left the Mormons more tolerant of "others" than most whites. Also Mormon theology held native Americans in special esteem, seeing them as a remnant of the lost tribes of

* Donald Jackson, ed., *Autobiography of Black Hawk* (Urbana, 1955), pp. 164–165.

Israel whom God had led to the New World and had destined to become someday a mighty and noble civilization. Mormon treatment of the Indians was more careful and diplomatic than that of most other whites. But as Brigham Young established Mormon farming colonies in southern Utah, Nevada, California, Arizona, Wyoming, Idaho, and Canada, and thousands of non-Mormon settlers came to the Salt Lake Valley in the 1850s, the white population increased and Indians lost much of their land. Construction of the transcontinental railroad through Utah Territory nullified more Indian land claims. In the end the Utes, Paiutes, and Shoshones were confined to reservations in some of the least hospitable regions of the Great Basin.

In 1848, when the Senate ratified the Treaty of Guadalupe Hidalgo with Mexico, the United States took sovereignty over the southwestern Indians and their lands. Americans had traded with the Spanish and Indians in the Southwest for years, and during the 1840s more white settlers came to work the silver mines and establish cattle and sheep ranches. The Pueblo Indians rebelled at Taos, New Mexico, in 1847 and killed several whites, but the uprising was quickly crushed. After that the Hopis, Zuñis, and Pueblos remained passively cooperative. Kit Carson and several hundred American troops attacked Navajos who had been raiding isolated white settlements in 1864, and eventually the Indians were marched several hundred miles to a reservation in eastern New Mexico, where they remained for three years until the government transferred them back to Arizona. Except for the Apaches, the Indians of the Southwest were defeated by 1865.

In the 1850s the tribes "removed" to the Great Plains twenty years before faced new problems. As white settlers poured into Kansas and Nebraska, the pressures on Indian land intensified just as the gold rush and the opening of Oregon was increasing the pioneer traffic. New treaties pushed the Indians north and south of the pioneer trails. During the Civil War some members of the Five Civilized Tribes of the South, hoping to regain their land, sided with the Confederacy, but after the war victorious northerners gave some of the Indians' land in Oklahoma to white settlers. They were then confined to much smaller, poorer tracts of land scattered over the territory. By 1865 only the Plains Indians and a few isolated tribes in the Southwest and the northern plateau remained free, and their days were numbered.

The Final Conquest

Beginning in the 1860s three developments sealed the Indians' future. First, Congress passed the Homestead Act in 1862, and after the Civil War hundreds of thousands of white settlers took up 160-acre tracts of free land in the Dakotas, Montana, Wyoming, Colorado, western Kansas, western Nebraska, and Oklahoma. The mass migration imposed extraordinary pressures on the Plains Indians. Second, the completion of five transcontinental railroads, linking eastern manufacturers with western markets, made their situation worse because the roads sold parcels of their federal land grants to white farmers. The Union Pacific–Central Pacific line from Omaha to San Francisco was finished in 1869; farther north the Northern Pacific and the Great Northern railroads were completed in 1883 and 1893, passing through the Dakotas, Montana, Idaho, and Washington to link the Great Lakes with Puget Sound. And by 1884 two southern routes were completed. The Atchison, Topeka, and Santa Fe ran from eastern Kansas to Los Angeles and the Southern Pacific connected New Orleans with the West Coast. Third, at the same time the railroads were being built, the buffalo slaughter became large-scale. Some public officials encouraged the hunts, hoping they would destroy the Plains economy and make it easier to force the Indians onto reservations. It worked. By 1883 the southern herd was wiped out and only remnants of the northern herd were surviving in Canada. The economy of the Plains Indians was in ruins.

Conflict began along the major trade and migration routes, and later erupted wherever white settlers encroached on Indian land. Late in 1862, after repeated acts of fraud by traders and a massive increase in settlers along the Minnesota River, the Santee Sioux rebelled and killed several hundred whites. Panic spread throughout southern Minnesota and thousands of people fled. Soldiers eventually dispersed the Sioux, capturing more than four hundred and driving others into Canada and the western Dakotas.

The southern Cheyenne in eastern Colorado also reacted to white settlers. After several skirmishes with whites in 1864, they agreed to a negotiated peace and quietly moved to a temporary camp at Sand Creek, Colorado. There, on November 29, 1864, soldiers under the command of Colonel John M. Chivington brutally attacked the Indians. In an orgy of violence they murdered three hundred Cheyenne, sparing none, not even women and children. A general war spread throughout eastern Colorado and western Kansas as enraged Cheyennes, Sioux, and Arapahos avenged the Sand Creek massacre. Not until 1868, when Lieutenant Colonel George A. Custer's Seventh Cavalry defeated the southern Cheyenne, did calm return temporarily to the Great Plains.

The wars intensified in the 1870s. In Idaho, Oregon, and Washington, troops extinguished the final resistance of the plateau tribes. The Modocs went to the Oklahoma reservations in 1872, and a few years later the Flatheads and Bannocks moved to reservations in the Northwest. In 1877, after a dramatic attempt to escape to Canada, Chief

Joseph and the Nez Percés were captured in northern Montana. In his surrender message to the United States Army, Chief Joseph said with tragic eloquence:

> I am tired of fighting. Our chiefs are killed . . . the old men are dead. . . . It is cold and we have no blankets. The little children are freezing to death. My people . . . have no blankets, no food. . . . I want to have time to look for my children and see how many I can find. Maybe I shall find them among the dead. Hear me, my chiefs, I am tired; my heart is sick and sad. From where the sun now stands, I will fight no more forever.*

The remnants of the Nez Percé tribe went to Indian Territory in Oklahoma.

In the Southwest the city-dwelling tribes and the Navajos were defeated by the 1870s, but the Apaches resisted fiercely. Between 1862 and 1886 they carried on a successful guerrilla war against white settlements, and not until 1886, when Chief Geronimo of the Chiricahua Apaches surrendered, did peace come to Arizona and New Mexico. Geronimo was sent to prison and the Apaches to reservations, where they depended for survival on supplies from the Department of the Interior.

Hostilities resumed on the Plains in 1874, when the discovery of gold in the Black Hills of South Dakota brought thousands of white miners. Only six years earlier the Sioux had been given "eternal" control of the area, but under intense political pressure the federal government hedged on its promise and asked them to leave. They refused, and the Department of the Interior ordered them out of the Black Hills. Still they refused, and government troops under Custer, now a general, and General George Crook left for the Dakotas. In one of the most famous battles in American military history, a combined force of Cheyenne and Sioux warriors, led by Crazy Horse and Sitting Bull, killed Custer and more than two hundred of his men at the Little Big Horn River in 1876. Inspired by revenge, white troops drove Sitting Bull into Canada and the Oglala Sioux to a South Dakota reservation. After more hopeless fighting, Crazy Horse surrendered in 1877 and the northern Cheyennes were moved to the Indian Territory. In fury and desperation Morning Star and Little Wolf led them off the reservation the following year and tried to make it back to ancestral lands in Montana. The flight captured national attention and touched the hearts of many whites, but troops soon returned those who were left to Oklahoma.

The last vestige of Indian resistance disappeared after the murder of Sitting Bull in 1890. Born to the Hunkpapa Sioux in 1834, he was perhaps

* Quoted in Angie Debo, *A History of the Indians of the United States* (Norman, Okla., 1970), pp. 215–216.

the most renowned native American of the nineteenth century. He returned to the United States from Canada in 1881 after government agents offered him amnesty. Under house arrest at Fort Randall for two years, he later moved to Standing Rock, Dakota Territory, before spending a year on tour with Buffalo Bill's Wild West Show. By 1888 he was openly opposing any further Sioux land cessions, and after resisting arrest in 1890 he was shot to death by Indian police on the reservation. News of his murder spread quickly through the Dakota Territory, and at Wounded Knee Creek, South Dakota, an angry Sioux warrior killed an army officer. In the ensuing melée enraged soldiers killed more than a hundred and fifty Sioux men, women, and children. That tragedy formally closed a chapter in American history. After 1890, with the buffalo herds gone and white homesteads throughout the "Great American Desert," Indian resistance would have been totally suicidal. Stripped of their land, the native Americans finally gave up and headed for the reservations. The wars were over.

Life was different on the reservations. Instead of deferring to tribal leaders, native Americans found themselves subject to the authority of Interior Department agents. Traditional attitudes toward power, authority, and responsibility were expected to change completely. Reservation Indians had to surrender the hunter-warrior ideal and accept passive roles as dependent wards of the state. All this upset the emotional balance of families and communities. They also had to accept the constant presence of white idealists and missionaries bent on converting them to Christian civilization.

With their independence lost, their cosmic rationale gone, and their culture under siege, thousands of native Americans turned to alcoholism and peyotism. Despite laws against it, local Indian agents often supplied liquor as a pacifier, and Indians readily accepted it as an escape from reality. Other Indians turned to peyote hallucinations. A derivative of the cactus plant, peyote found a ready audience among the hopeless hunters of the Indian Territory because it gave its users spectacular dreams and a heightened sense of personal value. The peyote cult had come from Mexico to the Mescalero Apaches, who passed it on to the Kiowas, Caddos, and Comanches. Quanah Parker, who was a mixed-blood child of a Comanche chief and a white mother and had resisted white settlement until his surrender in 1875, became a leader of the peyote cult and gained great influence over reservation Indians. By the 1880s peyotism had spread to the Cheyennes, Shawnees, and Arapahos, and by 1900 to the Pawnees, Delawares, Osages, and Winnebagoes. In the early 1900s peyotism reached the Omahas, Utes, Crows, Menominees, Iowas, Sioux, and Shoshones, and in the 1920s and 1930s it spread to the Gosiutes, Paiutes, Blackfoot, Creeks,

Cherokees, Seminoles, and Chippewas. Eventually peyotism was institutionalized into the Native American Church, which was designed to bring peace to people living a life over which they had no control.

Reservation life also produced a burst of supernaturalism. Sometime between 1869 and 1872 a Paiute prophet named Wovoka claimed to have received a special revelation from the Great Spirit:

> When the sun died, I went up to heaven and saw God and all the people who had died a long time ago. God told me to come back and tell my people they must be good and love one another, and not fight, or steal, or lie. He gave me this dance to give to my people.*

The Ghost Dance religion spread throughout the plateau, the Great Basin, and on to the Great Plains. The ceremony consisted of four straight nights of physically exhausting dances, and the religion offered a spiritual explanation for the native American dilemma. As a Paiute Indian explained it:

> All Indians must dance, everywhere, keep on dancing. Pretty soon in next spring Big Man come. He bring back all game of every kind. The game be thick everywhere. All dead Indians come back and live again. They all be strong just like young men, be young again. Old blind Indians see again and get young and have fine time. When Old Man comes this way, then all the Indians go to mountains, high up away from whites. . . . Then while Indians way up high, big flood comes like water and all white people die . . . nobody but Indians everywhere and game all kinds thick.†

According to this theology, God had punished the Indians for their sins by sending whites to rape the land and slaughter the people. Soon, however, with Indian repentance complete and sins atoned for, God would destroy whites, resurrect the Indian dead, and restore the buffalo herds. Although details varied from tribe to tribe, the Ghost Dance looked for the day when the promises would come true, and in the meantime the Indians wore sacred undergarments to protect themselves from danger. Not until 1890, when the slaughter at Wounded Knee proved the Ghost Dance would not protect the Indians from the soldiers' bullets, did the religion begin to decline.

Finally, a new version of an old Indian religion called the Sun Dance appeared. Before the conquest several tribes had used the Sun Dance to bring successful hunts, shore up personal courage, and guarantee victory over enemies. Days of dancing, fasting, and self-mutilation — men

---

* James Mooney, *The Ghost Dance Religion and the Sioux Outbreak of 1890* (Chicago, 1965), p. 2.

† Ibid., p. 26

slicing open the skin of their chests, passing rawhide skewers through the cuts, tying the rawhide to poles, and stepping back forcefully until the skewers ripped through the skin—were supposed to bring peace with the Great Spirit and prosperity in the world. On the reservations the Sun Dance became extremely popular with the Utes, Shoshones, and Goshiutes of the Great Basin, and changed fundamentally in character to a redemptive, individual religion. By participating in the Sun Dance, avoiding alcohol and sexual infidelity, and living a thoughtful, considerate life, an Indian could transform his personality. Where the Ghost Dance promised changes in reality, the Sun Dance promised only the possibility of individual virility and understanding of reality, a oneness with the universe that white people could never achieve.

Alcoholism, peyotism, the Ghost Dance, and the Sun Dance were hardly the conversion that white idealists were after. Native Americans still had little to do with white culture and remained as hundreds of distinct ethnic groups in the United States.

SUGGESTED READINGS

Andrist, Ralph K. *The Long Death: The Last Days of the Plains Indians*. New York: 1964.

Anson, Bert. *The Miami Indians*. Norman, Oklahoma: 1970.

Berkhofer, Robert F. *Salvation and the Savage: An Analysis of Protestant Missions and American Indian Response, 1787–1862*. Lexington, Kentucky: 1965.

Brown, Dee. *Bury My Heart at Wounded Knee*. New York: 1970.

Brown, Mark H. *The Flight of the Nez Percé*. New York: 1967.

Cook, Sherburne F. *The Conflict Between the California Indians and White Civilization*. Berkeley, Cal.: 1976.

DeRosier, Arthur. *The Removal of the Choctaw Indians*. Knoxville, Tenn.: 1970.

Fahey, John. *The Flathead Indians*. Norman, Oklahoma: 1974.

Faulk, Odie B. *Crimson Desert: Indian Wars of the Southwest*. New York: 1974.

———. *The Geronimo Campaign*. New York: 1969.

Fehrenbach, T. R. *Comanches: The Destruction of a People*. New York: 1974.

Freeman, John F. "The Indian Convert: Theme and Variation." *Ethnohistory*, 12 (Spring 1965), 113–128.

Fritz, Henry E. *The Movement for Indian Assimilation, 1860–1890*. Philadelphia: 1963.

Gibson, Arrell M. *The Chickasaws*. Norman, Oklahoma: 1971.

Gunnerson, Dolores A. *The Jicarilla Apaches: A Study in Survival*. DeKalb, Ill.: 1974.

Heizer, Robert F., and Almquist, Alan J. *The Other Californians: Prejudice and Discrimination Under Spain, Mexico, and the United States to 1920*. Berkeley, Cal.: 1971.

Jorgensen, Joseph G. *The Sun Dance Religion: Power for the Powerless*. Chicago: 1972.

Joseph, Alvin M. *The Nez Percé Indians and the Opening of the Northwest*. New Haven, Conn.: 1965.

La Barre, Weston. *The Peyote Cult*. New York: 1975.

Lurie, Nancy Oestreich. "The World's Oldest On-Going Protest Demonstration: Native American Drinking Patterns." *Pacific Historical Review*, 40 (August 1971), 311–329.

McKnitt, Frank. *Navajo Wars*. Albuquerque, N.M.: 1972.

Metcalf, P. Richard. "Who Should Rule at Home: Native American Politics and Indian-White Relations." *Journal of American History*, 61 (December 1974), 651–677.

Mooney, James. *The Ghost Dance Religion and the Sioux Outbreak of 1890*. Chicago: 1965.

Olson, James C. *Red Cloud and the Sioux Problem*. Lincoln, Neb.: 1965.

Phillips, George H. *Chiefs and Challengers: Indian Resistance and Cooperation in Southern California*. Berkeley, Cal.: 1975.

Price, John A. "North American Indian Families." In Charles H. Mindel and Robert W. Habenstein, *Ethnic Families in America*. New York: 1976.

Prucha, Francis Paul. *American Indian Policy in Crisis: Christian Reformers and the Indian, 1865–1900*. Norman, Oklahoma: 1975.

——. *The Sword of the Republic: The United States Army on the Frontier, 1783–1846*. New York: 1969.

Rogin, Michael Paul. *Fathers and Children: Andrew Jackson and the Subjugation of the American Indian*. New York: 1975.

Satz, Ronald. *American Indian Policy in the Jacksonian Era*. Lincoln, Neb.: 1975.

Sheehan, Bernard W. *Seeds of Extinction: Jeffersonian Philanthropy and the American Indian*. Chapel Hill, N.C.: 1973.

Strickland, Rennard. *Fire and the Spirits: Cherokee Law from Clan to Court*. Norman, Oklahoma: 1975.

Thrapp, Dan L. *The Conquest of Apacheria*. Norman, Oklahoma: 1967.

Trennert, Robert A. *Alternative to Extinction: Federal Indian Policy and the Beginnings of the Reservation System, 1846–1851*. Philadelphia: 1975.

Utley, Robert M. *Frontier Regulars: The United States Army and the Indian, 1866–1891*. New York: 1973.

Wallace, Anthony F. *The Death and Rebirth of the Seneca*. New York: 1970.

Washburn, Wilcomb E. *The Indian in America*. New York: 1975.

Wilkins, Thurman. *Cherokee Tragedy: The Story of the Ridge Family and the Decimation of a People*. New York: 1970.

Chapter Ten

Afro-Americans: From Slavery to Freedom

For Americans the first century of national life was tempestuous, marked by hope and despair, triumph and defeat, an era beginning with a burst of democratic euphoria and ending in 1877 after an agonizing civil war. Fundamentally the Civil War was an ideological and cultural crisis, an attempt to determine the real meaning of equality and freedom. Black people assumed a conspicuously public place in the national consciousness as the United States tried to carve out a philosophical place in Western civilization.

The American Revolution was more than a political separation from England; it also released a set of ideological forces that would ultimately lead to the Civil War. By 1776 the colonists were maturing politically, slowly becoming American nationals. From England they had inherited ideas of representative government, the evil nature of political power, and the unalienable rights of man, and when England violated those rights after 1763, the colonists became revolutionaries willing to resort to violence. By 1861 that spirit would ignite the Civil War.

Throughout the eighteenth century Philadelphia Quakers had denounced slavery because of their egalitarian theology. The antislavery movement was also strengthened by the Enlightenment emphasis on reason and natural rights which made legal justifications for slavery increasingly hollow. And evangelical Protestantism inspired a spirit of abolition in some northern circles by advocating charity toward all people. All these arguments had fallen on deaf ears until the Revolution.

But then the inconsistency of denouncing oppression while condoning slavery began to weigh heavily on the Founding Fathers. How could Americans criticize English oppression when 500,000 blacks were slaves? After 1776 Thomas Paine, Benjamin Franklin, Thomas Jefferson, James Otis, John Adams, Noah Webster, and John Jay all condemned slavery.

The military service of thousands of blacks during the Revoluation also pricked the conscience of America. Crispus Attucks, a runaway slave, was shot and killed during the Boston Massacre in 1770 and became the first American to die at the hands of British soldiers. Peter Salem and Salem Poore, both slaves freed to fight in the Continental Army, distinguished themselves at the Battle of Bunker Hill, as did Lemuel Haynes at the Battle of Ticonderoga and "Pompey" at the Battle of Stony Point. Manpower shortages forced state after state to free slaves who would volunteer to fight. Eventually more than five thousand blacks fought with colonial forces, participating in every major engagement from Lexington in 1775 to Yorktown in 1781. Their service further exposed the hypocrisy of slavery within a revolution.

Black People in the North

After the Revolution northern agriculture and industry became capital rather than labor intensive, relying on machines instead of people whenever possible. Because wheat, corn, and livestock farms as well as eastern factories did not depend on slave labor, the economic foundation of slavery crumbled. Nor was there a social rationale; the black population of the North was too small to threaten white society. There were only 75,000 blacks out of nearly 1.5 million northerners in 1776, and the ratio declined to only 250,000 blacks out of 20 million northerners in 1860. Not often frightened by the black minority, whites did not resist abolition; vested social and economic interests had little to lose from it.

For all these reasons a powerful movement arose in the North. Quakers organized the first antislavery society in 1775, and in 1780 Pennsylvania provided for the gradual abolition of slavery. Massachusetts abolished slavery by court order in 1783, and the next year Connecticut and Rhode Island passed general abolition laws. New York and New Jersey enacted similar laws in 1785 and 1786, and in 1787 the Northwest Ordinance prohibited slavery in the Ohio Valley. After fierce debate in 1787 the Constitutional Convention outlawed the importation of slaves after 1807. The American Revolution brought freedom from England and, for northern blacks, freedom from bondage.

Legal freedom, however, did not mean equality. In Ohio, Indiana, and Illinois white settlers from the South segregated free blacks whenever possible. White workers there feared economic competition from blacks, and black youths were often placed in long-term apprenticeships closely resembling slavery. Black adults could not serve on juries or vote, and immigration of blacks from other states was barred. Between 1807 and 1837 New Jersey, Connecticut, New York, Rhode Island, and Pennsylvania passed laws disfranchising blacks. And throughout the North black people were segregated in public facilities and widely discriminated against in the job market. The North was hardly the promised land.

Nevertheless, black people created meaningful lives for themselves. By 1860 there were more than 250,000 free blacks in the North; and although most were poor and restricted to menial jobs, several gained national recognition. Benjamin Banneker was a renowned astronomer and mathematician. Paul Cuffe, a black businessman from Massachusetts, became a wealthy shipbuilder and an advocate of black rights. Phillis Wheatley, Jupiter Hammon, and Gustavus Vassa were prominent black literary figures at the turn of the century. David Walker, a free black who had moved to Boston in 1829, wrote *Walker's Appeal*, which called on southern slaves to rise up against their masters. Robert Young, Theodore Wright, Sojourner Truth, Harriet Tubman, David Ruggles, and Charles Remond were all well-known black abolitionists.

Perhaps the most famous of all was Frederick Douglass. Born at Tuckahoe, Maryland, in 1817, Douglass escaped from slavery in 1838 and taught himself to read while working as a laborer. In 1841 he spoke at a meeting of the Massachusetts Antislavery Society, captivated the largely white audience, and immediately became one of the most popular abolitionists in the country. Writer, lecturer, and editor of the abolitionist *North Star*, Douglass went on to be active in Republican politics during the Civil War and, before his death in 1895, a Washington official and United States consul general to Haiti. His autobiography, published in 1845, was widely read.

Facing racial prejudice, Afro-Americans turn inward, relying on themselves for respect, recognition, and assistance. A number of early black organizations opposed slavery and campaigned for equal rights. The National Negro Convention, the American Moral Reform Society for Improving the Condition of Mankind, the General Colored Associations, the African Civilization Society, the American League of Colored Laborers, and the National Council of Colored People all demanded abolition and first-class citizenship for black people.

But the most important organizations in the black community were

Churches played a crucial role in Afro-American society. This engraving (1853) depicts a meeting in the African Methodist Church in Cincinnati, Ohio. (Culver Pictures, Inc.)

the fraternal, mutual aid societies and the churches. The African Union Society, the Free African Society, the Black Masons, and the Negro Oddfellows supplied medical, educational, and burial services to their members as well as a forum for recognizing achievements and resolving disputes. Even more important was the black church. Most blacks were Methodists or Baptists, probably because poor people generally joined those churches. But because of paternalism and forced segregation in white churches, black people began forming their own congregations late in the eighteenth century. In 1787, after being asked to occupy segregated pews at St. George's Methodist Church in Philadelphia, Richard Allen and Absolom Jones left and established the African Methodist Episcopal (AME) Church. In 1816 the independent AME churches in Pennsylvania, New Jersey, and Delaware joined into a national convocation and named Allen their bishop. Black Baptist churches also emerged in the North between 1805 and 1810. Independent of white influence, the black churches were influential forums where leadership could be developed and grievances freely expressed. In the process of selecting teachers, officers, ministers, and ecclesiastical representatives, black parishioners exercised a franchise power which the larger society denied them. The churches actively promoted educational and fraternal programs. Richard Allen, for example, played a leading role in the Free African Society and the Black Masons. Thus

when free blacks became active in their churches, they were also helping to build other social and economic institutions in their communities.
Even in our own time, the most influential black leaders—including
Martin Luther King, Jr. and Jesse Jackson—have come from the black
churches.

Black People in the South

The ideological revolution was stillborn in the South. A small but vocal
antislavery movement developed in the upper South during the Revolution, but it died out after 1800. To most white southerners abolition was
an ugly word. Slavery was still justified as providing cheap labor and a
means of controlling black workers.

Just as the economic need for slaves was disappearing in the North,
southern dependence on cheap labor was increasing. With their soil
exhausted and world markets glutted in the 1790s, tobacco farmers were
searching desperately for a more lucrative crop. The Industrial Revolution was stimulating demand for cotton, but the South could not fill it
because removing seeds from the fiber was too expensive. Eli Whitney
solved that problem in 1793 when he invented the cotton gin, a machine
which removed the seeds without destroying the cotton fiber, and
cotton quickly became the South's major cash crop. Production increased from 4,000 bales in 1790 to more than 5 million bales in 1860.
The southern plantation economy depended on having millions of black
slaves in the fields each day.

Southerners also opposed abolition for social reasons. By 1860 there
were 4 million blacks to only 7 million whites in the South. In Virginia,
Texas, and Arkansas, whites outnumbered blacks by three to one, but in
Mississippi and South Carolina blacks outnumbered whites. The population was divided almost equally in Louisiana, Alabama, Florida, and
Georgia. The size of the black population seemed ominous; whites were
obsessed with fears of slave uprisings, and only slavery gave them absolute control over black people. Emancipation was unthinkable.

Because the United States was in general a Protestant, capitalistic,
and states-rights society, there was no central authority—church or
state—to ameliorate the condition of slaves. Slave status imposed severe pressures on black people. The decisions of whites often invaded
the privacy of social and family life. Black men were not permitted full
decision-making power in their homes; black women had to work in the
fields even when their children were young and were sometimes
exploited sexually by white men; children had to go to work at an early
age; and family members could be sold separately at any time. Southern

states outlawed any education for slaves, hoping that illiteracy would keep them dependent on their white owners. Freedmen Bureau schools, established by the federal government during Reconstruction, provided most southern blacks with their first opportunity to learn to read and write.

Living conditions were primitive. At the age of ten or twelve, black children went to work in the fields and would perform backbreaking tasks all their lives unless they were among a tiny group of skilled workers or domestic servants. Typical food rations for field hands were four pounds of pork fat, a peck of corn meal, and a small amount of coffee and molasses each week; they usually had one dress or two shirts and one pair of trousers; and they lived in damp, small shanty homes in the "quarters." One slave song transcribed by Frederick Douglass pointed out the irony of slavery:

> We raise de wheat
> Dey gib us de corn;
> We bake de bread,
> Dey gib us de cruss;
> We sif de meal,
> Dey gib us de huss;
> We peel de meat,
> Dey gib us de skin;
> And dat's de way
> Dey takes us in.*

There were few rewards and few incentives.

But slave-owners had to provide a subsistence living for their property, if only to protect their own investment. Planters also had a vested interest in plantation stability because it boosted productivity; terribly unhappy slaves or slaves who hated an overseer were inefficient workers. Slaves resisted in many ways. To avoid field work, many convinced their masters that blacks were naturally lazy, clumsy, and irresponsible people from whom little could be expected. Other slaves injured farm animals, broke tools, and disabled wagons to postpone work. Some slaves even hurt themselves, inflicting wounds on their hands or legs, to avoid being overworked or sold. Feigning illness was common. Thousands of slaves also ran away, hoping to reach the North or Canada on the "underground railroad"—a group of whites and free blacks who assisted runaway slaves. And there were hundreds of slave rebellions. From the 1712 uprising in New York City, which killed nine whites, to Nat Turner's rebellion in 1831, which resulted in the death of sixty

* Frederick Douglass, *My Bondage and My Freedom* (New York, 1855), p. 253.

Virginia whites, discontented slaves often used violence to try to liberate themselves. Still, such rebellions were relatively rare; slave resistance was more often directed at ameliorating the conditions of slavery than at liberation.

Within the slave quarters, far from white society, was the world of Afro-America. "From sundown to sunup" a special slave culture appeared which eased the trauma of bondage, provided group solidarity and status, verbalized aggressions, and demonstrated love. The slaves' relationship with whites during the workday was secondary to their relationship with one another, and scholarly theories describing the slave personality only in terms of white society overlook the primary environment of the quarters. There blacks developed ethical and family values, positive self-images, and group unity. Recreation, religion, and family were the foundations of black society.

Leisure time permitted slaves to play social roles different from that of driven servants. In the evenings they gathered to visit and gossip, or to sing and dance; and on Sundays and holidays they hunted, fished, gambled, attended church, or had afternoon parties. Most excelled at something—racing, storytelling, singing, dancing, preaching, or teaching—and enjoyed prestige from such talents. Leisure activities offered a respite from the drudgery of the fields, a liberation from the emotional pressures of bondage.

Music was central to slaves' lives and accompanied daily activities—work, play, and church services. It was functional and improvisational, symbolically related to group solidarity and individual aspirations. In their songs the slaves retained the form and spirit of their African origins, fashioning expressive modes for dealing with the New World. Spirituals and secular songs helped them express anger or despair which whites would not have tolerated in speech. One slave song was:

> See these poor souls from Africa
> Transported to America;
> We are stolen, and sold in Georgia,
> Will you go along with me?
> We are stolen, and sold in Georgia,
> Come sound the jubilee!
>
> See wives and husbands sold apart,
> Their children's screams will break my heart—
> There's a better day a coming,
> Will you go along with me?
> There's a better day a coming,
> Go sound the jubilee!*

---

* W. W. Brown, *Narrative of William W. Brown, A Fugitive Slave* (Boston, 1847), p. 51.

Often whites had no idea what the lyrics of slave songs implied, but to blacks their meaning was quite clear.

Religion too liberated slaves from the white world and allowed them to express their deep feelings. Slave religion made few distinctions between the secular and the spiritual, between this life and the next, and symbolically carried slaves back in history to more glorious times and forward into a more benign future, linking them with the cosmos and assuring them that there was justice in the universe. Except for proud first-generation Africans tenaciously holding to the faiths of their fathers, most slaves converted to fundamentalist Protestantism, particularly that of the Baptists and Methodists because they sponsored the development of black clergies. Some white planters encouraged religion as a tool of social control, and white ministers preached bondage as the will of God. Patience, obedience, submission, gratitude—these were the themes of white-sponsored slave religion. Lunsford Lane, an escaped slave, recalled in 1848 that he had often heard white preachers tell slaves

> how good God was in bringing us over to this country from dark . . . Africa, and permitting us to listen to the sound of the gospel. . . . The first commandment . . . was to obey our masters, and the second was . . . to do as much work when they or the overseers were not watching us as when they were.*

But the slaves were not fooled, and they adapted Christianity to their own needs. In white churches they went through the motions of reverent attention, but they were rarely taken in by the joyless message of white preachers bent on molding them into submission. Instead they used white services to visit with friends and family from other farms or plantations, which they could rarely do at other times because the rigid pass laws confined them to their masters' property.

When permitted to worship on their own, the slaves reinterpreted Christianity and enjoyed an autonomy denied them everywhere else. Rejecting Calvinist notions of predestination, unworthiness, sin, and damnation as well as the Pauline doctrine of dutiful obedience, slave spirituals sang of redemption, glory, freedom, change, and justice. Black culture was not obsessed with guilt and depravity, and black preachers spoke of the spiritual equality of all people and God's uncompromising love for everyone. Threatened on all sides by a hostile environment, black slaves united the next world with this one and bound themselves into a single community, a "chosen people" loved by God. And this redemptive vision thrived in black America even though white society repeatedly tried to tell them that they were the lowliest of human beings. Slave religion allowed blacks to vent the frustrations of

* Lunsford Lane, *The Narrative of Lunsford Lane* (Boston, 1848), pp. 20–21.

bondage, united them in a sense of mission, and recognized them as individuals. Theirs was a spiritual world of deliverance, of Moses leading a special people out of bondage and Jesus saving them from a corrupt world.

Slave folk tales and beliefs in voodoo, magic, and the world of spirits reinforced the role of religion. African cultures had always assumed that all life had direction and that apparently random events were part of a larger cosmic plan, which could be divined by reading the appropriate "signs" in nature and human affairs. Man was part of a natural pantheon of life. All things had causes, and if one could figure them out they could be controlled. These ideas were not completely alien to Europeans either; beliefs in witchcraft, satanic influence, and magical healings were still widely held. Slaves used folk beliefs and folk medicine to heal the sick, and some folk practitioners were highly respected. Certain signs—an owl's screech, a black cat crossing one's path, the approach of a cross-eyed person—indicated bad luck ahead, which could be remedied by such devices as spitting, crossing fingers, turning pockets inside out, or turning shoes upside down on the porch. Dreams had great meaning. The world of magic and voodoo gave slaves a sense of power over their masters, for in the hexes, signs, and punishments of the supernatural they tried to control the behavior of whites and their own destiny. To blacks African folk culture offered a degree of power, a means of integrating life and transcending their enslavement.

Finally, in the slave family Afro-Americans found companionship, love, esteem, and sexual fulfillment—things the master-slave relationship denied them. Despite the breakup of families through the sale of slaves, white sexual exploitation of black women, and incursions on the authority of black parents, the family was the basic institution of slave society. Although antebellum slave society tolerated premarital sexual liaisons, adultery was strictly forbidden. Once two people had "jumped the broomstick," fidelity was expected. Typical slave households had two parents and were male dominated: the father exercised discipline and supplemented the family diet by hunting and fishing, and the mother was responsible for household duties and raising young children. That former slaves eagerly had their marriages legalized after the Civil War and searched the country over to reunite separated families confirms the loyalty of parents, children, and spouses.

Slavery and the Civil War

Since the colonial period economic interest and political philosophy had divided the North and the South. Committed to an agrarian economy and international export markets, the South had never seen the need for a national bank, high tariffs, internal improvements, or any other measures designed to stimulate industry. Most southern politicians preached laissez-faire, states' rights, and a strict interpretation of the Constitution to prevent preferential treatment of northern manufacturers. With a mixed economy of farming, commerce, and manufacturing, the North favored protective tariffs, a strong national bank, and federally financed internal improvements.

But when the issue of slavery was added to these differences, civil war erupted. Slavery was the structural foundation of southern society. It created a static caste system in the South, different from the more open class system of the North. And slavery went against the ideas of democracy, equality, and freedom. Some northerners attacked it as a moral evil, while many southerners defended it as a moral good, a way of preserving white culture and introducing black people to Christian civilization.

At first the national debate was limited. William Lloyd Garrison and Frederick Douglass called for the immediate abolition of slavery, but most northerners were unwilling to sanction such a radical disruption of southern life. Instead they opted for more gradual schemes. Formed in 1816, the American Colonization Society campaigned to resettle blacks in Africa, and before the Civil War the society sent several thousand blacks to Liberia. Most free blacks detested the idea, claiming the right of any other native-born American to dignity and equality *within* the United States. Other northerners wanted gradual abolition and compensation by the federal government to slaveholders for the loss of their property. The South would have none of it.

Most northerners realized that immediate abolition, gradual abolition, and colonization were naïve, unworkable approaches to the problem. They decided just to oppose the extension of slavery into the western territories, hoping to contain the "peculiar institution" in the Old South, where it might expire gradually. The Liberty party of 1840 and 1844, the Free-Soil party of 1848, and the Republican party— organized in 1854—committed themselves to that objective. But southerners believed that for slavery and the plantation system to survive they would have to have access to fresh soil in the West.

The sectional strife also reflected attitudes toward the composition of American society. A minority of northern whites opposed the expansion of slavery into the territories because they believed slavery was immoral and that any measures strengthening it were similarly evil. But they were joined by millions of others who opposed the expansion of slavery for economic reasons—free white workers could not compete financially with black slaves—or who disliked black people in general. Confining slavery to the South would guarantee free territories and a largely white society, where the entrepreneurial instincts of Yankee culture could flourish. Southern whites, convinced that containment of slavery was a first step toward its ultimate eradication, and terrified by the prospect of having 4 million free blacks in the South, insisted on the right to carry slaves into the territories, which the Dred Scott decision by the Supreme Court in 1857 permitted them to do. Southerners also realized that containment of slavery would guarantee the nationwide triumph of Yankee entrepreneurialism and its faith in technological change, material progress, and democratic egalitarianism. So in part the debate over free-soil politics was a cultural conflict between Yankee northerners and white southerners.

Between 1820 and 1860 every sectional crisis in the United States—the Missouri Compromise of 1820, the Mexican War of 1846, the Compromise of 1850, the Kansas-Nebraska Act of 1854, and the Dred Scott case of 1857—involved slavery in the territories. When the Republican candidate, Abraham Lincoln, won the presidential election of 1860 on a platform of free soil, protective tariffs, a national bank, and internal improvements, white southerners felt threatened socially, economically, and philosophically. The South panicked and seceded from the Union.

The Civil War ultimately destroyed slavery and resolved, legally at least, the status of black people. At first Lincoln's objectives were narrowly defined. The Civil War had broken out, he thought, only because southerners had insisted on carrying their slaves to the West; the North was fighting to prevent that and bring the South back into the Union. Preservation of the Union, not abolition, was the central issue. Suspicious of radical social change, Lincoln opposed abolition in the early months of the war. When General John C. Frémont entered Missouri in 1861 and freed the slaves, Lincoln angrily rescinded the order, and the next year he nullified General David Hunter's abolition order in Georgia, South Carolina, and Florida.

But a number of pressures transformed the Civil War into a struggle to preserve the Union *and* liberate the slaves. First, most northerners, including the president himself, had anticipated a brief, conclusive war in which superior northern forces would overwhelm the Confederacy. But after staggering defeats at Bull Run and in the Shenandoah Valley in 1861 and 1862, a war of attrition developed. Lincoln hoped abolition might disrupt the southern economy by depriving the Confederacy of 4 million slaves.

Political and ideological concerns also pushed Lincoln toward emancipation. Republican abolitionists were steadily gaining strength by denouncing the hypocrisy of proclaiming democracy while condoning slavery. Radical Republicans including Thaddeus Stevens, Charles Sumner, Wendell Phillips, and Benjamin Wade insisted that Lincoln abolish slavery and were outraged when he nullified military abolition orders. Lincoln was in political trouble. Military defeats had dissipated his popularity, and a powerful wing of his own party was condemning his insensitivity to the plight of black people. If he was to be renominated in 1864, Lincoln had to revive his popularity and attract Radical support. Abolition might do it. By appearing as a moral crusader rather than just a political leader, Lincoln hoped to shore up his crumbling political fortunes.

But regaining Radical Republican support posed another dilemma. Abolition would please the Radicals, but if Lincoln freed the slaves he would sacrifice the support of Democrats loyal to the Union in Delaware, Maryland, Kentucky, and Missouri—slave-owners who had opposed secession. Abolition might win renomination, but it would just as surely cost Lincoln the general election. Some way of satisfying Radical Republicans without alienating loyal slave-owning Democrats had to be found. Lincoln slowly moved toward partial emancipation. In the spring of 1862 he supported congressional abolition of slavery in the District of Columbia and in the territories. Finally, on January 1, 1863, Lincoln issued the Emancipation Proclamation, liberating only the slaves in the rebellious states. The 400,000 slaves in loyal border states remained slaves. Lincoln thus gained Radical support without estranging border Democrats. And in another brilliant political maneuver he selected Andrew Johnson, a loyal Tennessee Democrat, as his running mate in the election of 1864. He then went on to reelection.

In April 1865 the Union armies trapped General Robert E. Lee's troops near Appomattox Court House in Virginia. The Confederacy was finished and Lee surrendered. The national nightmare was over. More than 600,000 young men and $15 billion had disappeared in the smoke of destruction; dreams were broken, faiths shattered, and lives wasted. The South was a pocked no man's land of untilled farms, broken machinery, gutted buildings, fresh graves, worthless money, and defeated people. Schools, banks, and businesses were closed; inflation was spiraling; and unemployment was on the rise. Only southern blacks were hopeful that a new age of liberty and equality was dawning.

Reconstruction

The status of black people in American society had become a national obsession. Were they to remain beasts of burden, slaves in everything but name, or were they to become full citizens protected by the Constitution?

Radical Republicans wanted to elevate the political status of southern blacks. Supporters of high tariffs, federal internal improvements, free homesteads in the West, and free soil, the Republicans had been unpopular in the South long before the war, but to keep control of the federal government, they had to construct a southern political base. Former slaves would be the new constituency; the party of Lincoln, of freedom, would become the party of equality. By giving blacks the right to vote and hold public office, the Republicans intended to preserve their ascendancy. Only then could they be sure that Congress would pass the tariffs and subsidies the business community needed. Northern businessmen were also looking to the South as an economic colony, a source of raw materials and a market for finished products. Interested in the coal, iron, tobacco, cotton, and railroad industries of the South, northern investors wanted southern state legislatures to be Republican and pro-business. And many former abolitionists, now active among the Radical Republicans, wanted freedom converted into civil rights for the former slaves. Politics, economics, and ideology all combined to create a movement for black political liberty.

Thus during the Reconstruction period, the late 1860s and 1870s, Radical Republicans insisted on political rights for 4 million blacks. In March 1865 Congress created the Freedmen's Bureau to help blacks make the transition to freedom. The bureau sent thousands of doctors, nurses, lawyers, social workers, teachers, and administrative agents into the South to provide emergency food, jobs, housing, medical care, and legal aid to former slaves. Many white southerners hated the bureau and called its agents "carpetbaggers," but the bureau played an invaluable role in the South. The Thirteenth Amendment, ratified in December 1865, extended the Emancipation Proclamation to the border states. Slavery was ended. Early in 1866 Congress passed the Civil Rights Act outlawing discrimination on the basis or race, and two years later the Fourteenth Amendment gave black people citizenship and prohibited states from interfering with their civil liberties. In 1870 the Fifteenth Amendment gave blacks the right to vote.

White southerners fought back. Some states elected former Confederate authorities to local and state offices. Mississippi refused to ratify the Thirteenth Amendment and was joined by Georgia, Texas, and Virginia in postponing ratification of the Fourteenth Amendment. State legislatures enacted "black codes" segregating blacks in schools and public facilities, prohibiting them from carrying firearms or changing jobs, imposing strict vagrancy and curfew regulations on them, and making it virtually impossible for them to enter the skilled trades or the professions. In July 1866, when several hundred blacks and Unionists held a rally in New Orleans to protest the Louisiana black code, state troops moved in and shot two hundred demonstrators, killing forty of them.

Organized in 1865, the Ku Klux Klan relied on shootings, lynchings, torture, and intimidation to terrorize southern blacks into political submission.

The presence of Union troups guaranteed Reconstruction. More than 700,000 black adult males received the right to vote in 1870, and along with the "carpetbaggers" (northerners living in the South) and "scalawags" (white southerners in the Republican party), they took over every southern government except Virginia's. Sixteen blacks, including Hiram Revels and Blanche Bruce of Mississippi, entered the United States Congress, and hundreds of others took seats in the legislatures of South Carolina, North Carolina, Louisiana, Mississippi, Alabama, Arkansas, and Florida. Yet blacks never dominated any state government, even though this period has been called "Black Reconstruction."

Reconstruction governments in the South have sometimes been criticized as corrupt and incompetent. There was some corruption, to be sure, but the Reconstruction legislatures built the South's first public school system, eliminated debt imprisonment and property requirements for voting, repaired war-destroyed public buildings and roads, rebuilt railroads, repealed the black codes, enacted homestead laws, and tried to end discrimination in public facilities. Southern state governments were responding to the needs of poor people as well as rich, black as well as white.

Reconstruction collapsed as soon as Union troops left the South; blacks did not have the economic independence to survive politically. Radical Republicans had worried about black economic status and had even considered breaking up the plantations and distributing land among black families. But the confiscation schemes never made it through Congress, probably because they so clearly represented an assault on private property. Although blacks had gained the right to vote, they were economically dependent on propertied whites. When the troops left, whites exploited that dependence.

Nor were Republicans as concerned in 1877 about southern blacks as they had been in 1865. Politically they felt more secure about the future because new states were entering the Union. Nevada had become a state in 1864, and Nebraska followed three years later. Colorado received statehood in 1876, and the Dakotas, Montana, Washington, Idaho, Wyoming, and Utah would soon apply. Republican members of Congress from the new states would more than make up for the loss of the black vote in the South. Removal of federal troops, disfranchisement of black Republicans, and the resurrection of the white aristocracy no longer seemed so potentially disastrous. Northern businessmen began to think their economic interests might best be served by white Democrats. The momentum for black political rights evaporated. By 1877 the federal government had withdrawn its troops and whites were back in power in the South. Reconstruction was over, and black voters would soon fall victim to poll taxes, literacy tests, and white primaries.

During Reconstruction southern blacks had to adjust to their new freedom, and most did so simply by struggling to create a stable family life based upon legal marriages, reunions, the purchase of land and education. When the Union armies entered the South, they had established "contraband" camps where escaped slaves could live. Although the camps were makeshift and run by white soldiers who were often openly racist, blacks used the camps enthusiastically to begin their new lives. At the Fortress Monroe, Craney Island, and City Point camps mass ceremonies were held to legalize slave marriages. Blacks longed for the sanctity and stability of family life which legal marriage held out for them. They also wanted desperately to find family members who had been sold away. One slave song proclaimed:

> I've got a wife, and she's got a baby
> Way up North in Lower Canady—
> Won't dey shout when dey see Ole Shady
> Comin', Comin',! Hail, mighty day.
> Den away, Den away, for I can't stay any longer:
> Hurrah, Hurrah! for I am going home.*

Black newspapers abounded with personal classified ads of people trying to locate loved ones. One reason black people wandered so widely throughout the South after emancipation was not because they were irresponsible or did not want to work but because they were searching for parents, spouses, and children. Family reunion was the first task of freedom. Next came land and education. Thousands sacrificed to acquire their own farms, despite opposition from local whites, and tens of thousands supported Freedmen's Bureau schools to help educate their children. Emancipation held out the hope of a normal life in the United States, and southern blacks were determined to have it.

SUGGESTED READINGS

Absug, Robert H. "The Black Family During Reconstruction." In Nathan Huggins, ed. *Key Issues in the Afro-American Experience.* New York: 1971.
Belz, Herman. *A New Birth of Freedom: The Republican Party and Freedmen Rights, 1861–1866.* Westport, Conn.: 1976.

* Frank Moore, ed., *The Rebellion Record*, 11 vols. (New York, 1862-1864), 8:63.

Berlin, Ira. *Slaves Without Masters: The Free Negro in the Antebellum South.* New York: 1975.

Berry, Mary F. *Military Necessity and Civil Rights: Black Citizenship and the Constitution.* New York: 1977.

Berwanger, Eugene H. *The Frontier Against Slavery.* Urbana, Ill.: 1967.

Blassingame, John W. *The Slave Community: Plantation Life in the Antebellum South.* New York: 1972.

Brown, W. W. *Life of William Wells Brown, a Fugitive Slave.* Boston: 1848.

Cox, Lawanda, and Cox, John H. "Negro Suffrage and Republican Politics: The Problem in Reconstruction Historiography." *Journal of Southern History*, 33 (August 1967), 303–330.

Davis, David Brion. *The Problem of Slavery in the Age of Revolution: 1770–1823.* Ithaca, N.Y.: 1975.

Dillard, J. L. *Black English.* New York: 1972.

Douglass, Frederick. *Life and Times of Frederick Douglass.* New York: 1941.

Elkins, Stanley. *Slavery: A Problem in American Intellectual and Institutional Life.* Chicago: 1959.

Fischer, Roger. "Racial Segregation in Antebellum New Orleans." *American Historical Review*, 74 (February 1969), 926–937.

Fogel, Robert W., and Engerman, Stanley L. *Time on the Cross: The Economics of American Negro Slavery.* Boston: 1974.

Frazier, E. Franklin. *The Negro Family in the United States.* Chicago: 1939.

Frederickson, George M. *The Black Image in the White Mind: The Debate on Afro American Character and Destiny, 1817–1914.* New York: 1971.

Genovese, Eugene. *The Political Economy of Slavery.* New York: 1965.

———. *Roll, Jordan, Roll: The World the Slaves Made.* New York: 1974.

———. *The World the Slaveowners Made.* New York: 1971.

Gerteis, Louis S. *From Contraband to Freedom: Federal Policy Toward Southern Blacks, 1861–1865.* Westport, Conn.: 1973.

Gutman, Herbert G. *The Black Family in Slavery and Freedom, 1750–1920.* New York: 1976.

———. *Work, Culture, and Society in Industrializing America.* New York: 1976.

Levine, Lawrence W. *Black Culture and Black Consciousness: Afro-American Folk Thought from Slavery to Freedom.* New York: 1977.

Litwack, Leon. *North of Slavery: The Negro in the Free States, 1790–1860.* Chicago: 1961.

MacLeod, Duncan J. *Slavery, Race, and the American Revolution.* London: 1974.

Matthews, Donald G. *Slavery and Methodism: A Chapter in American Morality, 1780–1845.* Princeton, N.J.: 1965.

Muraskin, William A. *Middle Class Blacks in a White Society: Prince Hall Freemasonry in America.* Berkeley, Cal.: 1975.

Northrup, Solomon. *Twelve Years a Slave.* New York: 1853.

Owens, Leslie Howard. *This Species of Property: Slave Life and Culture in the Old South.* New York: 1976.

Quarles, Benjamin. *Black Abolitionists.* New York: 1969.

Rawick, George P. *From Sundown to Sunup: The Making of the Black Community*. Westport, Conn.: 1972.

Rice, C. Duncan. *The Rise and Fall of Black Slavery*. Baton Rouge, La.: 1975.

Robinson, Donald L. *Slavery in the Structure of American Politics, 1765–1820*. New York: 1971.

Sernett, Milton C. *Black Religion and American Evangelism: White Protestants, Plantation Missions, and the Flowering of Negro Christianity, 1787–1865*. Metuchen, N.J.: 1975.

Smith, Elbert B. *The Death of Slavery: The United States, 1837–1865*. Chicago: 1967.

Stampp, Kenneth. *The Peculiar Institution: Slavery in the Antebellum South*. New York: 1956.

Williamson, Joel. *After Slavery: The Negro in South Carolina During Reconstruction, 1861–1877*. Chapel Hill, N.C.: 1965.

Yetman, Norman. *Life Under the Peculiar Institution*. New York: 1970.

Zilversmit, Arthur. *The First Emancipation: Abolition in the North*. Chicago: 1967.

Chapter Eleven

Cultural Fusion: Mexican-Americans, 1519–1848

Mexican-American history began when Siberian hunters slowly scattered across the Western Hemisphere; those who settled central Mexico developed one of the most advanced cultures in the New World. When Hernando Cortez entered Tenochtitlán, he came upon the last in a series of sophisticated Indian cultures in Mesoamerica. Mayan civilization was the first. Between 1500 B.C. and 700 A.D. the Mayans developed a sedentary life based on corn cultivation, twenty-five city states, an effective medium of exchange, a fine transportation network, good educational programs, and an excellent water delivery system. Using slash-and-burn methods they cleared the dense tropical jungle and raised surpluses of corn, beans, peppers, tomatoes, and squash.

The Mayan social structure was specialized into priest, noble, warrior, free farmer, and slave classes. Mayan achievements included a hieroglyphic writing system, use of the zero in mathematics, several accurate calendars, water reservoirs, causeways, temples, pyramids, roads, and astronomical observatories. The Mayans mined gold and silver, cut and polished precious gems, wove cotton into richly elaborate textiles, and created expressive pottery, murals, and mosaics. During the years of Mayan ascendancy Mesoamerica stood with the Near East, West Africa, and the Indus River Valley as a cradle of civilization.

Around 800 A.D., because of overpopulation, soil exhaustion, or both, Mayan cities declined, roads fell into disrepair, and tropical jungles reclaimed the corn fields. The Toltecs then rose to power. In architecture and metallurgy, if not in mathematics and science, they rivaled the Mayans, and their serpent god Quetzalcoatl was worshiped throughout Mexico and South America. Brilliant at its peak, Toltec civilization declined as quickly as it had developed. In the fourteenth century the Aztecs, coming from a region in northern Mexico (the fabled Aztlán), conquered the Toltecs, settled in the valleys, and built the city of Tenochtitlán. Eventually the Aztec empire had several urban centers and governed nearly 9 million people. The Aztecs flourished by clearing the land, irrigating the fields, terracing the hillsides, and constructing artificial islands in lakes. They raised corn, beans, tobacco, squash, tomatoes, potatoes, chili, and cotton; collected mangoes, papayas, and avocados; and domesticated dogs and turkeys. When Montezuma II assumed the throne in 1502, Aztec civilization was among the most advanced in the world.

The Spanish Origins

Spain was then one of the most dynamic nations in Europe. The marriage between Isabella of Castile and Ferdinand of Aragon in 1469 had created a national dynasty, and over the next twenty years they subdued the nobility and united Spain. After a final victory at Granada in 1492, they expelled the Moors from the Iberian peninsula, ending an ethnic, religious, and political crusade which had lasted for 800 years. They then looked beyond Spain to new opportunities for wealth and prestige.

During the 1400s Portugal controlled commerce along the African coast and Italians monopolized the Near East trade. Spain considered diplomacy and even war to break those cartels until geographers suggested circling the globe. Reach the East, they said, by sailing west. To assert its national glory, outdo the Portuguese, and destroy the Italian monopoly, Spain conducted worldwide explorations. Columbus discovered the Bahamas, Cuba, and Haiti in 1492, and in three subsequent voyages explored Central America and the northern coast of South America. In 1499 and 1500 Alonso de Ojeda, Juan de la Cosa, and Peralonso Niña went to northern Venezuela and the Gulf of Maracaibo, and in 1513 Vasco de Balboa discovered the Pacific Ocean and Juan Ponce de León entered Florida. In 1519 Ferdinand Magellan began the circumnavigation of the globe, and Hernando Cortez and seven hundred men invaded Mexico. Spanish guns and horses gave Cortez military advantages, and Indian belief in the return of a bearded white deliverer provided an awesome, if temporary, psychological advantage. The Aztecs' policy of exacting tribute and their practice of human sacrifice had left them with bitter enemies throughout Mexico. Cortez shrewdly exploited these enmities, using Aztec foes against Montezuma's forces. In two years Montezuma was dead and the Aztec empire crushed. Between 1521 and 1540 Spain extended its authority throughout central and southern Mexico.

Spanish Catholicism was a complex affair, reflecting the nationalism of the new monarchs, the missionary zeal of humble friars, and the fanatical commitment of the *Reconquista* (the reconquest of Spain from the Moors). Ferdinand and Isabella ordered the Spanish clergy to purify themselves and preach the gospel for the glory of God and Spain. Claiming divine authority in the New World, they hoped to convert Indians and glorify Spain.

The Spaniards also hoped to take Indian land and use their labor. The *encomienda* and the *hacienda* dominated the economic relationship between Spaniards and Indians. Technically the encomienda was a feudal covenant in which a Spaniard provided military protection and religious instruction to Indians in return for work. Encomienda Indians became an exploited lower class in Mexico, laboring on farms, ranches, sugar mills, construction projects, and mines. Catastrophic declines in the native population, however, destroyed the encomienda. Between 1519 and 1600 measles, smallpox, diphtheria, whooping cough, and influenza reduced the Indian population from approximately 25 million to about 1 million. With less labor to exploit, Spaniards shifted from a labor-intensive to a land-intensive economy, gradually taking abandoned Indian property. Haciendas, or landed estates, replaced the encomiendas in the seventeenth century. Native civilization deteriorated, with Indians living at subsistence levels, tied to the haciendas by economic dependence and debt peonage, and by force when necessary.

The class structure reflected ethnic divisions. At the top were white European families, divided into Spanish-born *peninsulares* and Mexican-born *criollos*. At the bottom were Indian and black slaves, peons, and encomienda laborers. In between were *mestizos*—offspring of Spanish and Indian parents. In the 1500s less than 10 percent of the colonists were women, so sexual contact between Spanish men and Indian women was common. The few mestizos born in wedlock were raised as Spaniards, part of the first criollo generation. Illegitimate mestizos remained in the Indian villages. They were ethnically distinct, neither Catholic nor Aztec, Spanish nor Indian. During the sixteenth century a mestizo middle class gradually emerged, caught between the white peak and the Indian base of the social structure. Mestizos eventually became the largest group in Mexico. Children of Spanish and mestizo parents were known as *castizos*, and functioned on the periphery of the upper class; mestizos married mestizos, enlarging the middle class; and other mestizos married Indians and stayed in the lower class.

In the towns and cities mestizos were domestic servants to criollos and peninsulares or unskilled dock and construction workers. Some became overseers on the haciendas, or cowboys, sheepherders, or miners. Others were artisans. Thousands more became soldiers, salesmen, and small businessmen. Not as rich as whites but not as poor as Indians, they were a unique consequence of the New World colonies—a new ethnic group.

The Borderlands: Expansion Northward

Late in the sixteenth century New Spain began expanding north and northwest. Catholic missionaries, mestizo soldiers, and Mexican-Indians carried out the borderlands colonization. Expeditions searched for gold, and conquest of local Indians became the first stage in the settlement process. Priests then moved in and established missions, taught Spanish and Catholicism to the Indians, and started farms. The final stage began when soldiers remained in the north after their tour of duty. To service them, artisans and merchants settled near the missions and *presidios* (military outposts). Upper-class criollo or peninsulare women did not migrate, so mestizos became dominant, in numbers at least.

What is now New Mexico became the first borderlands colony. Rumors of the fabulously wealthy "Seven Cities of Cibola" had circulated in New Spain since 1519, and when Cabeza de Vaca returned from his ill-fated expedition to Florida in 1536, he amplified the excitement by spreading stories of gold-laden Indian societies to the north. In 1539 Fray Marcos de Niza explored western New Mexico in search of the cities, and Francisco Coronado searched between 1540 and 1542. In 1581 several Franciscan friars began proselytizing the Indians in the north, and their labors continued well into the nineteenth century. Finally, geopolitical concerns inspired expansion. The Pacific voyages of Sir Francis Drake in the 1570s convinced Spain that England had located the legendary Northwest Passage; and to forestall any English presence in the area, New Spain sent colonists to New Mexico.

Dominican missionaries established the city of Santa Fe in 1609. When rich mineral deposits were not discovered, the missionary impulse became dominant. By 1680 New Mexico had more than twenty-five missions, encompassing nearly a hundred villages and seventy-five thousand Indians. But Chief Popé and the Pueblos slaughtered hundreds of colonists and captured Sante Fe in 1680, which retarded the development of New Mexico for decades. Not until 1692, after twelve years of bitter fighting, did the Spaniards reconquer New Mexico, and it was not until 1706 that they founded Albuquerque. More than a thousand colonists died in the Yaqui rebellion of 1740.

Because of the danger of Indian attacks, the colonists lived in villages along the major rivers where water and presidios supported life. A cultural symbiosis occurred there. Like the Indians, the *nuevos mexicanos* (Mexican settlers) cultivated corn, beans, squash, and chili, but they added cotton and fruit, which the Indians quickly adopted. From the Indians the Spanish learned about irrigation and in return taught the Indians to raise sheep. Spaniards built churches in the Indian communities, and the Indians learned to speak Spanish and worship Christ. Still, life was provincial in' New Mexico, and in 1800 there were only eight thousand Mexican settlers there—a well-to-do landowning class and an impoverished class of mestizo workers.

Present-day Arizona was settled more slowly because of the hostility of the Apaches and Navajos and the lack of water. The Jesuit priest Eusebio Francisco Kino led a missionary expedition deep into western Arizona in 1687. He worked closely with the Pima Indians and established a mission near Tucson after the turn of the century. The Arizona economy depended on subsistence agriculture and sheep grazing, and the people lived in fortified towns, but with only two thousand colonists the settlement remained underdeveloped throughout the Spanish colonial period.

Spanish colonization in what is now Texas began after the French explorations of the Jesuit Father Marquette and Louis Joliet in 1673 and of Sièur de La Salle in 1682 had opened the Mississippi River. To counter French influence, New Spain founded Nacogdoches in 1716 and San Antonio in 1718. Cattle and cotton became the bases of the Texas economy; and because of the weakness of local Indians, the colonists (known as *tejanos*) were more scattered than in New Mexico. A tense rivalry existed in Texas until 1763, when Spain took Louisiana from France. Without the French threat, Spain's desire to colonize Texas waned, and as late as 1800 only 3,500 Mexican settlers lived there.

The Spanish moved into California after hearing of Russian and English interest. José de Galvez, a royal official who visited Mexico in the 1760s, decided to colonize California and discourage England and Russia. The Franciscan priest Junipero Serra then left New Spain and founded San Diego in 1769. Franciscans had established twenty other missions by 1823, including Los Angeles, Santa Barbara, San Jose, and San Francisco. California's rich natural resources and temperate climate made it the most prosperous borderlands colony. With the avail-

An early Spanish mission in California. The Catholic church played a key role in the colonization of the borderlands. (Brown Brothers)

ability of good land and the Spanish inclination to make large land grants, the *ranchos* became powerful, independent economic units, much like the Mexican haciendas. Catholic missions and private ranchos dominated the California economy, producing corn, wheat, cotton, grapes, fruit, beans, hogs, sheep, and cattle. The *californio* upper class consisted of large landowners and the clergy; the *cholo* middle class of mestizo workers, soldiers, small farmers, and new settlers; and the lowest class of impoverished California Indians.

Borderlands society differed substantially from that of New Spain. A sparse population of only 25,000 people were living there in 1800, and the criollo and mestizo classes were quite small. In comparison, New Spain had over 3 million Europeans, as did the United States, and in both places Europeans vastly outnumbered native Americans. Compared to New Spain and the North Atlantic colonies, the borderlands were provincial, subsistence outposts of civilization.

The church was more dominant there than in New Spain. Lacking rich mines and encomiendas, the borderlands developed a subsistence economy under the control of the Catholic missions. The church was the primary educational institution as well. In California, New Mexico, and Texas the Indians spoke dozens of languages, and the priests were unable to master them all. Unlike the priests in Mexico, who had learned the Aztec dialects, borderlands friars had to teach Indians Spanish before theology, and their language instruction was as intense as their religious indoctrination.

The church was also the major agent of social change. Since the fifteenth century Spain had looked upon religious conversion as a civilizing force in the New World; but in the borderlands, native Americans appeared so "uncivilized," at least when compared to the Aztecs, that the "civilizing" role of the church assumed new importance. In California and Texas, where the Indians were nomadic, the mission congregated them in residential communities near the church, and they learned to raise crops and livestock, work in industry, speak Spanish, and become Christians.

From Spain to Mexico
to the United States, 1810–1848

During the colonial period an immense social chasm developed between peninsulares and criollos. Resentment of peninsulare Spaniards was so intense in New Spain that Indians, criollos, and mestizos subordinated their own ethnic differences in a united assault on European imperialism.

Indians had always resented the power, insensitivity, and self-righteousness of the Spanish settlers. The Zacatecas led the Mixton Rebellion in 1541 and 1542, killing hundreds of colonists; food riots among the Indians led to the burning and looting of government buildings in Mexico City in 1624; the revolt of Popé in 1680 nearly destroyed New Mexico; the Indians in Nuevo León rebelled in 1704, as did the Yaquis of New Mexico in 1740; Mayans revolted in the Yucatán in 1761; and in 1802 the Mariano Rebellion broke out in Tepic province. When the general uprising against Spain began in 1810, Mexican-Indians participated enthusiastically.

Criollo resentment was both social and political. For centuries peninsulares had considered criollos crude and unsophisticated and denied them political power. Although criollos obtained land and succeeded commercially, economic power did not translate into social or political influence because peninsulares controlled most positions in the government, army, and clergy. Despite their numerical superiority, criollos felt powerless, and late in the 1700s they began forming insurgent groups and talking of political separation from Spain.

Mestizos too were weary of Spanish domination and yearned for important civil and religious positions. Peninsulares, they believed, had no real interest in Mexico beyond enhancing their political careers. Resentful of elites, some mestizos looked upon peninsulares as the backbone of an exploitive upper class; removal of Spanish authority might lead to male suffrage, separation of church and state, and full civil liberties. Some even hoped for an economic revolution that would break up the large estates and distribute them among the poor. Mestizo cooperation with criollos was expedient at best, since the criollos too were seen as part of the upper class, but mestizos were nevertheless willing to join forces against Spain.

In 1810 Father Miguel Hidalgo, the criollo son of a hacienda manager, led a revolt against Spain. As a parish priest in Dolores, Mexico, Hidalgo had grown close to the Indians and empathized with their plight. Frustrated at the gap between the rich and the poor and the arrogance of peninsulare rulers, Hidalgo led a march of fifty thousand people southward toward Mexico City. Along the way several criollo landowners were killed. Although Hidalgo's army reached the outskirts of the capital, Spanish troops defeated them; and because of the antirich sentiments of some of his supporters, he received no support from conservative criollos. In 1811 he was executed.

José María Morelos, an associate of Hidalgo, took up the revolutionary banner one year later. An uncompromisingly liberal mestizo, Morelos declared independence from Spain after taking military control of much of southern Mexico. He convened a congress which called for universal suffrage and the abolition of slavery, racial discrimination, and Indian tribute taxes. But like Hidalgo, Morelos angered criollos who worried more about revolution from below than repression from above, and Catholic prelates who sensed a threat to the church's vast property holdings. Without the support of criollos or the church, Morales was doomed, and in 1815 Spanish authorities captured and executed him.

An army revolt at Cádiz in 1820 precipitated a liberal revolution in Spain, and the new government abolished the Inquisition, took control of church tithes, outlawed ecclesiastical courts, granted civil liberties, ordered new elections to the Cortes (Spain's national legislature), and nationalized much church property. Conservative criollos and church leaders in Mexico awakened from their apathy, joined with the Indian and mestizo remnants of the older revolutionary movements, and called for independence from Spain. Augustine de Iturbide emerged as the criollo leader; his was a counterrevolution designed to preserve aristocratic privileges, and in 1821 he proclaimed Mexican independence. But Iturbide's coalition was too volatile: Indians and mestizos despised his conservatism. He wanted to stop the revolution after the expulsion of Spanish officials and had no desire to see it extend into economic affairs. In fact, Iturbide wanted to install a native monarchy. Facing intense liberal opposition, Iturbide resigned in 1823, and Guadalupe Victoria then came to power.

Rebellion was already brewing in the borderlands. Mexican liberals and conservatives had cooperated politically to destroy peninsulare dominance, but success exposed their differences. The conservatives were wealthy landowners, a political and social elite who believed in rule by the rich, the unity of church and state, and a strong central government. Liberals, mostly new businessmen and the lower classes, favored a weak federal government, strong provincial governments, separation of church and state, and extension of the suffrage. After Iturbide's resignation, the liberal government secularized the missions, nationalized church property, outlawed mandatory tithe paying, and suppressed ecclesiastical courts. These reforms spurred conservatives to depose the liberal government in 1834 and install Antonio López de Santa Anna. He weakened the provinces by abolishing their legislatures, restricting the powers of municipal governments, and ousting local officials. Upset about the loss of local power, provincial leaders in the borderlands began considering rebellion against Mexico.

Their restlessness coincided with Anglo-American expansion. Between 1820 and 1848 thousands of Americans settled in the Southwest. The Santa Fe trail opened in 1822, and the economic relationship between the borderlands and central Mexico changed dramatically; it was easier now to obtain goods from the United States than from central Mexico. Nuevos mexicanos began drawing closer to the United States. A similar situation developed in California during the 1820s and 1830s, when American settlers established farms in the rich central valleys and merchants and shippers crowded into San Francisco to profit from the Pacific trade. Mexico encouraged American immigration during the 1820s by giving large land grants in Texas to men such as Stephen Austin. There were more than twenty-five thousand Americans in eastern Texas by 1830. Some married into local families, but most looked down upon Mexicans as inferiors. American political loyalties flowed east to Washington, D. C., not south to Mexico City.

A coalition of discontented mestizos and Americans developed in all the borderland colonies. Texas was the first province to revolt against Mexico, and the rebellion there set in motion a chain reaction that eventually brought New Mexico and California into the United States. Attracted by the rich bottomlands of east Texas, thousands of settlers crossed the Louisiana border during the 1820s and started hundreds of cotton plantations. Mexican officials had encouraged the early settlers, but they became alarmed at the size of the immigration. To discourage American settlement, Mexico prohibited the importation of slaves into Texas and established customs houses and military presidios along the Texas-Louisiana border in 1830. But it was too late. After the conservative revolt of 1834 in Mexico City, Texans declared their independence. Despite an initial defeat at the Alamo mission in San Antonio in March 1836, a combined Texas army of Anglo-Americans and tejanos, under the command of Sam Houston, defeated Santa Anna at the Battle of

San Jacinto a month later. The subsequent Treaty of Velasco, which Santa Anna was forced to sign but Mexico never recognized, granted independence to Texas.

The Republic of Texas was not admitted to the Union for nine years, however, because many northern congressmen feared that five slave states might eventually emerge out of the area and give the south control of the Senate. But by 1845 the new expansionist Manifest Destiny ideology, which called for American sovereignty over the entire continent, had overcome all reluctance to accepting Texas. In 1845, in a joint session of Congress, the United States annexed the Lone Star Republic. Texas became the twenty-eighth state of the Union.

Mexico immediately severed diplomatic relations with the United States, but despite the breach between the two countries, late in 1845 President James K. Polk decided to try to purchase New Mexico and California. When Mexico bluntly refused, Polk ordered American troops into Texas south of the Nueces River hoping to create a military emergency. It was a pretext for acquiring the rest of the Southwest. After a brief clash between Mexican and American forces in a disputed area of southern Texas in May 1846, President Polk claimed that "Mexico . . . shed American blood upon American soil," and Congress declared war.

California and New Mexico became United States territories soon afterward. On the eve of the war a group of Anglo-American and Mexican leaders in California, upset about the conservative triumph in Mexico, declared independence and launched the Bear Flag Revolt. When American military forces entered California, the revolt merged with the larger conflict, becoming one theater in the war with Mexico. American businessmen in Santa Fe convinced nuevo mexicano colleagues that the province would be more prosperous under American control, and when General Stephen Kearny arrived in 1846 he met no resistance.

After months of bitter fighting, triumphant American troops entered Mexico City; and on February 2, 1848, the two nations signed the Treaty of Guadalupe Hidalgo. For $15 million the United States acquired California, Arizona, New Mexico, Nevada, Utah, and part of Colorado, and Mexico recognized American title to Texas. Manifest Destiny had triumphed.

Eighty thousand more people now lived in the United States. Concerned about the fate of Spanish-speaking mestizo Catholics in a white Protestant society, Mexican officials had inserted several guarantees into the Treaty of Guadalupe Hidalgo. Mexicans in the ceded territory had a year to decide their loyalties; if at the end of the year they had not declared their intentions, they would automatically receive United States citizenship. Only two thousand crossed the border; the others became Mexican-Americans. Article IX, as well as a statement of protocol issued later, guaranteed their civil liberties, religious freedom, and title to their property. Despite the guarantees, however, the Fourteenth Amendment was still twenty years in the future. Although the federal government had promised a great deal, it had little authority to enforce its will in the states. An ethnic and religious minority in the Southwest, Mexican-Americans would have difficulty enjoying their promised liberties.

SUGGESTED READINGS

Acuña, Rodolfo. *Occupied America: The Chicano Struggle Toward Liberation*. San Francisco: 1972.

Barker, Eugene C. *Mexico and Texas, 1821–1835*. New York: 1965.

Bolton, Herbert E. *Rim of Christendom*. New York: 1936.

————. *The Spanish Borderlands*. New Haven, Conn.: 1921.

Burland, C. A. *The Gods of Mexico*. New York: 1968.

Carter, Hodding. *Doomed Road of Empire*. New York: 1971.

Caso, Alfonso. *The Aztecs: People of the Sun*. Norman, Oklahoma: 1958.

Faulk, Odie B. *The Land of Many Frontiers*. New York: 1968.

Forbes, Jack. *Apache, Navaho, and Spaniard*. Norman, Oklahoma: 1960.

Gibson, Charles, *The Aztecs Under Spanish Rule*. New York: 1964.

————. *Spain in America*. New York: 1966.

Gladwin, Harold S. *A History of the Ancient Southwest*. Portland, Me.: 1957.

Grebler, L., Moore, J. W., and Gusman, R. S. *The Mexican American People*. New York: 1970.

Hallenbeck, Cleve. *Spanish Missions of the Old Southwest*. New York: 1926.

Hammond, George P. *The Treaty of Guadalupe Hidalgo, 1848*. Berkeley, Cal.: 1949.

Jones, Oakah L. *Pueblo Warriors and Spanish Conquest*. Norman, Oklahoma: 1966.

Lang, James. *Conquest and Commerce: Spain and England in the Americas*. New York: 1975.

Leon-Portilla, Miguel. *The Broken Spears*. Boston: 1962.

Lowrie, Samuel H. *Culture Conflict in Texas, 1821–1835*. New York: 1932.

Marshall, C. E. "The Birth of the Mestizo in New Spain." *Hispanic American Historical Review*, 19 (February-December 1939), 161–184.

Meier, Matt S., and Rivera, Feliciano. *The Chicanos: A History of Mexican Americans*. New York: 1972.

Meinig, Donald W. *Southwest: Three Peoples in Geographical Change, 1600–1970*. New York: 1971.

Moquin, Wayne. *A Documentary History of the Mexican Americans*. New York: 1971.

Paz, Octavio. *The Labyrinth of Solitude*. New York: 1961.

Perrigo, Lynn. *The American Southwest*. New York: 1971.

Peterson, Frederick. *Ancient Mexico*. New York: 1959.

Price, Glenn W. *Origins of the War with Mexico: The Polk-Stockton Intrigue*. Austin, Texas: 1967.

Ramos, Samuel. *Profile of Man and Culture in Mexico*. Austin, Texas: 1962.

Riesenberg, Felix. *The Golden Road: The Story of California's Mission Trail*. New York: 1962.

Sanchez, George I. *Forgotten People: A Study of New Mexico*. Albuquerque, N.M.: 1940.

Simpson, Leslie B. *Many Mexicos*. Berkeley, Cal.: 1967.

Spicer, Edward H. *Cycles of Conquest: The Impact of Spain, Mexico, and the United States on the Indians of the Southwest, 1533–1960*. Tucson, Arizona: 1961.

Stoddard, Ellwyn R. *Mexican Americans*. New York: 1973.

Vaillant, George C. *The Aztecs of Mexico*. Garden City, N.Y.: 1962.

Chapter Twelve

Asia in America: The Chinese Immigrants

Emigration has long been a part of Chinese history. As early as the seventh century farmers looking for new land crossed the Taiwan Strait and settled on the island of Taiwan. During the Ming period (1368–1644) people from the coastal provinces of South China fanned out to the Philippines, Southeast Asia, and the East Indies. And as the New World opened, they went to Mexico, Brazil, Peru, and Canada. Eventually perhaps 10 million Chinese scattered throughout the world, and between the gold rush of 1849 and the Chinese Exclusion Act of 1882 nearly three hundred thousand, most of them from Kwangtung (Canton) Province in southeastern China, came to the United States. Ostracized socially, isolated culturally, and faithful to their values, the Chinese immigrants would have an extraordinary experience in the United States, one marked by pain as well as triumph.

Most of the nineteenth-century Chinese immigrants came from the Sunwui, Toishan, Hoiping, and Yanping districts of Kwangtung. Kwangtung is noted for hot monsoon summers and cool winters. With most of the soil arable. Kwangtung farmers raised rice on the wet, flat coastal plain, where seventy inches of rain fell annually. Sugar cane was an important cash crop, and so were mulberry leaves for the silk industry. Pears, organges, plums, mangoes, peaches, and pineapples grew in the mountains. Except for the cities of Canton (Kwangchow), Hong Kong, and Macao, Kwangtung was a rural, agrarian society where peasant families had tilled the land for millennia.

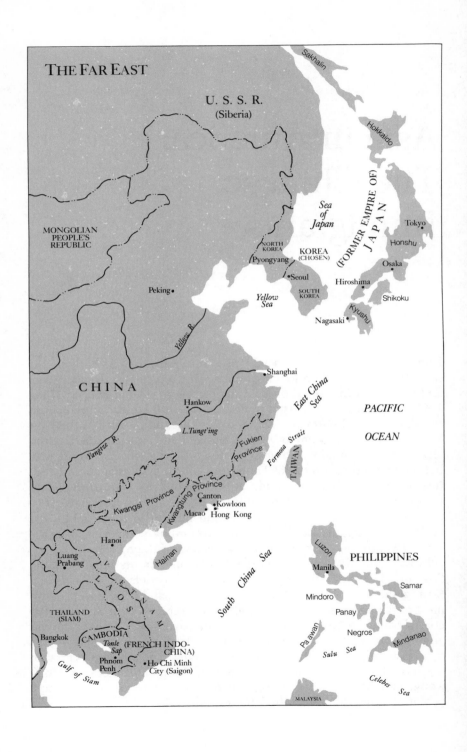

In spite of the land's fertility and its intensive use, life was a struggle. There were more than 400 million people in China in 1850, and population density along the coast averaged more than a thousand people per square mile. Agricultural techniques were primitive, and with only one-third of an acre to feed each person, production never satisfied demand. Even when the harvest was good, rice had to be imported. Frequent river flooding and periodic crop failures further beset peasant life.

There were ethnic problems as well. The Cantonese were natives of the Kwangtung delta who considered themselves superior to other groups. They controlled the economic and political machinery of the province. The Hakka (guest people) had immigrated from North China in the thirteenth century and were culturally and linguistically distinct from the Cantonese. They lived in separate villages, resented the patronizing attitudes of the Cantonese, and had competed with them for hundreds of years. Finally, there were the Tanka, chronically poor fishermen, smugglers, and ferrymen despised by Cantonese and Hakka alike. Social outcasts, the Tanka were prohibited from attending school or entering the civil service.

European imperialism created new problems. Since the seventeenth century, when Dutch merchants introduced opium to China, European traders had competed to supply the huge Asian demand for the drug. In the 1830s English merchants dominated the opium traffic, but Chinese officials wanted it to stop because they felt it was undermining the fiscal and moral base of China. When Chinese officials seized the English opium supplies at Canton in 1839, the British government sent military forces and occupied the city. After three years of intermittent conflict, the First Opium War ended when China signed the Treaty of Nanking. England imposed huge indemnities to pay for the war; took control of Hong Kong; and, on the principle of extraterritorialty, claimed the right to try all English criminals in China by British rather than Chinese law. It was a humiliating blow to Chinese pride.

The European presence disrupted traditional society. Christian missionaries preaching Jesus Christ and the church as a social institution challenged the Confucian emphasis on family authority. British textiles entered Kwangtung, ruined local producers, and vastly increased unemployment. Anglo-Chinese wars stimulated racial violence between the English and the native peasants. And the Taiping (Heavenly Peace) Rebellion in the 1850s devastated southeastern China. In one of the largest of China's many peasant revolts, Hung Hsiu-ch'üan, a Hakka student and a Protestant Christian convert, proclaimed himself the younger brother of Jesus Christ and led a mystical religious-military revolt against the Manchu authorities of Kwangsi Province, just north of

Kwangtung. Quickly spreading to Kwangtung, the rebellion turned into a general uprising of discontented scholars denied admission to the civil service (and thus consigned to a life of menial work); merchants resentful of taxes imposed by British officials; Cantonese residents suffering from economic disruptions; troubled peasants wanting land reform; democrats hoping to destroy political tyranny; and Hakkas planning to blunt the power of the Cantonese. It was a social catastrophe; the rebellion and its suppression completely destroyed the rural economy and killed more than 20 million people. Desperate peasants began looking beyond China for new opportunities.

But amidst all these upheavals the Chinese family continued to order peasant life. A basic institution of social control, the clan tied families together in village economies where property was held in common, graveyards administered, and ancestral halls maintained. Individuals subordinated their personal interests to the authority of the extended family, and kinship patterns of elder male dominance continued throughout life. Peasants were intensely loyal to the family: it supplied their reason for being. The disruptions of the mid-nineteenth century tested that loyalty, as peasant farmers became more and more hard-pressed to support their families. In the end, family devotion pushed hundreds of thousands of peasants overseas.

Just as all these social and economic problems were developing in China, American merchants brought news of gold in California. Rumors spread, and the "Golden Mountain" and high wages in California seemed the answer to peasant troubles. The Chinese became sojourners, temporary immigrants who planned to work in America until they were fifty or sixty years old. Then they would return home bringing wealth and respect. During their years abroad, they hoped to make return visits to China several times, marry a woman selected by the clan, father many children, and help the family make ends meet. In America they would live frugally and send most of their money home to China. Emigration was not a turning away from their homeland but a defense of the family and the village, the only way to preserve the traditional order.

Chinese-American Society

By 1855 there were 20,000 Chinese immigrants in the United States, most of them in California. Of the 63,000 Chinese in America in 1870, more than 50,000 lived in California and nearly 10,000 in Idaho, Nevada, Oregon, and Washington. Ten years later there were 105,000 Chinese in America, 75,000 of them in California and 24,000 scattered throughout the western states. A few thousand Chinese immigrated to the Kingdom of Hawaii after the 1840s, and when the United States annexed Hawaii in 1898, they became Chinese-Americans.

Although a few Chinese merchants found work supervising American trade with Asia, most early Chinese came looking for gold and worked in the mines. But whenever they made a large strike, jealous white miners drove them off their claims. As mining became more expensive with the shift to hydraulic extraction, Chinese took jobs with the large mining companies. Thousands worked gold mines in Oregon, Idaho, and Montana; silver mines in Nevada and Arizona; and coal mines in Utah and Wyoming. Many Chinese were domestic servants, laundry workers, and restaurant owners; others were the backbone of the woolen, shoe and boot, and metal industries. After the Civil War the Central Pacific Railroad hired more than ten thousand Chinese workers to build the line from San Francisco to Utah. The Southern Pacific Railroad later employed them throughout the Southwest. Chinese could also be found building dams, levees, and irrigation systems in the San Joaquin and Sacramento River valleys. On the large wheat and fruit farms of California they were seasonal workers, the first generation of migratory laborers. Chinese truck gardeners and horticulturists were common in the West, and Chinese fishing villages dotted the Pacific coast, where they processed and sold salmon, sturgeon, halibut, bluefish, redfish, flounder, shrimp, and abalone.

Because the Chinese saw their move as temporary rather than permanent, they brought few women along—only one immigrant in twenty was female. It was not customary for a Chinese woman to leave her family, and the men believed they would soon be returning anyway. Theirs was a "bachelor society." Not surprisingly, because of the lack of women and because of their reasons for leaving home, the Chinese returned home far more frequently than European immigrants. But most conspicuous was the resiliency of their social structure—the central place afforded the family. The Chinese sense of identity was powerful. Family and kinship relations were far more personal and important than in European societies. In Kwangtung whole villages were often inhabited by one family. The patriarchal order was strong, and clans were the basic unit of the economy, society, and local government. Even in death, through ancestor worship, family lineage continued. Individuals, in terms of their origins and destiny, were indistinct from their family backgrounds.

Once in America the Chinese did everything possible to reconstruct familiar social and political institutions, not only to ease their adjustment to the New World but to maintain emotional ties to China. Traditional clans became important in America too. Because there were only 438 distinct family surnames in China, it was relatively easy for immigrants to identify their clan, and those who shared the same surname associated closely. Wei Bat Liu, an immigrant resident of San Francisco in 1913, remembered that

> all the cousins from the Liu family . . . had one big room . . . we slept in that room, cooked in that room, one room. Anybody who had a job had to sleep outside the room, because he could afford to rent space . . . for himself. Anybody who couldn't find work slept . . . in this room. At the end of the year, all the members would get together and figure out all the expenses . . . even the ones who didn't sleep were willing to pay . . .*

Leadership in China rested on village elders and the scholar-gentry; but since they did not migrate, the dominant figures in the immigrant communities were usually wealthy merchants. Stores were social centers for clan members as well as shelters for newcomers; merchants also offered charity to the old, the indigent, and the handicapped. Family elders in America served as proxy parents for new immigrants, and family associations provided guidance and discipline for the young. Clan ties directed settlement, and in the scattered colonies one or a few clans controlled local affairs. In San Francisco the Chan, Lee, and Wong families were dominant, as the Ong family was in Phoenix and the Chin family in Seattle. After World War II the Moi family rose to prominence in Chicago, and the Yee clan in Detroit and Cleveland.

Overlapping and transcending clan authority were *hui kuan* associations whose membership was determined by dialect and regional origins. Many different clans participated in each hui kuan, and these mutual aid societies played an important judicial role by mediating disputes between clans. In 1851 Cantonese immigrants in San Francisco formed the Sam Yup Company, a hui kuan association, and later in the year another group from Kwangtung established the See Yup Company. Chungsun immigrants formed the Yeong Wo Company and Hakka settlers the Yan Wo Company in 1852. The most powerful hui kuan association, the Ning Yeung Company, was formed in 1854, and in 1862 others organized the Hop Wo Company. Known as the Six Companies, these hui kuan functioned as a quasigovernment in Chinatown. They constructed large buildings to house their operations, and representatives of each company, after greeting new immigrants, would take them to the company's headquarters. During the immigrants' first weeks in America the companies found places for them to live, lent money, found jobs, cared for the sick, adjudicated disputes, and helped return

*Victor Nee and Brett deBarry, *Longtime Californin'* (New York, 1973), pp. 64–65.

the dead to China for burial. One immigrant recalled his greeting from the Six Companies upon arrival in San Francisco:

> One valuable lesson . . . which you will soon appreciate is that we must stick together . . . even though we are not kin. That is why we have formed . . . the Six Companies representing the six districts which most of us come from. . . . You will always find food and shelter here among us. . . . When you have earned money . . . you will pay dues into the company fund. This fund helps us to maintain the company headquarters and helps us set up an orderly system to take care of our own.*

In an age when public welfare was unknown, the Six Companies helped meet the social needs of Chinese immigrants.

Finally, there were the *tongs*. For more than a thousand years these secret associations had provided a form of social order independent of clan and hui kuan. Because of the tremendous loyalty expected in Chinese families, the country was atomized into hundreds of local elites lacking central direction. The Chinese could not unify because they were unable to transcend kinship, linguistic, and geographic differences. Secret societies, however, organized people without regard to these differences. People who failed civil service examinations joined tongs to get back at the government; angry tenants joined to punish landlords. During economic distress poor farmers, workers, and merchants joined to strike back at those who exploited them. In nineteenth-century China the tongs were a powerful social infrastructure—a clandestine linear system of political power organizing China along horizontal lines and helping to overcome family and language differences.

In America tong members chafed at the power of the merchant elite, whether clan or hui kuan leaders. The Suey Sing Tong repeatedly challenged the Wong family in San Francisco, and bloody battles between the On Yick Tong and the Yee clan were common. The secret societies were often involved in organized crime. In San Francisco's Chinatown the Hip Yee Tong, Chee Kung Tong, Wa Ting Tong, and On Leong Tong controlled gambling, prostitution, heroin, and opium traffic. Rival tongs fought wars to control illegal businesses, resisted bitterly when the Six Companies tried to stamp out crime, and at times violently confronted prominent clan leaders who opposed their activities. Where clans or hui kuan were weakly organized, tongs provided health care and life insurance, and welfare assistance to the sick, disabled, and unemployed. Along with the clans and hui kuan, the tongs

---

*Betty Lee Sung, *Mountain of Gold* (New York, 1967), pp. 24–25.

provided Chinese America with an invisible government based on district and family loyalty, fear, and piety.

The Chinese formed one of the most self-contained immigrant communities in America. Clans, hui kuan, and tongs exerted great authority, nearly as much as in China. At the same time, most Chinese lived in urban ghettos where they were physically as well as culturally isolated. Not permitted to naturalize, they could not vote and had little power in local politics. Without the need to court their votes, local politicians ignored them. As a result, the Chinese had extraordinary control over their own affairs; the clans, hui kuan, and tongs were the real political power in Chinatown. While other immigrants struggled to gain access to the political establishment, the Chinese lived in a social and political island.

The Anti-Chinese Crusade

As nonwhite, non-Christian, and non-Western immigrants, the Chinese frightened many Americans. Treated as "colored" people, they experienced the discrimination meted out to blacks, Indians, and Mexicans, and as a religious minority suffered the same indignities as German, Irish, and French-Canadian Catholics. And in addition, as non-Western people they seemed strange, different from all other immigrants. Despite the general decline of nativism during the Civil War, an anti-Chinese movement developed soon afterward.

In the early nineteenth century American traders and missionaries had passed on negative images of the Chinese. In addition to ridiculing Chinese tastes in food and music, Yankee traders living in China between 1780 and 1840 looked upon the Chinese as a backward people who were cruel, dishonest, immoral, and superstitious. And through sermons, books, magazines, and newspapers Protestant missionaries in China reinforced those images. To many Protestants the Buddhism, Taoism, and Confucianism of China were depraved religions and the Chinese faithful were heathens. Western society, with its emphasis on competitive individualism, embraced a monotheistic God and took an emotional, evangelical approach to religion, seeing human affairs as a struggle between good and evil. Coming from a communal, ascetic culture, the Chinese were polytheistic, accepting many gods and relying periodically on different ones for assistance; there were gods and goddesses of war, wealth, fertility, agriculture, and rain. The Chinese found devotion to one and only one God a particularly narrow-minded perspective. They were not at all in tune with sectarianism; instead they tolerated all faiths and were even able to accept the deities of other people. Ignored by most Chinese, the missionaries only became more convinced of "Oriental paganism." Finally, many missionaries spread pornographic rumors, saying that sexual licentiousness was widespread throughout the country.

During the Opium War Americans had sided with England and many rejoiced when China was defeated. The Taiping Rebellion reinforced the idea that the Chinese were uncivilized barbarians; so did the murder of Christian missionaries in Tientsin in 1870. These events in Asia served to increase American suspicions about the Chinese in the United States.

Nativism existed for economic reasons as well, especially among workers convinced that Chinese immigrants would depress wages and make jobs scarce. Businessmen, on the other hand, favored Chinese immigration as a source of cheap labor, and in 1868 business triumphed when Congress ratified the Burlingame Treaty, which permitted unrestricted immigration of Chinese laborers to work on the transcontinental railroad. But when the Union Pacific–Central Pacific Railroad was completed in 1869, ten thousand Chinese workers had to look for other jobs and competed directly with American workers. Many Americans believed all Chinese were "coolies," slave laborers controlled by contractors who had "shanghaied" them to the United States. To be sure, most Chinese did come under contract because they could not afford the passage, just as indentured servants had in the eighteenth century. But while many Chinese laborers who left Hong Kong and Macao for South America and the West Indies did work as slaves, contract workers in the United States were permitted complete freedom of movement as long as they paid monthly installments on their passage debt. Whenever there were wage cuts or unemployment, native workers held the Chinese responsible. Labor unions began demanding immigration restriction.

Social and cultural misgivings also surfaced. Many Americans believed stereotypes about Chinese proclivities for gambling, prostitution, and opium smoking, and the crowded, physically deteriorating conditions in San Francisco's Chinatown seemed a source of crime and unrest. The lack of Chinese women frightened people who believed Chinese men were sexually attracted to white women. The Chinese were believed to be spreading leprosy, venereal disease, and other illnesses. Finally, Chinese culture seemed strange. The immigrants believed China was the center of the earth, the highest expression of human civilization, and that Westerners were the barbarians. Not that they said so, but Americans were outraged anyway. They were also suspicious about the tongs, clans, and hui kuan that made the Chinese communities so autonomous. Most Americans viewed the Chinese as an alien group that would never assimilate. Demands for immigration restriction grew more intense.

Discrimination became more common. Between 1852 and 1860 several counties in northern California expelled Chinese miners; and as the mining frontier moved north into Oregon, Washington, and Idaho, similar measures were passed there as well. In the 1870s labor unions in California conducted anti-Chinese propaganda campaigns, and early in the 1880s the state legislature denied the use of California employment bureaus to the Chinese and prohibited them from working on dam, levee, or irrigation projects.

The Chinese encountered widespread social and civil discrimination. In 1854, for example, a white man was convicted of murder on the eyewitness testimony of a Chinese worker, but the California Supreme Court overturned the decision on the grounds that "Mongolians" could not testify against whites. After that it was difficult to prosecute whites for anti-Chinese violence, and the Chinese had no legal avenues to express grievances. California prohibited Chinese children from attending public schools in 1860; and although state courts later ordered "separate but equal" facilities, local school districts refused to build new schools for Chinese children. Harassment laws were common. One San Francisco law prohibited carrying baskets on long poles, a common practice in Chinatown, and in 1873 an ordinance required jailers to give short haircuts to all prisoners, cutting off the queues of Chinese men. Such laws resulted in second-class status for the Chinese in America.

Sporadic violence also occurred. On October 23, 1871, as Los Angeles police tried to end a feud about the status of a woman contractually bound as a worker to a hui kuan, two policemen were killed. Hearing the news, more than five hundred whites entered Chinatown, burned dozens of buildings, and lynched fifteen people. In 1876 a mob in Truckee, California, burned several Chinese homes and shot fleeing occupants. Ten months later vigilantes known as the Order of Caucasians murdered several Chinese in Chico, California. The 1877 riots in San Francisco destroyed thirty Chinese laundries. The worst race riot took place at Rock Springs, Wyoming, on September 2, 1885, when rampaging white miners murdered twenty-eight Chinese-Americans. Another riot occurred at Log Cabin, Oregon, in 1886. And individual muggings, beatings, and destruction of property were common.

As nativist fears mounted, the immigration restriction movement grew stronger. The Know-Nothing party called for an end to Chinese immigration, and in 1855 the California legislature passed a tax of fifty dollars for each Chinese worker brought into the state. Although difficult to enforce, the law's intent was clear. In 1870 California prohibited the immigration of Chinese women unless they could prove good char-

Anti-Chinese riots erupted in Denver, Colorado, in 1880. (Brown Brothers)

acter, and other western states passed similarly punitive laws to drive out the Chinese. Demands for exclusion were especially intense during the depression of the 1870s, when a lull in railroad construction brought thousands of unemployed Chinese workers back to California. The Workingmen's party demanded restriction of the Chinese. All this occurred just as immigration was swelling dramatically. More than 115,000 Chinese arrived on the West Coast in the 1870s, and another 50,000 came in 1881 and 1882. Under enormous pressure from western politicians and labor unions, Congress approved the Chinese Exclusion Act in 1882 prohibiting future immigration from China.

From then until 1943, when China was once again permitted to send immigrants, the Chinese-American population declined as tens of thousands returned to Kwangtung. And for those remaining in the United States, the melting pot did not exist; assimilation was impossible. Most Americans were too suspicious of the Chinese, and the immigrants lived in their own world anyway. Politically inactive, culturally distinct, and economically independent of the general economy, Chinese America was an isolated entity in the United States.

SUGGESTED READINGS

Barth, Gunther. *Bitter Strength: A History of the Chinese in the United States, 1850–1870*. Cambridge, Mass.: 1964.

Cattell, Stuart H. *Health, Welfare, and Social Organization in Chinatown*. New York: 1962.

Chen, Han-Seng. *Agrarian Problems in Southernmost China*. Shanghai, China: 1936.

Cheng, David Te-Chao. *Acculturation of the Chinese in the United States*. Hong Kong, China: 1949.

Ch'u, T'ung-tsu. *Law and Society in Traditional China*. Paris, France: 1961.

Chu, George. "Chinatowns in the Delta: The Chinese in the Sacramento–San Joaquin Delta, 1870–1960." *California Historical Society Quarterly*, 49 (Spring 1970), 21–38.

Coolidge, Mary Roberts. *Chinese Immigration*. New York: 1909.

Harrison, John H. *China Since 1800*. New York: 1967.

Hoyt, Edwin. *Asians in the West*. New York: 1974.

Hsu, Francis L. K. *Americans and Chinese*. New York: 1970.

———. *The Challenge of the American Dream: The Chinese in the United States*. Belmont, Cal.: 1971.

Hundley, Norris, ed. *The Asian American: The Historical Experience*. Santa Barbara, Cal.: 1976.

Kashima, Tetsuden. *Buddhism in America*. Westport, Conn.: 1977.

Kingston, Maxine Hong. *The Woman Warrior*. New York: 1976.

Kung, S. W. *The Chinese in American Life*. Westport, Conn.: 1962.

Lee, Rose Hum. *The Chinese in the United States*. Hong Kong, China: 1960.

Light, Ivan H. *Ethnic Enterprise in America: Business and Welfare Among Chinese, Japanese, and Blacks*. Berkeley, Cal.: 1972.

Lin, Hazel. *The Physician*. New York: 1951.

Lin, Yueh-hwa, *The Golden Wing: A Sociological Study of Chinese Familialism*. London: 1948.

Loewen, James. *The Mississippi Chinese: Between Black and White*. Cambridge, Mass.: 1971.

Lyman, Stanford M. *Chinese Americans*. New York: 1974.

———. "Conflict and the Web of Group Affiliation in San Francisco's Chinatown, 1850–1910." *Pacific Historical Review*, 43 (November 1974), 435–447.

McClellan, Robert. *The Heathen Chinese*. Athens, Oh.: 1971.

Melendy, H. Brett. *The Oriental Americans*. New York: 1972.

Miller, Stuart. *The Unwelcome Immigrant: The American Image of the Chinese, 1785–1882*. Berkeley, Cal.: 1969.

Nee, Victor G., and de Bary, Brett. *Longtime Californ'*. New York: 1973.

Olin, Spencer C., Jr. "European Immigrant and Oriental Alien: Acceptance and Rejection by the California Legislature of 1913." *Pacific Historical Review*, 35 (August 1966), 303–317.

Sandmeyer, Elmer. *The Anti-Chinese Movement in California*. Urbana, Ill.: 1973.

Saxton, Alexander. *The Indispensable Enemy: Labor and the Anti-Chinese Movement in California*. Berkeley, Cal.: 1973.

Sung, Betty Lee. *The Chinese in America*. New York: 1972.

———. *Mountain of Gold: The Story of the Chinese in America*. New York: 1967.

Wakeman, Frederick. *The Fall of Imperial China*. New York: 1975.

Summary

Ethnic America
in 1890

As the 1880s opened, American life seemed stable. People had resumed the normal business of life. After seventeen years of military conflict and political instability, the Civil War and Reconstruction were over. The Union was preserved, the states' rights philosophy defeated, and the noble experiment of black civil equality ended. Americans were taking up where they had left off in 1860, conquering the continent and transforming the environment into material wealth and security. Approximately 60 million people were living in the United States by 1890, and the end of one era and beginning of another would have enormous consequences for all of them, for the 23 million people of British descent as well as for the other European and racial minorities.

Afro-Americans were immediately affected by changes in the political and social climate. For thirty years they had been the focal point in the national debate over free soil, abolition, and equality. When the last federal troops left Florida, South Carolina, and Louisiana in 1877, there were approximately 7 million black people living in the United States, 85 percent of them still in the South. Black communities existed in most northern states, and thousands of black farmers and cowboys had moved west, but most Afro-Americans were still attached to the soil of the rural South. For fourteen years, between the Emancipation Proclamation of 1863 and the election of 1876, the Republican party had experimented with black equality, trying through the Fourteenth Amendment, the Fifteenth Amendment, and the civil rights laws of

1866 and 1875 to give blacks power at the ballot box. And as long as federal troops patrolled the South, the white descendants of the early English, Scots, Scots-Irish, and German settlers had put up with the reforms. But by 1877 northern Republicans had tired of their "southern strategy." New GOP votes were pouring in from the western states and the need for black votes was declining. Tired of the political instability generated by army troops and the Ku Klux Klan, and anxious to invest in the resources and labor of the South, northern businessmen had called for an end to the experiment. The troops left, conservative white "Dixiecrats" resumed their former positions of power, and black Republicanism was dead. With neither capital nor land, southern blacks were poor and dependent once again on the power of the white upper class. Jim Crow laws were already appearing.

Changes were also affecting native Americans. The advance of Christian missionaries, environmental change, disease, and hundreds of thousands of white settlers had devastated the Indian population. By 1890 there were only about 250,000 native Americans, most of them barely surviving on government reservations. Contemptuous of white values but unable to defend their traditional ways, some Indians were turning to pan-Indian spiritual movements to deal with their new lives. From the Great Basin the Sun Dance religion of the Utes and Shoshones was spreading into the rest of Indian America; the gospel of the Ghost Dance was still affecting Indians throughout the Plains; and from Mexico via the Mescalero Apaches the peyote cult was gaining thousands of native American converts.

On the West Coast, nativism had resulted in the Chinese Exclusion Act of 1882. Because of rumors from missionaries and traders traveling in China and fears of their own, local officials were passing harassment laws against the Chinese, and the Workingmen's party in California was demanding deportation. For their part, the Chinese were working hard on railroads, commercial farms, construction projects, factories, and in their own businesses, governing their own community while earning enough money to return to the "Celestial Kingdom," where their families would forever live in prosperity and honor, free of the poverty and pain of peasant life.

And throughout the Southwest nearly 300,000 Mexican-Americans were trying to keep hold of their land despite the influx of thousands of Anglo settlers. By 1890 the tejanos and californios were vastly outnumbered by Anglo farmers and were rapidly losing their land through fraudulent decisions by local judges, state legislatures, and public land commissions. In New Mexico the nuevos mexicanos still retained most of their land and a good deal of power in the territorial legislature, but large-scale Anglo immigration would soon develop, as it had earlier in

California and Texas. Mexican-Americans tried to save their land, but like native Americans, they would lose it, and like blacks, they would become a low-income laboring people.

Disfranchised and poor, these minorities were on the defensive. In the South people of British and German descent had wrested political power from black Republicans; on the Great Plains British, German, and Scandinavian farmers had pushed Indians onto reservations; in California English, German, and Irish workers had discriminated against the Chinese; and hundreds of thousands of white farmers, mostly of British and German descent, had acquired Mexican-American land.

Except in their attitudes toward nonwhites, there was little unanimity among white Europeans in the United States; they too were divided along ethnic lines in 1890. Scattered throughout urban American but concentrated in the Northeast were more than 6 million Irish Catholics. Still poor, ostracized socially because of their religion, and largely confined to poor housing downtown near the docks, warehouses, and railroad terminals or in peripheral shantytowns and "Paddy's Villages," they were a distinct ethnic community. Every major city had an Irish population, and the immigrants took great pride in being Irish and Roman Catholic. From the coal fields of Pennsylvania where the Molly Maguires had fought discrimination to the great railroad strikes of 1877, the Irish immigrants were working for a better standard of living. And from urban political machines they were about to strike back against Protestant assaults on their saloons, parochial schools, and Catholic charities.

Throughout rural and urban America there were more than 8 million people of German descent. A diverse group of Lutherans, Calvinists, Catholics, and pietists from various provinces in Germany, they had possessed neither nationalistic nor religious unity, but by 1890 they were nevertheless becoming more conscious of their German nationality. Mostly concentrated into rural villages and urban centers of the German belt and German triangle and linguistically isolated from the rest of America, they too constructed their own ethnic world and exhibited an overwhelming inclination, in the first generation at least, to marry other Germans.

The Norwegian, Swedish, Danish, Finnish, Dutch, Swiss, and French immigrants were too recent arrivals in 1890 to be threatened by assimilation. Of the 1.2 million Scandinavians living on the farms and in the towns of Michigan, Wisconsin, Illinois, Minnesota, Iowa, and the Dakotas, more than 900,000 of them and their children had arrived since 1870. Although many of the New York and New Jersey Dutch had deep roots in the colonial period, most of the 80,000 Dutch in Michigan and Wisconsin had come to America since 1870, as had 110,000 of the 200,000 Swiss settlers in the Midwest. And the French community in the United States—500,000 French-Canadians in New England and the Great Plains, 200,000 Cajuns in Louisiana, and 150,000 immigrants from France—was still separated by religion and language from the larger society.

For all these people the melting pot did not really exist in 1890. In schools, shops, and churches the Old World languages and customs were still flourishing; time and the passing of generations had not yet blurred the European past. Ethnic America in 1890 was still that—a nation of ethnic communities.

The most distinguishing feature of ethnic America in 1890 was the rise of the ethnic city. Rural, agrarian America was disappearing into the urban, industrial complex of the twentieth century. Cities were attracting all kinds of people with promises of jobs, freedom, anonymity, and excitement. It was an extraordinary time. New York City grew from 60,000 people in 1800 to more than a million in 1860, and cities like Buffalo, Chicago, Cleveland, and Cincinnati were doubling their populations every decade. But American cities were totally unprepared to absorb millions of new inhabitants. Housing, sanitation, transportation, water and utilities, and police and fire services were far from adequate; as a result, crime, disease, crowding, and vice were common. Entrepreneur landlords began building tenements and converting stables, cellars, sheds, and warehouses into multifamily housing. Even in smaller cities Irish and French-Canadian shantytowns appeared on the outskirts as the immigrants found work in the mills and factories. Poverty, unemployment, and sickness were a rude shock for the immigrants as well as for the more well-off Americans. Whether it was the Chinese in San Francisco, the Scandinavians in Minneapolis, the Germans in St. Louis, the Irish in New York, or the French-Canadians in Boston, urban life was new and strange to them.

In Holyoke, Massachusetts, for example, the Irish immigrants of the 1840s worked in the city's textile and industrial economy, and soon after settling they had established a Roman Catholic parish in what was once a center of English Congregationalism. Then in the late 1850s French-Canadians began moving in to take up jobs in the textile mills, and so did a few hundred German Lutherans. Soon there was a French Catholic parish in Holyoke as well as a German Lutheran church, and a Catholic hospital, orphanage, and parochial school. Similar patterns occurred in other mill towns—Lowell, Lawrence, Fall River. In larger cities ethnic diversity increased between 1776 and 1890. In Rochester, New York,

Irish Catholics had a parish in the 1820s; German Catholics, Lutherans, and Reformed in the 1830s; and a French-Canadian parish, a Reformed German-Jewish synagogue, and a Dutch Reformed church all came in the 1870s. In major metropolitan areas like Boston the massive influx of the Irish in the 1840s transformed the physical landscape. They were followed by other immigrants who crowded into downtown Boston near the piers, warehouses, markets, and factories while the English, Scots, and Germans fled for quieter suburbs in the West End, South End, and Charlestown. Eventually, as the street railways reached into every area of the city, prosperous immigrants or their children headed for better homes in the suburbs, leaving the downtown slums for poorer, newer immigrants to fill. In a few years they too would be moving toward the suburbs and replaced by southern and eastern Europeans, then by southern blacks in the 1920s, 1930s, and 1940s, and by Puerto Ricans after World War II. In 1890 most Americans were still living in a rural, agrarian world, but the outlines of the future were clearly drawn.

Assimilation among these people was almost nonexistent in 1890 because a third immigrant generation had not yet appeared. Except for the Irish, the mass migration from Europe did not begin until the 1850s, and not until after the Civil War did it reach flood-tide proportions. Immigrants and their children were tightly bound into their own ethnic families, churches, and associations, and social contact outside work and business was infrequent. Still, acculturation was well underway by 1890. Despite vigorous attempts to preserve Old World ways, the adoption of some dimensions of American culture was inevitable. For the second generation the use of English became the rule, and the Old World tongue became a relic used only in speaking to parents or grandparents. As historian Marcus Hansen has written, the second generation often worked at acquiring at least the appearance of American culture. They spoke English with relish, quickly shed Old World costumes for the utilitarian, mass-produced clothing of America, and celebrated such holidays as the Fourth of July and Thanksgiving with patriotic fervor. They were also affected by the ideological flavor of American life, and imbued with the American faith in progress, at least after the initial shock of migration and settlement had passed. They became enthusiastic supporters of Manifest Destiny, American democracy, and natural rights and popular sovereignty.

By 1890 the immigrants were also expanding their contacts with other white ethnic groups. They had long worked and done business with a wide variety of people, but their family and social contacts had been narrowly defined. That was slowly changing. As the immigrants made the transition to English, some contact with other groups occurred in the churches. When the German and Scandinavian churches switched to English-language services, some of the immigrants and their children began attending the Lutheran or pietist church closest to home. And as the public school movement spread throughout the country in the 1870s and 1880s, the Protestant ethnic parochial schools gradually disappeared and English, German, Scots, Danish, Norwegian, and Swedish children began attending the common school together. As the "streetcar suburbs" expanded out from the cities, the Germans, English, Irish, and Scandinavians fanned out to newer homes and apartments. Income, rather than just ethnic group, came to determine residential patterns, and people from different cultural backgrounds found themselves living together as neighbors. That too encouraged cultural assimilation and led to the full assimilation which would occur in the twentieth century.

Finally, political controversy helped integrate the immigrant communities into the larger society. Across the United States—from the Irish ghettos of the East to the German Catholic centers in the Midwest and the tiny Dutch Catholic settlements in Michigan—Roman Catholics supported the Democratic party in 1890. English Protestants, Welsh Methodists, Scandinavian Lutherans, Irish Protestants, and Dutch Reformed, on the other hand, were more likely to vote Republican. German pietists also voted Republican, while German Lutherans and Reformed broke the pattern by narrowly supporting the Democrats. In part, the ethnic cleavage in American politics had an economic base. The Whigs and Republicans had traditionally reflected the interests of business and commerce, and—in an economy just beginning to industrialize—those of skilled craftsmen who were still either small businessmen themselves or the elite of the labor force in mining and manufacturing. Generally, businessmen of British descent believed the Republican party would best promote their economic needs. And in the 1860s and 1870s, when most of the Dutch, German, and Scandinavian farmers poured into the Midwest, the Republican party had favored free land through the Homestead Act. So among businessmen, skilled workers, and northern farmers the Republican party enjoyed strong support.

But in 1890 cultural values were as effective a barometer of political behavior as economic interests. Ethnic groups supporting the Republican party were usually pietistic or evangelical in religion and more formal, ritualistic groups tended to support the Democrats; that is, the Baptists, Methodists, Presbyterians, Quakers, Scandinavian Lutherans, and Scandinavian and Dutch Calvinists in the North were often Republicans, while Roman Catholics and high church Lutherans were generally Democrats. Emphasizing formalism and priestly authority, the

Catholics and German Lutherans viewed the world skeptically, as if secular affairs really were distinct from religious ones and man could do little to purify the world of corruption or make it perfect. Instead of perfecting the world, they usually wanted to ameliorate some of society's worst conditions, particularly to ensure that people's standard of living was sufficient to make family and religious life fulfilling. The Irish poet John Boyle O'Reilly condemned poverty and class differences in his writings; the journalist Patrick Ford bitterly described urban poverty and unemployment in the pages of the *Irish World*; Henry George, author of *Progress and Poverty* (1879), proposed a "single tax" on all profits from the sale or rental of land; and Irish political machines freely distributed food, fuel, and jobs to poor people in the cities.

The evangelical Protestants, on the other hand, felt an intense need to purify the world of sin, to change people's minds and behavior. While the ritualists turned to the parish and parochial school to preserve their values, the evangelicals ultimately tried to legislate their morality. Because Catholics and conservative Lutherans would not abandon their saloons and parochial schools voluntarily, the evangelicals sought to force them to do so. To achieve their objectives, they turned to the Republican party, which in the middle of the nineteenth century had promoted strong government, free land, and abolition. Ritualists turned to the Democratic party for just the opposite reasons, because it opposed a strong central state and respected the prerogatives of local communities.

Throughout the nineteenth century evangelical Republicans advocated change while ritualistic Democrats supported tradition and stability. The Protestants opposed the parochial schools because they preserved Old World traditions and Catholic values, so they promoted public schools. The Catholics saw the public schools as "Protestant" schools: Protestant ministers served on school boards, Protestant prayers were repeated each morning, and the King James Bible was used for instruction. The Protestants supported prohibition as a means of purifying the world, but the ritualists viewed liquor as a harmless diversion and opposed the temperance movement. The Protestants supported Sabbath laws to close stores and taverns on Sunday, and the Catholics opposed them as unnecessary invasions of their privacy. So while the Protestants in the Republican party worked to create a homogeneous America free of sin, the Catholics and high church Lutherans in the Democratic party tried to create a stable world where family and religious values could flourish. After 1900, as industrialization continued its inexorable transformation of the social structure, economic issues would become more important, but in 1890 culture still shaped political loyalties and group relations in the United States.

SUGGESTED READINGS

Berthoff, Rowland. *An Unsettled People: Social Order and Disorder in American History*. New York: 1971.

Billington, Ray Allen. *The Protestant Crusade, 1800–1860*. New York: 1938.

———. *Westward Expansion: A History of the American Frontier*. New York: 1974.

Bruchey, Stuart. *The Roots of American Economic Growth, 1607–1861*. New York: 1965.

Buel, Richard, Jr. *Securing the Revolution: Ideology in American Politics, 1789–1815*. New York: 1972.

Cawelti, John G. *Apostles of the Self-Made Man: Changing Concepts of Success in America*. Chicago: 1965.

Chudacoff, Howard P. *The Evolution of American Urban Society*. Englewood Cliffs, N.J.: 1975.

Curran, Thomas. *Xenophobia and Immigration, 1820–1930*. Boston: 1975.

Davis, Lawrence B. *Immigrants, Baptists, and the Protestant Mind in America*. Urbana, Ill.: 1973.

Esslinger, Dean R. *Immigrants and the City: Ethnicity and Mobility in a Nineteenth-Century Midwestern Community*. New York: 1975.

Gutman, Herbert G. *Work, Culture, and Society in Industrializing America*. New York: 1976.

Hansen, Marcus Lee. *The Atlantic Migration, 1607–1860*. New York: 1940.

Jones, Maldwyn. *American Immigration*. Chicago: 1960.

———. *Destination America*. New York: 1976.

Kleppner, Paul. *The Cross of Culture: A Social Analysis of Midwestern Politics, 1850–1900*. New York: 1970.

Leonard, Ira M., and Parmet, Robert D. *American Nativism, 1830–1860*. New York: 1971.

Marty, Martin. *Righteous Crusade: The Protestant Experience in America*. New York: 1970.

Merk, Frederick. *Manifest Destiny and Mission in American Life: A Reinterpretation*. New York: 1963.

Nichols, Roy F. *The Disruption of American Democracy*. New York: 1948.

North, Douglass C. *The Economic Growth of the United States, 1790–1860*. New York: 1961.

Pessen, Edward. *Riches, Class, and Power Before the Civil War*. New York: 1973.

Potter, David. *The Impending Crisis, 1848–1861*. New York: 1976.

———. *People of Plenty: Economic Abundance and the American Character*. New York: 1954.

Potter, J. "The Growth of Population in America, 1700–1860." In D. V. Glass and D. E. C. Eversley, eds. *Population and History*. New York: 1965.

Rischin, Moses. "Beyond the Great Divide: Immigration and the Last Frontier." *Journal of American History*, 55 (June 1968), 42–53.

Schultz, Stanley K. *The Culture Factory: Boston Public Schools, 1789–1860.* New York: 1973.

Smith, Elwyn A., ed. *The Religion of the Republic.* New York: 1971.

Smith, Henry Nash. *Virgin Land: The American West as Symbol and Myth.* New York: 1950.

Somkin, Fred. *Unquiet Eagle: Memory and Desire in the Idea of American Freedom.* New York: 1971.

Taylor, Philip. *The Distant Magnet: European Emigration to the U.S.A.* London: 1971.

Thernstrom, Stephen. *Poverty and Progress: Social Mobility in a Nineteenth Century City.* Cambridge, Mass.: 1964.

Vecoli, Rudolph J. "European Americans: From Immigrants to Ethnics." In William H. Cartwright and Richard L. Watson, Jr., eds. *The Reinterpretation of American History and Culture.* Washington, D.C.: 1973.

Ward, David. *Cities and Immigrants: A Georgraphy of Change in Nineteenth Century America.* New York: 1971.

Warner, Sam Bass. *Streetcar Suburbs: The Process of Growth in Boston, 1870–1900.* Cambridge, Mass.: 1962.

Index

i

DATE DUE

DEMCO 38-297